NORA EPHRON

a biography

KRISTIN MARGUERITE DOIDGE

CHICAGO
REVIEW
PRESS

Copyright © 2022 by Kristin Marguerite Doidge
All rights reserved
Published by Chicago Review Press Incorporated
814 North Franklin Street
Chicago, Illinois 60610
ISBN 978-1-64160-375-1

Select portions of this book have previously appeared in articles published by the author in *Bustle* and the *Los Angeles Review of Books,* and in the author's 2015 master's thesis at the University of Southern California.

Library of Congress Control Number: 2022933004

Typesetting: Nord Compo

Printed in the United States of America
5 4 3 2 1

For Mom and Dad, my first readers

Don't be frightened: you can always change your mind.
I know: I've had four careers and three husbands.

—From Nora Ephron's 1996 commencement speech
at Wellesley College, her alma mater

CONTENTS

Act V: In the End (2000–2012)

AUTHOR'S NOTE
Why Nora Ephron (Still) Matters

ALL ROADS lead to Nora.

I have said this many times over the years as I dug into the life and work of Nora Ephron—first as a graduate student and later as a reporter. When I first came across a quote from Nora's 1996 Wellesley commencement speech—"Don't be frightened. You can always change your mind. I know: I've had four careers and three husbands"—I wondered: how could this fascinating woman have been the same person who wrote both the scathing novel *Heartburn* and the warm and earnest film *Sleepless in Seattle*?

The answer? As her dear friend and longtime collaborator Dianne Dreyer said to me, "She would always surprise you." During the past seven years I spent working on this book, one way or another an inevitable connection to Nora would emerge: an actor or actress she'd worked with early on or who'd sought her advice or counsel, a writer she'd mentored, a book or show she'd adapted or had ultimately inspired. (For some recent examples, see such diverse productions as the hit AppleTV+ show *Ted Lasso*, Hulu's *Only Murders in the Building*, and HBO's *Succession*.)

But one of the most "delicious" things about writing a biography, as Nora might have put it, is that you're still living your own life right alongside the person you're studying, learning about, and writing about. As you change and grow and evolve, so too does your understanding of what that person went through in various stages of her life, and how she must have felt when she faced decisions both small and large as a feminist, filmmaker, foodie, writer, friend, sister, daughter, wife, and mother.

I discovered that new Nora sources, stories, and materials would emerge. Details became clearer—and at the same time, somehow more complicated.

Embrace the mess and the complications, she'd once said, but also, seek out joy in the simplicity of life's greatest treasures: good books, good friends, good food. Most of all, find what makes you happy and give it all you've got.

What she found in husband Nick Pileggi was a real-life love story, and I think she wanted women (and men) to know that true love *is* out there. And it's possible their Sam Baldwin is not a husband but rather beautiful children who warm the house with their stories, music, or jokes, or sisters who fill your soul with memories and speak a language only you understand.

I was naive and perhaps ignorant enough to have the blind ambition necessary to take on a task of this magnitude. I approached it with the love, admiration, and critical eye of what communications scholar Henry Jenkins calls an "aca-fan." And I hope that in doing so, I have captured in the pages of this book a nuanced portrait of a woman who taught us how to live—who reminded us not to take ourselves too seriously, no matter how many punches life may throw at us.

So why does Nora Ephron still matter? Because she gives us hope.

The intelligent, self-described cynic was the one who helped us see that it's never too late to go after your dreams, or to change direction in the pursuit of reinvention: she was thirty-two when she got her first column with *Esquire*, and she was fifty when she became a film director in an industry and an era that often rewarded youth over talent. Drawn to chef Julia Child's work as a young woman, she realized that Child, too, came to be who she was later in life. (Child didn't publish her book or get her first cooking show until she was fifty as well, and Julie Powell, the blogger who made up the other half of the biopic *Julie & Julia*, was thirty when she started blogging about Child.)

As the writer Meg Wolitzer so poignantly explained, Nora's legacy lives on "because in the great rushing loneliness of the world, when a writer's voice makes you feel befriended, you want more of it even after the person is gone."

Nora shared the same anxiety about death we all do: she wanted to have a "good death" as much as she wanted to have a good life. She spoke about her friend having organized a file on the computer labeled EXIT, and how he'd died in his sleep peacefully after living a full life.

She once said that she hoped to die at eighty-four years old, peacefully in her sleep, "after dinner at L'Ami Louis" in Paris. But Nora didn't get that chance, at least not at eighty-four years old—but after living a full life, yes. As much as Nora had shown us how to live, she also showed us how to die.

"One of the things you discover about parents is that you learn things about them after they die," her son Jacob said at a 2019 talk called "All About Nora" at the TCM Festival in Los Angeles. "[Things] that you didn't know about them when they were alive. And that's both sad and . . ."

"And like a gift," actress and friend Rita Wilson added.

Thank you so much for reading *Nora Ephron: A Biography*. It has been the gift of a lifetime to get to write it.

There's a reading guide in the back of the book that should be both fun and useful for book clubs and students alike. I also invite you to visit my website at www.kristinmarguerite.com.

As you rewatch her films, read or reread her essays and articles, and consider her unique point of view, you might find that many, if not all, roads worth taking somehow lead back to Nora.

Nora called on us to make a little trouble on behalf of women; I hope this book will help galvanize us all to be a little braver. And to order more than one dessert.

PROLOGUE

Not An Heiress

IT ALL STARTED with a telephone call between a father and his daughter in 1987.

"Nora?"

"Yes, Dad, hello."

"Nora, did I tell you I finished my memoirs?"

"That's great, Dad."

"I just called Kate Hepburn and I told her the name of my memoirs," he added. "She loved it."

On this particular day, screenwriter Henry Ephron—Nora Ephron's ailing father, who by that time had some forgetfulness—had another, juicier tidbit to add to one of his trademark brief but colorful phone calls: Uncle Hal—the estranged brother of Nora's late mother and a once-left-leaning government official who had caused problems during the days of the House Un-American Activities Committee and the Red Scare in Hollywood—was going to leave her a fortune in his will.

Nora was going to become an heiress. She'd never have to write again.

The twice-divorced newlywed was happily embracing her new career as a screenwriter following the success of famed director Mike Nichols's *Silkwood*, starring Meryl Streep and Cher, which earned Nora and cowriter Alice Arlen an Academy Award nomination for Best Original Screenplay in 1984. (Pulitzer Prize–winning playwright and screenwriter Horton Foote took home the trophy that year for *Tender Mercies*.)

But that didn't make the act of writing any easier when it came down to it. "The hardest thing about writing is writing," she'd once wryly noted. At the time, the recovering journalist and one-time novelist was working on a script called *How They Met*, and later, *Harry, Meet Sally*. But it really wasn't working.

This could be her way out, she thought. This could save her from a life of toiling away at the computer using up hundreds of pages for a single article lede or trying to find the right dialogue for the right moment. No one would ever have to know about Harry, Sally, or the wagon-wheel table, for that matter.

Still, she had no reason to believe any of it was even real until one warm summer day when another phone call revealed Hal was indeed ill, and Nora was listed as his next of kin. "We need you to be prepared to make an end-of-life decision," the voice on the other end of the phone said. Stunned, she called her sister Delia.

"Get ready to be an heiress," Nora told her.

Nora shut off the computer and took a walk around her new East Hampton home. She started to imagine what she might plant and grow with her new-found wealth. Some hydrangeas, perhaps, and a big dogwood tree. Definitely a dogwood, she and her husband, fellow screenwriter Nick Pileggi, agreed.

"In fifteen minutes, did I pass through the first two stages of inherited wealth: Glee and Sloth," she later wrote.

But alas, a real estate misadventure in Puerto Rico had drained much of Hal's estate, and he left half of what was left to his faithful housekeeper, Louise, who had worked for him for forty years. The fortune that was to be Nora's and Delia's simply never came to be.

And so, she was left with the pesky unfinished screenplay:

EXTERIOR. NEW YORK STREET CORNER – DAY
Downtown near Washington Square. The car pulls up and HARRY hops
out, grabbing his stuff. SALLY also walks to the back of the car.

                    HARRY
          Thanks for the ride.

                    SALLY
          Yeah. It was interesting.

                    HARRY
          It was nice knowing you.

                        SALLY
            Yeah.

SALLY nods. Harry nods. An awkward moment.

SALLY holds out her hand. They shake.

                        SALLY
            Well, have a nice life.

                        HARRY
            You too.

Two years later, upon the release of that screenplay's film with its finalized title, *When Harry Met Sally . . .* , Nora earned her second Academy Award nomination for Best Original Screenplay—this time all by herself. The iconic film, directed by Rob Reiner, grossed nearly $93 million worldwide and was placed firmly in the history books as a model that would come to define the romantic comedy genre for years to come.

"We bought a dogwood," she later wrote. "It's really beautiful. It blooms in late June, and it reminds me of my sweet uncle Hal."

Of course, had she become an heiress, would Nora Ephron have *become* Nora Ephron? Perhaps she would have become interested in some other profession (highly unlikely, but still), or taken an altogether different path. Thankfully, instead she would spend the next twenty-five years writing some of the most poignant, hilarious, and unforgettable words of our time.

This is her story.

ACT I

GROWING UP EPHRON (THE EARLY YEARS: 1941–1958)

1 | THE GODDESS

> You're born. You die. Everything in between is up
> for interpretation.
>
> —*Lucky Guy*

IT COULD BE SAID that Nora Ephron never cried.

Born Nora Louise in New York City in May 1941 to playwrights (and later screenwriters) Henry and Phoebe Ephron, she "learned to write in the womb." But a crier she was not. She was fierce and strong and fearless—except, perhaps, when it came to showing vulnerability.

But before there was Nora, there was Phoebe.

Phoebe Ephron was a mysterious, mythical figure even to her own daughters. A child of immigrant parents, Phoebe Wolkind was born on January 16, 1914, in the Bronx. She attended James Monroe High School and Hunter College in New York City, where she majored in English.

Even as a little girl, Phoebe felt she was responsible for the family. She consoled her mother as she cried over her father's infidelity, and later helped her brother, Dickie (Harold), land a job with Walt Disney. As she built a career for herself with Henry in Hollywood in the 1940s, she took care of her parents financially—and kept their bankruptcy secret.

Her own biggest secret? A fear of crying. A fear of losing control. A fear of failure. If she told the story, it could be funny—and not scary. If she controlled the narrative, she could be the hero.

Phoebe instilled in Nora, her eldest daughter, this ethos via her famous credo: "Everything is copy." But she also bequeathed to her a deep love of reading and writing from a young age.

"I remember her teaching me to read when I was three or four, and the almost giddy pleasure that I felt that she had passed this secret art on to me before anyone else in my class knew about it," Nora said.

The first of four girls, she and her sisters really had no choice in the matter; her parents were both successful playwrights and screenwriters who saw the family dinner table as an opportunity for the young girls to learn the art of storytelling and practice their material. Phoebe especially delighted in telling her daughters the story of their first date: "By the end . . . Daddy asked me to marry him. And I said, 'Can I read your work?'"

For Phoebe, words were just as divine as dessert. She was so mesmerized by them, in fact, that she gifted them to her four daughters like heirlooms.

Take good care to use your words wisely, Phoebe Ephron might have said, before adding, *because it's important to remember: everything is copy.*

Of the four girls—who each took that adage to heart in her own unique way—it was her oldest daughter, Nora, who did it most famously, often collaborating with younger sister Delia. The written word became not only a means of financial survival for her after divorce but also a means of processing some of the most painful events of her life.

And what choice did she have? She was literally born into a movie—or at least into a play. Nora Ephron was named after Henrik Ibsen's Nora in *A Doll's House,* the wife who famously eschewed the notion of becoming a mere plaything for her husband. Life for Nora from birth could easily be understood in terms of the extraordinary or imaginary—especially when her own story was borrowed and remixed by her parents in some of their most famous works, such as *Three's a Family* and *Take Her, She's Mine.*

But Phoebe, too, eschewed most anything that seemed traditional or ordinary at the time: most women were home cooking, cleaning, and taking care of the children. Phoebe was not.

"Nora was lovable and quick even as a baby," Henry later wrote in his memoir. "But Phoebe, who had always held interesting jobs, found the long hours of walking the carriage around and sitting on a park bench extremely irksome."

With Nora's early learned resilience came a toughness that often rubbed some people the wrong way and outright alienated others. Her first opportunity for mischief? Baby sister Delia, born in 1944.

By the time Delia arrived, Nora had just turned three years old, and Henry and Phoebe had their first hit play in *Three's a Family: A Comedy in Three Acts*—running in New York, Chicago, and London. Delia's arrival signaled the beginning of a beautiful friendship between sisters. It was also the beginning of a successful second-generation writing partnership that bridged old Hollywood and new—and one that would last their entire lifetimes through illness, divorce, loss of loved ones, movie hits, movie misses, and sisterly disagreements.

One summer, Phoebe asked young Nora to help with a vital task that in many ways changed Nora's life for the better.

"Nora, won't you help the cook with creating the menus?"

Ever the high achiever, Nora wasn't about to let this opportunity sneak by without mastering the craft of cooking. "It was a great way to learn," she said later.

But in her own way, Phoebe was teaching Nora about resilience too. The confusion and everyday tragedy of alcoholic but once-brilliant parents, of the cheating but once-loving husband, of the weakening but once-vibrant body—it could all somehow be overcome if "butter" is your religion. When almost nothing can be counted on to stay the same, a twirl of the spoon and a flip of the page could, at least temporarily, make it seem like everything would be all right.

"What I love about cooking," Nora writes in *Heartburn*, "is that after a hard day, there is something comforting about the fact that if you melt butter and then add flour and then hot stock, *it will get thick!*"

These were Phoebe's greatest gifts, perhaps, that Nora carried on to share not just with her own friends and family but with readers and filmgoers the world over: a love of language and literature, and of vibrant conversation around a dinner table.

Food—one of Nora's longest-running love affairs—was one of her favorite ways to bring people together. It's fitting that the culinary-flavored biopic *Julie & Julia*, released in 2009, was her last film. It has a warm, maternal instinct to it that is so charmingly Nora, and it embodies the way her words can travel through time to bring new meanings for each generation.

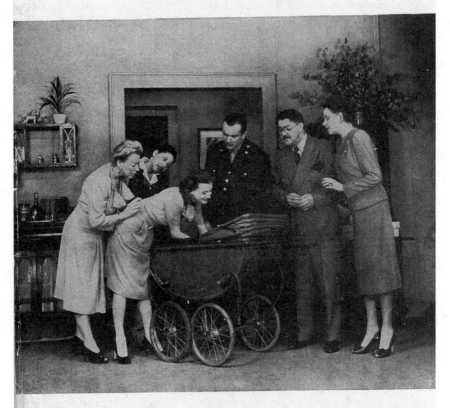

3 IS A FAMILY

THE PLAYBILL

FOR THE LONGACRE THEATRE

Nora's "theater debut": her birth inspired her parents' play *Three's a Family*, which premiered on Broadway at the Longacre Theatre in New York on May 5, 1943. *Playbill Inc. / author's collection*

LONGACRE THEATRE

SELECT OPERATING CORPORATION

THE · PLAYBILL · A · WEEKLY · PUBLICATION · OF · PLAYBILL · INCORPORATED

Week beginning Sunday, December 12, 1943   •   Matinees Saturday and Sunday

JOHN GOLDEN

presents

(IN ASSOCIATION WITH JOHN POLLOCK AND MAX SIEGEL)

"3 IS A FAMILY"

A Farce Comedy

By PHOEBE and HENRY EPHRON

Staged by MR. EPHRON

Setting by STEWART CHANEY

CAST

(In the order of their appearance)

SAM WHITAKER .... ROBERT BURTON

IRMA DALRYMPLE .... ETHEL OWEN

ADELAIDE .... EDITH GRESHAM

The inside of the original playbill for *Three's a Family* that shows Phoebe listed first (as she requested) alongside Henry (who directed). *Playbill Inc. / author's collection*

"It is about the passion of the supposedly passionless middle-aged man and woman, love arriving not late, but right on time," Richard Cohen writes in *She Made Me Laugh: My Friend Nora Ephron*. "It is about Paris. It is about writing and it is, in all those themes, about the life Nora made for herself with Nick."

Of course, it's also about Phoebe. It was one of Nora's last opportunities to reconcile the important but complicated relationship she had with her mother, notes film scholar Liz Dance, and also a chance to rewrite it. Indeed, a commitment to revision—*and* contradiction—was perhaps what connected them the most.

"She is her mother's daughter," Dance writes. "Her art is the space she uses to record and consider her life and the world around her. It is where she tells the stories of her life."

Many of those stories ultimately have become the stories of our own lives, transcending time and place. Today, the greatest gift Nora left for *us* is the freedom to choose our own destiny, and to realize we have personal agency in creating or even recreating our own narrative, thus shape-shifting and reinventing ourselves in the process.

"Above all, be the heroine of your life," she once said.

With the resilience of an auteur like Nora, whatever the tragedy is, you can get through it with your wit and intelligence. You can write your way out of any problem. You can even make it funny. These are the gifts of Phoebe.

But as it turned out, Phoebe's own story was just as complex as the heroines of her favorite Jane Austen novels or the real-life women who would later figure into some of Nora's most acclaimed films, such as *Silkwood* and *When Harry Met Sally* . . . So who was Phoebe, really?

"What was the truth?" Nora asked herself.

It was a question she asked time and time again as a journalist and essayist driving the New Journalism wave of the 1960s and '70s, and one she grappled with throughout her film and theater career as well. The notion that one story could have a number of layers, heroes, and versions was one that intrigued her, and one that gave her great creative freedom to mix the real with the imaginary in entirely new and interesting ways.

But when it came to Phoebe, the truth mattered. Because, Nora wrote, "I was invested in the original narrative; I was a true believer. My mother was a goddess. But my mother was an alcoholic."

2 | THE CAMP YEARS

> What I think she gave us, most of all, was the sense that we could do anything, anything at all, that anything was possible. Being women had nothing to do with it, just as it had had nothing to do with it for her. That is a remarkable thing to pass on to daughters.
>
> —Nora Ephron, eulogy for Phoebe Ephron,
> October 13, 1971

IT WAS MAY 26, 1950: Nora's ninth birthday. Her thick brown hair and short bangs framed her big brown eyes and sweet-but-slightly-mischievous smile. Her lilac-colored dress was offset by a lemon-yellow cardigan, and a pair of black Mary Jane shoes and white socks. In the big grassy backyard at the house on North Linden Drive, she's proudly carrying a new toy lawn mower as the family movie camera rolls. At nine, Nora had become the big sister—a.k.a. the big boss—of not only Delia but two-year-old Hallie Elizabeth as well. (Over her lifetime, Nora's trademark bossiness became legendary. As high school classmate and future media magnate Barry Diller recalled later, "Nora has always been Nora.")

Each morning, Henry and Phoebe would take separate cars to the Twentieth Century Fox lot for work, which was a total of some three and a half miles from their Beverly Hills home. Phoebe would speed off in her chic, newly redesigned 1947 Studebaker, and later, in her smooth, luxurious new 1955 Ford Thunderbird. It was as if Phoebe was "out of a Tracy-Hepburn movie," Nora told the author Rachel Abramowitz in 1993. "She had an offbeat, tomboy great look."

As contract writers at Fox, Henry and Phoebe "wrote one movie after another," Nora said, "and what they wrote got made."

It seemed like a Hollywood dream come true for almost anyone—but not to Nora. Just four years earlier, when the family had moved to Los Angeles, "everything had gone downhill as a result," she would say later of the traumatic event in which she was "ripped" away from her beloved New York. "I had been in a place that I knew was welcoming and safe for smart women, and I had a very clear sense that Hollywood was not that place."

That sense, she said, came from what she perceived as her mother's alienation from her own community, a sentiment shared by Delia too.

"The thing that really breaks my heart about my mother was that she had no close girlfriends," Delia remembered. "The phone simply never rang for her. And I think the cost of this, both the person she created—this very confident working woman—as well as the other side—the dark, self-destructive side— she was keeping herself apart from them as a successful woman, and she was keeping herself apart from them as a woman who wasn't in any way together. So she was isolated, I think; deeply isolated." It was rare, if at all, that Phoebe showed her true, vulnerable self to anyone.

Still, there were moments of great joy as the young Ephron daughters grew up. Eventually, there were four, and the littlest one, Amy, was named for her literary counterpart in *Little Women* when she arrived in 1952. If Nora's religion was "butter," Phoebe's was decorum at the nightly dinner table. A certain schedule and elegance was maintained each and every day: Phoebe and Henry would arrive home at four thirty, and while they sipped cocktails in the den, the children would join them for crudités. Dinner would follow promptly at six thirty—prepared by the family cook—and by seven fifteen, they'd be on to the next of their evening activities: playing charades, reading poetry, perhaps, or singing rounds. (Nora later invited esteemed guests to participate in running charades, a more fast-paced version of the game, and enjoyed challenging her son Max to a game of Scrabble.)

"It was all very civilized, though," Nora remembered. "Very, very civilized, and very sweet, and we all had fun."

As for her younger sisters, they remembered the dinner hour a bit differently.

"The competition for airtime was Darwinian," Hallie recalled. "My instinct was to step back from the fray—I didn't have the stomach to fight to be heard."

In August, Nora and Delia headed to Camp Tocaloma in Flagstaff, Arizona, for the first time. As she remembered it, Nora eventually attended camp "every single summer for about 300 years," and it was another chance to try out her jokes on a new audience, to explore, and to gain more confidence. For Delia, it felt like she was being sent away.

As the sisters arrived at Union Station in downtown Los Angeles with their trunks in tow, they hugged their parents goodbye for the last time before a month's worth of bonding and skill building in the great outdoors.

"Don't forget to write home," Phoebe said.

"And remember to call—but only with important news or good stories," Henry added.

With that, they were off. Their fearless leader was Gertrude Dietz, a decorated WWII US Air Force veteran. She'd come door-to-door with her slides-and-carousel presentation to show parents in Beverly Hills and other areas around L.A. about the new camp experience she was creating.

"The ethos of this camp was a happy, healthy atmosphere," fellow camper and second-generation Hollywood writer Victoria Riskin told me. "It was a fantastic experience."

Gertrude recommended "cheerful" letters from home "at least twice a week," and asked parents not to send more than five dollars of spending money. Once they arrived in Arizona, the girls climbed into a big, open truck and rode across the dirt into camp. No, this was not exactly glamping. But the property that housed Camp Tocaloma was stunning nonetheless. There were open meadows surrounded by big trees, and a feeling of being out in the middle of nowhere, away from the city lights and hustle and bustle—and all the worries that went along with it.

But when Nora first arrived at Camp Tocaloma, she quickly learned she wasn't special. All the girls were meant to feel equal, and in the trenches of the great outdoors, they truly were. Modeled after the army, summer camps like Camp Tocaloma came into vogue after World War II when parents worried that their suburban children had lost connection with nature. Each summer, about one hundred girls between the ages of eight and eighteen participated in activities like horseback riding, swimming, archery, riflery, canoeing. There were hikes, crafts, and baseball games. Through local field trips to nearby villages, Gertrude encouraged the campers to appreciate and learn not only about the great outdoors but also about Native culture from the local Navajo, Hopi, Havasupai, Kaibab-Paiute, and Hualapai people by visiting and spending time with them.

CAMP TOCALOMA
Foxboro, Arizona

Home Address 10784 Santa Monica Blvd. Los Angeles 25, Calif.

L. A. Phones GRanite 9-6955   GRanite 8-1271

July 23, 1959

Dear Parents:

With camp just a few weeks away, we have a few suggestions to make, that we feel will prove beneficial to your daughter as well as the camp.

1--We ask you not to visit during the four weeks. The risk of exposure to colds and other communicable diseases will be lessened by the exclusion of all outsiders. Let's be fair to all of the campers.

2--Write cheerful letters at least twice a week, and don't worry if you should receive a homesick letter the first few days. If you don't hear often enough, it's probably because she's having an especially good time.

3--Send three or four good books plus games--please help us stamp out comic books. Do not send edibles.

4--Be sure and send high rubber boots, rain coat and hat.

5--We request $5.00 spending money per camper. Please do not give your daughter over that amount. This should be turned into camp office the day the luggage is delivered to club-house.

6--Stamps and stationery should be sent with each camper.

As a final reminder: The campers from the Los Angeles area will leave August 7th. Please have your daughter at the clubhouse, 10784 Santa Monica Blvd. by 11:30 A.M. We request the parents drive to the front gate, where a counselor will meet the girls. Please say your goodbyes at the gate. Campers should have had lunch at home. For this group, luggage should be brought to the clubhouse on Saturday, August 1st until 5:00 P.M., or Sunday, August 2nd during day until 4:00 P.M.

Campers outside of the Los Angeles area but living in towns on Santa Fe's route will receive complete information concerning luggage, tickets and arrival time of train from Mr. Ralph Fell, Santa Fe representative.

We're looking forward to a wonderful four weeks camp, and we are happy to have your daughter with us.

Sincerely yours,

Gertrude Dietz

Gertrude Dietz--Director

The new camp telephone number is ATwater 2-3329 -- through Sedona, Arizona. Please note change in arrival at clubhouse, 11:30 A.M.

Letter home to parents from Gertrude Dietz. *Courtesy of Audrey Lord-Hausman*

"One of the most wonderful things about camp was evening campfire," Audrey Lord-Hausman told me. "Out where that picture of Nora and Karen ('Pokey') were in that field is where the campfire was. We sat on logs by tribe. We would sing and sing."

One evening, Riskin recalls getting to sit next to Nora. "She was always a natural leader," she told me. "She was funny and talented, and we just loved her."

Still, the camp experience was fraught with some of the challenges that inevitably come up when a group of girls get together and stay together for a month straight. This was especially true for those who were coping with the realization that as bad as things might get at camp, it was still better than going back home.

"There are ups and downs, and there are rivalries—misunderstandings and all kinds of luggage that kids brought—emotional luggage," fellow camper Nancy Krim told me. "And a lot of that was from kids whose parents were too busy to really listen to them. They found the listening at camp."

Junior counselors Nora and Karen "Pokey" Hokenson pose on the field as they play a team sport around 1957. *Courtesy of Audrey Lord-Hausman*

The Main Lodge at Camp Tocaloma where the campers had all their meals and where the stage and talent shows were held. *Courtesy of Audrey Lord-Hausman*

Among some of the other famous campers over the years was Liza Minnelli, the impressionable daughter of the talented but troubled screen legend Judy Garland. Even as a young girl, she had an air of sophistication, much like Nora.

"Liza was a great example of someone who was starved for attention," Krim added. "She was going back and forth between New York and L.A."

Other famous campers, such as actor Burt Lancaster's daughters, Susan and Joanna, and later, Victoria Sellers, daughter of actors Britt Ekland and Peter Sellers, also arrived at Camp Tocaloma feeling a bit lost and unsure of why they'd been left to essentially fend for themselves for the summer.

"Gertrude was aware of that, and she was very clear with the families and monitored it with letters coming in," Audrey Lord-Hausman recalled. "She was watching out for the kids in so many different ways."

But even for those who came from troubled, or at least unconventional households (i.e., with parents in "The Business" of Hollywood) like Nora's, camp could be a place of solace and adventure. Talent night was when Nora and her better half, Marcia Levant, really got to shine.

"With Nora and Marcia, they were really a duo," Lord-Hausman told me. "Their getting dressed up and creating words to Broadway songs and singing and dancing was an amazing thrill. Most of us didn't have a clue who their parents were."

Marcia and her famous father, the multitalented actor and musician Oscar Levant—whose schtick of neurosis and mournfulness informed his witty one-liners—had a significant influence on young Nora as she developed her own comedic voice. As the girls gathered around the campfire, Nora and Marcia would lead the group in song—but not just any old campfire song. They'd cleverly rewritten the lyrics to favorite Broadway tunes (some of which have controversial or offensive origins) to be about specific, comedic observations of happenings at camp:

> Happy talk, keep talking happy talk
> Talk about things we like to do
> Going down red rock slides,
> Damaging our hides,
> As the rushing water passes by,
> Come to Tocaloma,
> Where we're never blue,
> And where all your dreams will soon come true
>   —After Richard Rodgers and Oscar Hammerstein
>   II's "Happy Talk" from *South Pacific*

At night, they'd cozy up in their sleeping bags in small cabins—some of them doing so for perhaps the first time. And that left them feeling homesick.

"Don't worry if you should receive a homesick letter the first few days," Gertrude had warned parents in a letter home before camp started. "If you don't hear often enough, it's probably because she's having an especially good time."

Ten-year-old Nora was beginning what would become a saving grace from more than just homesickness later in life—though it could be argued that a sense of homesickness lingers for children of alcoholic parents forever. But writing letters home to Phoebe meant she'd receive one back. And in the process, she was becoming a writer—a real writer with her own voice.

"What kind of letters?" her youngest sister Amy asked her later on. "Were they personal letters?"

No, not exactly. But then again, nothing with Phoebe was really that personal—or at least not too sentimental—when it came to her daughters.

"[My mother] wrote the most fantastic letters," Nora explained in her eulogy for Phoebe in 1971. "My friends—first at camp, then at college—would laugh and listen, utterly rapt at the sophistication of it all." But Nora was rapt, too. It was in sending and receiving those letters at camp that she began to gain confidence in her writing and a lifelong connection to her mother and her mother's work.

"Nora had that edge and sarcasm that's evident in her essays," Krim remembered.

Decades later, in a piece written for the *Huffington Post* in 2006, two sentences appeared that one might not have ever thought would come from the pen of Nora Ephron, the sophisticated Manhattanite: "I would just like to say that I have fired a shotgun. What's more, I used to teach riflery at Camp Tocaloma."

Now we know the backstory.

As Nora grew older and became a junior counselor herself, she was asked to help with another unusual task: secretly unsealing some of those letters home before they made it to the mailbox. Even when she was a teenager, her instincts told her this was an inappropriate invasion of privacy—and she wouldn't stand for it. As she remembered it, she was given a teakettle and a hot plate in order to steam open letters home from new campers. (The skill came in handy later when she'd steam open a certain unfaithful spouse's credit card bills.)

From 1957 when Nancy was a camper
and Nora (left) was her junior counselor.
Courtesy of Nancy Cohen Krim

"Nora was furious," her camp pal Audrey remembered. "She did not like that, but I do understand why Gertrude did it. Nora just did not think it was the right thing to do."

Nora did, however, appreciate Gertrude for who she was: a strong, adventuresome female mentor who more than anything else wanted the young women to learn how to be kind and fair. The counselors and junior counselors were older and wiser, and therefore could help the younger and less experienced campers feel comfortable. During the burgeoning women's movement across the nation, that kind of cooperative spirit was more than just a mission statement; it was a key to survival.

In the late 1990s, Nora was scheduled to speak in San Francisco as part of a series of distinguished women talking about those critical years of progress for women. Audrey and a fellow Camp Tocaloma alumna decided to purchase tickets to hear their old friend speak.

Soon thereafter, she was interviewed on a radio show in the city, and they stayed afterward while Nora signed books for a long line of fans. Not wanting to interrupt, the women decided to slip her a note:

"Hi Nora, loved being here tonight and hearing you talk. Signed, the Tocaloma girls"

They folded it up and placed it on the table behind her—and waited.

"She opened it, turned around, stood up, left all these people standing there and came over with a big smile on her face and gave us a hug," Audrey told me. "We chatted briefly and then she went back. It was really touching. Deep down, that tells you who she was."

A decade or so later, as Nora prepared for the release of what would be her last film, *Julie & Julia*, she received an e-mail. It was from Audrey: one of her dearest friends from childhood, Anita, was dying from lung cancer, and she'd had the crazy idea that if she somehow got in touch with Nora, she might be willing to make arrangements for Anita to see the film at home. On a whim, Audrey thought she might just give her old camp friend a call. Perhaps she'd remember her, and perhaps she'd be willing to help.

"I looked up Nora's New York office and I e-mailed her," Audrey said. "I told her about my friend and how much she loved Julia Child, and would it be an imposition to ask to have the film sent because I was going down to visit her, and then I would send it right back."

Nora replied right away. "Absolutely," she wrote. "Please call J.J. and give him the address and dates . . . xx, Nora."

The next day, the disc showed up in the mail. "My friend Anita was just stunned and was so excited," Audrey said. "She and her daughter got their Julia Child cookbook out and made a whole picnic and we watched the movie. . . . I've just been forever indebted to Nora for her warmth and kindness."

For Audrey, it was a wonderful reminder of what the whole camp experience had been about: even after all those years, the friendship and the memories mattered—and the love for one another endured.

3 | BEVERLY HILLS HIGH

IT WAS DURING THEIR FIRST DAYS of working in Hollywood that Phoebe and Henry Ephron got the call.

"Mr. Lubitsch wants to see you," the voice on the phone said. "He has a story he wants you to read."

The legendary, charming German writer-director Ernst Lubitsch had taken an interest in the young writers. He thought they could help translate a book called *All-Out Arlene* into a screenplay. There was just one problem: the pair of playwrights didn't exactly know how to write for the screen yet.

But it didn't matter. Ernst, as he liked the Ephrons to call him, was a gentleman and, by all accounts, a genius. Leland Hayward, their venerable bicoastal agent, had set them up with a place to stay and even let the young family borrow his car until they were settled. Hayward's other clients at the time included Fred Astaire, Greta Garbo, James Stewart, Katharine Hepburn, and Judy Garland, among hundreds of other stars—several of whom ended up starring in Ephron-scripted films over the years.

"Read the book and think about the central situation," Lubitsch said. "An engaged couple are in the Army. She is a lieutenant and he is a private. Their love affair has been interrupted by the war. The rest is up to us."

Ten years earlier, the Ephrons had begun their own love affair that was interrupted by war—not to mention the challenges that come with balancing increasingly demanding work, family, and the occasional accusation of being Communist sympathizers.

But that all came later. For now, the Ephrons were just two bright, young dreamers with no idea that they'd one day find their place in the movies. One night in 1933, as Henry tells it, he was invited by his then-girlfriend to go to a party given by a girl named Phoebe Wolkind. At the time, Phoebe was dating a minor league baseball player for the Jersey City Giants—but she was looking for someone smart.

"I don't know at what moment in the evening I fell in love," Henry later recalled in his memoir, *We Thought We Could Do Anything*. To him, the beautiful dark-haired Phoebe looked like a movie star, like Katharine Hepburn—and they made a date for the very next night.

Henry, who'd been working days at his father's rug store, was a playwright by night after dropping out of Cornell University, while Phoebe, who'd been an English major at the top of her class at Hunter College, was busy helping her father at his dress shop.

A year later, they were married in Kingston, New York, near the summer camp where they'd both been counselors. Soon after that, they began writing and working together—Phoebe would be at the typewriter, and Henry would pace around the room as the pair talked through scenes and dialogue. Even during off hours, they'd spend hours talking and thinking about ideas for a play. He'd lie around reading James Joyce, while Phoebe preferred Jane Austen.

After seven years of marriage, their best idea arrived in the form of a new baby. Just over six months before the attack on Pearl Harbor on December 7, 1941, Phoebe went into labor with her first child—a girl, to be named Nora. It was a difficult labor, lasting for twenty hours. When Nora was finally born, Henry took one look at her and fell in love.

By the age of two, Nora had already provided much of the inspiration for her parents' first big hit play on Broadway, *Three's a Family*. It was written about the real-life situation that Phoebe's favorite aunt had found herself in: she was the dentist at Lord & Taylor while her husband stayed home and took care of the family. "It was truly an upside down household," Henry later remarked.

One night, the First Lady herself came to a performance. As Eleanor Roosevelt, in all her glory, walked down the theater aisle in a long Eleanor Blue gown while the audience cheered, Phoebe wept. The show ran for 495 performances and played for a year and a half in London. It also inspired a 1944 film of the same name.

Meanwhile, as thriving young parents and busy screenwriters, Phoebe and Henry were hopelessly devoted to two things: narrative and comedy. Later in life, they each became devoted to decidedly separate things: for her, the drink, and for him, the drink—and other women. It's important to understand these two ideas side by side because the earlier Ephron ideals informed the later Ephron denial.

They'd hired a nanny for the children, and Phoebe would go to the bookstore on La Cienega to pick up books for them. After work, she'd read her favorite books to Nora, Delia, Hallie, and Amy over and over—*Little Women*, the *Spanish Fairy Tales*, the Oz books, *A Little Princess*, *The Secret Garden*— not unlike the ones shown some fifty years later in *You've Got Mail*, the elder sisters' update of Lubitsch's *Shop Around the Corner*. Henry would take the girls everywhere with him. He considered them some of the smartest and funniest people he knew—and greatly enjoyed their company.

In the evenings, they'd discuss politics and how the New Deal had saved the country—fostering, for Nora, "a lifelong love of the Democratic Party." And while Henry and Phoebe had the occasional disagreement—and there were apparently some that ended up with dishes being broken—life was good. They were living their dream in Hollywood.

Three years before Nora's arrival, Senator Joseph McCarthy's House Un-American Activities Committee (HUAC) was formed and began actively summoning any and all potential Communist sympathizers to testify in Washington and Los Angeles. By 1944, a conservative group of Hollywood leaders formed the Motion Picture Alliance for the Preservation of American Ideals. The group decried "communist sympathy among members of the film industry" and called for a congressional investigation.

By 1947, when the HUAC hearings were being held, the Ephrons had settled into their new, grand 1920s Spanish-style home at 703 North Linden Drive in the flats of Beverly Hills. The home boasted five bedrooms and more than 6,800 square feet of living space on a lot covering nearly one-third of an acre—plenty of room for the growing Ephron family—and ample space for parties in the evening, where the girls could sneak out and peek over the balcony in their pajamas to see Hollywood stars as they drank, danced, and sang the night away at the living room piano.

The Ephrons were active in their local labor union, the Writers Guild (then known as the Screen Writers Guild), and had supported Norman Thomas, the Socialist Party of America's candidate for president. They'd never gone further left than socialism, Nora later wrote, but the era of "naming names" was frightening all the same.

One day, Nora's parents were called into the office of Spyros Skouras, the pioneering Greek American who ran Twentieth Century Fox for four decades. In his hand was a piece of paper about Phoebe's brother, Hal, and his potentially questionable political affiliation.

"Phoebe, vy you a Communist?" Skouras asked, to which Phoebe replied that she was not, and, as Nora later wrote, "that was pretty much the end of it."

Still, many of the Ephrons' friends were called on to testify. Some became what would be known as "friendly witnesses" as they complied with the request, while other accused writers and directors became "unfriendly witnesses" when they refused to testify—ten of whom became known as the "Hollywood Ten." Cited for "contempt of Congress," they were fined and sent to jail for a year. More painfully, industry executives issued the Waldorf Statement, censuring the Ten and blacklisting or graylisting them for the rest of their careers. For many, including Dalton Trumbo (*Roman Holiday*), their screenwriting credits weren't restored until fifty years later, in 1997.

In 1956, Republican president Dwight Eisenhower was reelected by a landslide, and most of White middle-class America was settling into an era of prosperity. But for the Ephrons, it was anything but business as usual at Fox. HUAC had destroyed what was left of the golden era of Hollywood's studio system, and American households were changing too: the suburban living room television set had become a hot commodity, drawing audiences away from the once-bustling city centers where movie palaces had brought people together for big movie spectacles, like some of the films the Ephrons helped create.

Still, the Ephron household was changing in such a shocking and painful way that Nora and Delia were ready for almost any chance to get away—and camp provided a welcome outlet. Nora was fourteen years old and Delia was eleven when Phoebe's after-work scotch turned into a regular routine of all-night rage, and Henry's philandering became more apparent and harder for Phoebe to ignore. Secretly, the girls grew scared and worried.

The feature film screenwriting work was drying up, and the Ephrons were becoming more drunk more often. As Nora and Delia grew older and went to school, Phoebe's more positive influence was felt in the choices they made in choosing which subjects to study (Latin and French, and ideally, no science) and where to go to college (anywhere without sororities). The girls were to go to New York one day and become writers. And that was all there was to it, no matter that it was the era of the career housewife.

"She had contempt for women who didn't work," Nora later recalled. "There was none of that stuff which is fashionable now which is to pretend to respect any choice that people make. My mother did not respect the choices that most women had made. We all grew up knowing that she expected us to work, and, of course, there was no sense in our house that [that] excluded getting married and having children. She had done that too."

The influence of Phoebe's own mother, Kate, was also strong. In fact, as Henry points out in his memoir, she was the one responsible for Phoebe's— and therefore Nora's—clever wit. Kate ("Katie") and her husband, Louis (from whom Nora received her middle name, Louise), moved in with the young couple after Louis's heart attack prevented him from continuing to work. Phoebe taught her mother, a Russian immigrant, how to read and write in English, and looked after her parents for the rest of their lives. In fact, she'd been taking care of her family since she was a little girl. She essentially raised her little brother, Harold ("Dickie"), from the time he was a baby, and she was the one who comforted her mother when she was distraught over Phoebe's father's infidelities.

"Mother, *why* won't you divorce him?" she'd beg of her.

"I can't," Kate would reply. "I love him too deeply, and besides, who else would want to marry me?"

By the mid-1950s, America was changing, and so was Hollywood. And that spelled trouble for many of those who had been a part of the old studio system regime. In fact, it was in 1955 that Marilyn Monroe became the first woman since Mary Pickford to start her own production company. She challenged the Ephrons' studio, Twentieth Century Fox, to meet her demands—and won.

"At a time when the studios wielded absolute power, this was revolutionary," journalist Elizabeth Winder later wrote. "Monroe hadn't just won her autonomy—she'd made history."

As for Nora, the most important thing on her teenage mind was getting her first bra—and real menstrual cramps so she could stop faking them. She'd skipped a grade by then, and was always a bit more petite than the other girls in her class. For all her intellectual maturity and athletic prowess, she'd failed to produce the one thing she wanted: breasts.

One night, she climbed into bed with Phoebe, who was reading.

"Mother, I want to buy a bra," Nora said.

"What for?" Phoebe replied.

"Because I am too *old* for an undershirt!"

"Then don't wear one."

There was screaming. There was shouting. There was weeping. Then, in an act that would surprise no one, Nora resolved to go down to the glamorous Robinson's department store in Beverly Hills to purchase her first bra by herself. The newly built shopping palace was covered in head-to-toe white marble and offered nearly a quarter million square feet of fine items, such as luggage, furs, and stationery.

But Nora was on a mission.

"Lean over," the saleswoman said once Nora got inside the fitting room. She hoped that miraculously, she would be somehow able to fill in the pockets of the 28 AA bra. But alas, no dice.

When she got her period for the first time, her mother burst into tears. Nora had seen her cry only maybe two times in her whole life. It was Henry who'd get weepy over his daughters most often. But for Phoebe, it was a rare moment of true vulnerability: her oldest daughter was becoming a woman, and she'd have to one day go out and make her own mistakes in life and love. Worst of all, she might get hurt.

But Nora knew the rules well by now: it's all copy. When something bad happens to you, write it funny—or at least make it into a good story. "Slip on a banana peel, and people will laugh at you," she once explained of her mother's famous axiom, "but tell people you slipped on the banana peel, and you become the hero, rather than the victim, of the joke."

She described the whole experience of first-bra-buying agony in hilarious, poignant detail in what would become a seminal piece of New Journalism, "A

Few Words About Breasts," published in *Esquire* in May 1972. From her first confession of faking cramps to fearing that she might never find a husband (indeed, she ended up finding three), now it was Nora who was showing how fearless she was in her vulnerability during what she recognized was a traumatic experience for almost every young girl. She also realized the moment was symbolic of the way gender norms and expectations permeated culture over the years.

Other classmates in high school and college recalled how self-conscious she could be about her appearance, especially her bustline. She did worry others might notice her slightly closed left eye, which was still not fully repaired from being injured at birth. (She and Delia had both gone for surgery as little girls at Children's Hospital Los Angeles.)

"There wasn't a whole lot that was feminine about Nora," her Beverly Hills High School classmate Barry Diller recalled. But it didn't matter. Nora had lots of dates—and she was at the top of her class. She was voted "most likely to succeed" alongside her classmate Steve Pauley. She was a member of "Girls' League," the purpose of which was to "foster friendship and spirit among the girls at Beverly," according to the yearbook description. She was also an active member of student council and was voted the "biggest politician." And in the summertime, she'd become a junior counselor at Camp Tocaloma. Her future in leadership was clear.

In her yearbook photo, she sports a large toothy smile and a short haircut. On the outside, Nora was confident and energetic. On the inside, though, it would be hard not to feel at least a *little* insecure. "I don't think Mom ever said to any of us, you know, 'you're so beautiful' . . . 'you're adorable'—any of that," Delia later explained. "I think if your mom never tells you that, how would you ever know it?"

By 1958, Nora would graduate first in her class from Beverly Hills High, and she had earned the highest academic honors a graduating senior can receive, as a member of Ephibians, Alphas, and the California Scholarship Federation as well as Lektos in English, which stood for the "epitome of success in one field." In the spring semester of her senior year, she was the coeditor of *Highlights*, the school newspaper, from which Diller said she once fired him.

One night after a date, Nora knocked on her mother's bedroom door. "There she was, reading *The Wizard of Oz*," Nora remembered. She climbed in bed once again, and nervously asked her mother about sex.

"Mother, could I please have some advice?" Nora asked.

"Nora, you're sixteen-years-old," Phoebe replied. "If I haven't raised you to make your own decisions, it won't do me any good to tell you what I think."

ACT II

THE WELLESLEY YEARS (1958–1962) & NEW JOURNALISM (1962–MID-1970s)

4 | TAKE HER, SHE'S MINE (NORA AT WELLESLEY)

However many roads you travel, I hope that you choose not to be a lady. I hope you will find some way to break the rules and make a little trouble out there.
—Nora Ephron at Wellesley in 1996

ON A WARM DAY in the summer of 1958, a petite, dark-haired girl stepped up to the dorm sign-out sheet and neatly wrote "Ephron" in cursive.

"Are you any relation to Phoebe Ephron?" one of the other young women nervously asked.

"Yes, indeed, I am," Nora replied.

She was flattered—and a friendship burst into bloom on the spot. Having skipped a grade, Nora was one of only a few other young women—or "girls" as they were called back then—who was a full year younger than everyone else starting their college careers at Wellesley.

"Wellesley was one of the best places you could go to and most of the very bright women in the United States went to Wellesley, or Radcliffe, or Stanford," Nora explained later. "It was an unbelievably bland time in America. It was the end of the '50s, the happy homemaker—Betty Friedan was about to publish *The Feminine Mystique* [in 1963], and the women's movement was about to begin as well as quite a few other social movements in the '60s. It was about to really break free, but we didn't know that in 1958."

Still, getting to study with other smart women meant exposure to new perspectives on the important issues of the day, and she got to cover many of them as a writer and editor at the *Wellesley News*.

For Nora, freshman year was full of exciting opportunities and a few unexpected surprises. After falling in love with the school's beautiful campus during a slide show presentation in high school, she knew she was finally on her way to starting a life as a writer. Ever since her mother had given her the anthology *A Treasury of Great Reporting* for Christmas, ever since being exposed to fictional women journalists Lois Lane and Brenda Starr and attending vocational day in high school, Nora knew she wanted to be a reporter. She came to Wellesley with ideas about what she wanted to write (journalism, film, stage plays, and fiction)—and a strong point of view.

In fact, back home, she'd already grown up quite a bit more than some of her new classmates. Her first job was at a bookstore when she was fourteen, and she'd also picked up a job calling in the scores from girls' basketball games and published stories under the byline N. Ephron at the *Los Angeles Times*.

At the time, Phoebe and Henry were eager to build on the success of their 1955 French-themed musical film *Daddy Long Legs*, which starred Fred Astaire and Leslie Caron in the lead roles. Henry wanted to do more. He asked Darryl Zanuck if he and Phoebe could produce in addition to writing their next film.

But Zanuck had other plans. He thought it would be best if Phoebe stuck to writing while Henry produced on his own in a decision that would mark a sort of beginning of the end for the writing team. Ironically, Zanuck claimed he was trying to save the relationship by keeping the pair apart.

Every so often, Phoebe would mention how she longed to return to New York. "The kids are growing up, and soon there won't be two cars in the driveway, there will be four," she once told Henry over a 2:00 AM nightcap. "I know I should be grateful, but it isn't quite how I planned my life."

She'd grown restless—and as the drinking worsened, she'd begun to lose her hearing.

———

Nora was adjusting to living in the dormitory on campus and away from her parents for the first time as Phoebe's play *Howie* was premiering that September at the 46th Street Theatre in New York. The original comedy about a jobless man who drives his family crazy—and ultimately ends up on a game show, where hilarity ensues—ended up running for only five performances despite receiving big laughs from audiences, some strong reviews, and a write-up in the Sunday *New York Times*. Phoebe was crushed when it closed so swiftly.

Meanwhile, even though Nora had found a roommate and a few friends who were just as bright as she was—she found that living in Navy, the barracks-style dorm on the edge of campus, wasn't ideal. She and several classmates were also displeased that they failed to get an exemption from freshman English— something they complained about constantly.

Having left home at a slight 106 pounds, Nora returned twenty pounds happier (as many college freshmen do) on account of the delicious sticky buns, scones, and other baked goods at the dorm cafeteria. And there was a milk machine that, according to Nora, dispensed the "coldest, most delicious milk you've ever tasted." It was glorious. When her parents came to pick her up, her father took one look at her and joked to her mother, "Well, maybe someone will marry her for her personality."

But her mind wasn't on marriage—at least not yet. Nora was determined to make herself a success. She returned to campus with a renewed spirit and eagerness to learn. Sophomore year, she moved into the six-story baronial Tower Court dormitory, which stood high above all the other buildings on campus. She made lifelong friends in classmates Louise Connell Mills, Melissa Travis Mohlman, and Carol Tropp Schreiber. Nora and her roommate Jennifer Carden (later Rogers) lived across the hall from another lifelong friend, Susie Levine Dworkin, who shared a triple dorm with Kathy Taylor and Nancy Greenamyre. Also on the hall was their classmate Brent Goo.

If skits were being written or if there was a gathering, Susie, the future fellow *New York Times* bestselling novelist and playwright, was dazzling everyone right alongside Nora, though they each had their own unique talents and viewpoints.

Nora was passionate about the political issues of the day. A young Democratic senator from Boston, John Fitzgerald Kennedy, was elected to be president of the United States in a closely contested election on November 8, 1960. At forty-three years old, he was the youngest president ever to be elected, and his idealism, accessibility, and bold interest in human rights were, to many, a sign of a new beginning for the nation—and most especially, a new beginning for the nation's youth. (The cover of the *Wellesley News* that week, however, showed support for Kennedy's opponent: WELLESLEY ELECTS DICK NIXON, the headline read.)

Nora could be found picketing with her classmates in front of the local store, Woolworth's on Central Street in "the Vil," as they called the town of Wellesley, to protest the racist lunch-counter policies at the chain's southern locations. She covered Fidel Castro for a *Wellesley News* cover piece in April 1961, while colleague (and future editor-in-chief of *Good Housekeeping*) Ellen Levine gave fair coverage of Malcolm X's campus visit. In a piece that hit perhaps too close to home, Nora and her colleagues Rosalind Epstein and Jennifer Carden wrote a piece about a controversial HUAC film presented on campus in a cover story a week later.

"Don't forget, most of her parents' friends were blacklisted," a classmate explained on a recent Zoom call with the Wellesley '62 class. "She was very, very aware of what was going on politically in the world."

When the classic 1961 film *Breakfast at Tiffany's* premiered, Nora covered it and gave it a glowing review. She also fell in love with Audrey Hepburn's black turtleneck and chic style. As for the now-iconic, Oscar-winning film *West Side Story*, Nora's analysis was that it was "good, not great," as she expressed her frustration that it didn't uphold the important social implications that the play presented in a strong enough fashion. She could be a tough crowd.

"The Romeo and Juliet theme is at times embarrassingly sappy," she wrote, but noted that Rita Moreno's performance was "excellent."

During her senior year, Nora became involved in student government alongside her dear friend, fellow poli-sci major, and future roommate Marcia Burick, who headed it up. As the news liaison, Nora "helped to stir up issues that really needed to be stirred up," as Burick put it.

Just as tensions were building across the United States, so too were tensions in the dormitory at Wellesley. Some of the disputes were about the civil rights issues of the day (as Nora recalled later, several students were asked to leave Wellesley because they were lesbians), while other disputes were about who hadn't replaced the toilet paper when it ran out.

Once at the Well, the college snack bar, Nora accidentally tipped an entire chocolate malt into her purse. "Oh, why am I such a klutz?" she said, the first of countless times the girls heard her say it. She could be competitive about things as seemingly insignificant as the Sunday crossword puzzle. She could be blunt and a bit too honest for some.

Roommate disputes notwithstanding, many of Nora's classmates grew to be in awe of her and of Susie. And there was plenty of time for fun when they weren't busy studying. Sometimes, Susie, Nora, and Ruth Anne Thran would get together at Tower Court. Ruth Anne would come back after having washed the dishes for different faculty parties, and the girls would then have their own sort of party where they could talk and gossip over snacks and leftover cake.

On other nights, there would be music. They'd gather around the piano, or Susie would play the guitar (Susie, a talented songwriter, later inspired a character in *Take Her, She's Mine*—the play and the movie). "We'd go through the *Great American Songbook*," classmate Marcia McClintock Folsom remembered. "These were very exciting early days. Susie had a great, even motherly warmth, and generous wisdom. She still does. You can see it in her writing."

On the weekends, Nora would sometimes have a visitor: her mother would meet up with her at the Ritz-Carlton in Boston and they would catch up over what Nora remembered as "fabulous" crab-salad sandwiches.

"I was more different than the same," she said later of her time at Wellesley. "I was a spiky Jewish girl, not a little WASP with a circle pin and McMullen blouse. That just wasn't me."

She was also ambivalent about sex. At nineteen, she was still a virgin, and she confided in a friend that she felt having sex would upset her parents and violate their faith in her. As she explained to her friends at the time, her father was the lovable teddy bear while her mother was one of her best girlfriends with whom she would faithfully share every last detail of her dates.

But Nora would sometimes come back to her dorm room upset after a Sunday night phone call from Henry, who was weeping about how Phoebe was berating him, calling him a failure or a wimp. As for Henry, he was drinking and womanizing.

Nora was clearly under a lot of stress, but she hid her tears from her classmates. She secretly worried about her weight and her hair. And she worried about her family unraveling back home—she especially worried about her little sisters. But by her third year, she'd seemingly come into her own, and she'd even become quite fond of Wellesley. As a senior, Nora was named associate editor of the *Wellesley News*, where she worked alongside managing editors Jennifer Carden, Linda Seltzer, and future ABC News correspondent Lynn Sherr, while Rosalind Epstein served as editor in chief.

Nora (center) smiles as she works. She was named associate editor of the *Wellesley News* in her senior year (1962). *Photo by Wellesley News photographer 1961–62 / courtesy of Wellesley College Archives, Library & Technology Services*

Finally, Nora settled in both academically and socially. Writing and editing for the *Wellesley News* helped her find her purpose, and the Junior Show gave her a reason to get creative in a throwback to her camp days on stage. Susie and Nora were both central parts of the team producing the show—an important tradition at Wellesley.

Nora and Marcia Burick were in charge of writing the lyrics for the big production, while Susie came up with the tunes. A group of girls went to Cape Cod for the week to work on the show. Even though a hurricane came through, they had a wonderful time. "That was the beginning of our friendship," Marcia remembered fondly.

The Junior Show that year was called *Orchids by Wire*, and Nora served as a writer/creator, and as an actor in the show in the part of "Nails."

"It was brilliant . . . at least we all thought so," fellow classmate Martha Bewick remembered. "She was funny and sarcastic as Nails, one of the gang of female crooks trying to become famous."

But she could be restless too. In her junior year at Wellesley, Nora had thought about transferring to Barnard College—and was engaged to be married. She was eager to get to the rest of her life in New York City. On Saturdays, she'd often visit Harvard in Cambridge, and one day, she came back with an

Junior Shows were put on by the junior class (a tradition started in 1936) and had original music, choreography, and scripts. The Class of 1962's Junior Show was titled *Orchids by Wire*, and Nora (center, seated) is listed in the cast of characters as one of the "Orchid's Eleven," named Nails.
Photo by Wellesley News photographer 1961–62 / courtesy of Wellesley College Archives, Library & Technology Services

engagement ring. The lucky young mystery man? He was an up-and-coming lawyer she later referred to as "Stanley J. Fleck."

When she asked for advice from her class dean at the college, she was surprised by her response. "You've worked so hard at Wellesley, when you marry, take a year off," the dean told her. "Devote yourself to your husband and your marriage."

Nora was stunned. She thought about what she would do with herself for an entire year as a wife—iron?

That summer, she applied for and accepted a prestigious summer internship at the White House in the office of the press secretary, Pierre Salinger. He'd been a key figure in President Kennedy's 1960 presidential campaign after gaining recognition for his work as a journalist covering organized crime. Nora was thrilled to be in the center of the action—although she later found out she was likely the only woman to roam the halls and *not* get any attention from JFK, likely due to her bad wavy haircut and dyed Dynel dresses that "looked like distilled Velveeta cheese," she surmised.

Perhaps even more frustrating, interns didn't have desks or typewriters, and that meant that by her estimate, some forty-eight thousand words were going unwritten every single day she was there. It was painful. Still, Marcia's mother was incredibly impressed when Nora's first letter to her arrived with a return address of the White House. "Nora had quickly found the stationery drawer," Marcia told me.

And Nora did get at least one moment of glory one beautiful Friday afternoon in the Rose Garden. Well, sort of. The president's helicopter was there waiting to take him to Hyannis Port for the weekend. The noise from the chopper blades was deafening—and the wind was blowing all around. Just then, Kennedy was there, and he recognized Nora. As far as she could tell, he asked, "How are you coming along?" to which she replied, "WHAT?"

She took her fiancé, "Stanley," around for a tour of the White House, proudly displaying her credentials for anyone who asked. She showed him all her favorite rooms, and he responded with the comment "No wife of mine will ever work in a place like this." And that was the end of that. Curtains for Stanley J. Fleck.

Needless to say, she didn't end up going through with the marriage, nor the transfer, nor the plan to iron for a year, so when it came time to graduate in June of 1962, Nora was both anxious and excited.

As Nora remembered it, her mother drank a bottle of scotch every night. "One day she wasn't an alcoholic, and the next day she was a complete lush," she wrote later. "My father drank too, but he was a sloppy, sentimental drunk, and somehow his alcoholism was more benign."

Just before Christmas in 1961, the Ephrons' play *Take Her, She's Mine* opened on Broadway at the Biltmore Theatre. Nora's classmates knew all about it—about how her letters home had inspired the story (and were actually quoted in the play), and how her "remarkable mother" could pretty much do anything.

A few days before graduation, Phoebe called to let Nora know that she and Henry had decided to come. They would fly in from California for the ceremony. The image of Phoebe was one of a glamorous, successful working woman. The reality of Phoebe was one of an alcoholic who was losing her hearing and her dignity all at once.

When she arrived on campus, she was dressed to the nines—she wore a crisp suit, three-inch heels, and shiny earrings that matched her brooch. As far as Nora's friends knew, Phoebe was the epitome of grace and style: an accomplished, funny, smart, beautiful woman who definitely "had it all." One day, they hoped, they could be just like her.

But as Phoebe slept in the dorm room next to Nora's for two nights, Nora lay awake worried. Would Phoebe's drunken mutterings destroy her image and embarrass her in front of her friends? Would she stumble into the hallways of Tower Court and reveal the ugly truth of what had become of her? It was all too much. And it wasn't fair.

"Alcoholic parents are so confusing," Nora wrote later. "They're your parents, so you love them; but they're drunks, so you hate them. But you love them. But you hate them."

As for her friends, Phoebe's feminist outlook was a big influence.

"She is not just the mother of my dear friend, but she really had a tremendous effect on all of us," Nora's friend and roommate, Jennifer Carden Rogers, wrote in her letter to Nora after Phoebe's death. "You know how dazzled we were by the career, by the working with her husband, by the four children, by the approach to life."

Jennifer shared how as a mother herself, she'd often thought she was practicing "the Phoebe Ephron family plan"—the "let's-do-everything-in-life attitude." Somehow, she and the other young women at Wellesley had considered Phoebe their own.

The commencement speaker that day was the writer Santha Rama Rau, a Wellesley alumna whose first book, *Home to India*, started out as an assignment for her senior year English composition class and was published by HarperCollins a year after her own graduation.

Nora desperately wanted to hear words of wisdom from Santha. She was terrified to be leaving one of the only safe places she had ever known. What would become of her when she arrived in New York? Would she ever meet anyone? Or would she die alone—in that fabled New York death where no one would notice?

Just a few months later on August 5, 1962, the world was stunned to learn that actress and Hollywood icon Marilyn Monroe was found dead in her home in the Brentwood neighborhood of Los Angeles. She was only thirty-six years old. Just eight years earlier, she'd been the star of Henry and Phoebe Ephron's musical film *There's No Business Like Show Business*. For some, it might have signaled the beginning of the end for her in Hollywood.

Though the film was a commercial and critical failure, the Ephrons were nominated for a Writers Guild of America award for Best Written Musical, and the film earned three Academy Award nominations as well.

Still, the performance of the ensemble cast was largely panned, and costar Johnnie Ray never starred in another Fox film again. As for Monroe, she was coming off a months-long "suspension" by Fox for not complying with her contractual obligation to star in another film for the studio. She'd still go on to star in one of her most famous roles of all time in Billy Wilder's comedy *The Seven Year Itch*, but her newly formed production company, Marilyn Monroe Productions, has been credited as being "instrumental" in the collapse of the studio system.

5 | MAIL GIRL

> I believed that I was temperamentally suited to journalism because of my cynicism and emotional detachment; I sometimes allowed that these were character flaws, but I didn't really believe it.
>
> —Nora Ephron, "Journalism: A Love Story"

EVEN AT THE TENDER AGE of four and a half, Nora knew what she wanted. More precisely, she knew what she needed. *If I can just get back to New York*, she thought, *I'll be fine.*

Surrounded by sunlight and "happy laughing blond children" on the playground of her nursery school in Beverly Hills, she wondered how in the world she ended up there.

But it would take more than sixteen years before she was able to make her fantasy come true. After graduating from Wellesley in June 1962, she was finally off to the city she'd end up calling home for more than five decades: New York City.

Upon her arrival that summer, she and a roommate moved into a small apartment at 110 Sullivan Street in what she described as a "horrible, brand-new white-brick building" in what's now referred to as SoHo. At the time, the rent was $160 a month with the first two months free—and the real estate agent assured her it was an up-and-coming neighborhood. (It wasn't just yet.)

There was a moment before she arrived, though, when she thought she might be lost forever—literally—and might never find her way back. Nora was prone to getting lost sometimes. After leaving Wellesley and piling her books, records, clothes, and new white scalloped sheet sets into a rental car, she'd somehow ended up on the George Washington Bridge and on her way to New Jersey—and she thought she "might never find a way to make a U-turn," she later recalled.

Thankfully, she did. And when she arrived in Manhattan at long last, the Festival of St. Anthony was taking place on her street—there were delicious fried things (zeppole, to be exact), colorful cotton candy, games, and laughter. (She later made a point to show the street fair in *You've Got Mail*, and yes, she was sure to have the young actors get some cotton candy.)

That fall, Nora and her dear friend from college, Marcia Burick, found a small apartment in a three-story, prewar brownstone building at 428 West Forty-Fourth Street in the Hell's Kitchen (or Midtown West) neighborhood on the West Side of Manhattan. Naturally, Phoebe made up stationery for the girls to make it clear that the area of their new abode was *not* "GU," or geographically undesirable, as some might have called it, by situating it near the theater district:

428 West 44th Street (Just south of Lincoln Center)

As far as Phoebe was concerned, this actually was an up-and-coming area— and Nora and Marcia, too, were on the cusp of transformation from curious college girls to serious working women. A mention of your proximity to the newly developing Lincoln Center for the Performing Arts on your beautiful handmade stationery? Essential.

Not that there wasn't any time for fun. For a while, a third roommate moved in, and as Marcia tells it, the trio had an absolute blast.

"I loved being with Nora," Marcia told me. "We lived in a fashionable building in an unfashionable neighborhood and loved it. It was just a wonderful time."

Eager to make her mark as a journalist, before graduation Nora had already secured a job at *Newsweek* as a "mail girl" for fifty-five dollars a week. In the first of a string of events that Nora later deemed to be simply good luck, she was made an "Elliott Girl"—meaning her job wasn't just to deliver mail, but to deliver it personally to the magazine's managing editor, Osborn "Oz" Elliott, just as he was on the verge of helping the traditional news magazine transform into a must-read publication that rivaled *Time* and, importantly, was taking a stand on important issues of the day, such as civil rights and the Vietnam War.

But behind the scenes, the old guard still stood strong against progress.

"Why do you want to work here?" the man interviewing her had asked.

"Because I hope to become a writer," she replied.

"Women don't become writers at *Newsweek*," he said.

"I see," she replied, kicking herself later for not instead blurting out, "You're going to be wrong about me!"

Three months into the job, she was promoted to clipper, then researcher (a.k.a. fact-checker). The job entailed working Tuesday through Saturday when the magazine closed its issue each week. Marcia, meanwhile, had taken a job at the office of the US Mission to the UN when Adlai Stevenson was the ambassador.

"She always said she felt like she was rooming with Adlai Stevenson," Marcia remembered. "My first job was doing mail and I would bring home bags of mail. It wasn't confidential so I could bring it out of the office."

On her days off, Nora was writing, writing, writing. And reading. She'd curl up on her new, wide-wale corduroy couch with a cup of hot tea and her dog-eared paperback copy of Doris Lessing's *The Golden Notebook* and delight in "epiphany after epiphany."

"I was electrified by Lessing's heroine, Anna, and her struggle to become a free woman," Nora later recalled. "Work, friendship, love, sex, politics, psycho-analysis, writing—all the things that preoccupied me were Lessing's subjects, and I can remember how many times I put the book down, reeling from its brilliance and insights."

That December, the great newspaper strike of 1962 began. It lasted for 114 days.

"At the center of the strike was really fear of technology and fear of com-puters," said Scott Sherman, who wrote about the strike for *Vanity Fair*. Union leaders feared that automation would cost jobs—and in their efforts to fight it, there was an enormous shift in how people came to find the news each day—and how reporters came to write about it.

Sherman writes that during the strike, six hundred million newspapers went unprinted as seventeen thousand employees—everyone from reporters to photoengravers—were out of a job at the seven local city papers in New York.

"It was like the city's lifeblood was cut off," Nora had told him.

With no full-time jobs in traditional news, long lead times, and more time to report and write longer features, future figures of the New Journalism movement like Nora, along with Tom Wolfe, Pete Hamill, and Gay Talese, were essentially forced into freelancing for magazines. As a result, a new style of writing emerged that utilized the storytelling techniques of novelists to give context to news after it happened.

———————

Though she'd once feared she might never meet anyone in New York, she eventually met and briefly dated Victor Navasky, a young Yale Law School graduate. (Navasky would provide the last name of the fictional Frank Navasky, played by Greg Kinnear in *You've Got Mail* decades later.)

While at Yale earning his law degree, he and a friend, Richard Lingeman, started a magazine of political satire, *Monocle*, which they continued through mail subscription after graduation in 1959. Nora became a contributor.

Monocle would throw wonderful parties, and that's where Nora met fellow writers John Gregory Dunne and Calvin "Bud" Trillin, and literary agents Lynn Nesbit and Amanda "Binky" Urban, who also became dear friends, as did Victor and his future wife Annie. They enjoyed evenings at the Algonquin Hotel, where they'd share drinks and stories, and Nora, frequently it seems, was the only woman at the table—just like her clever heroine Dorothy Parker had been decades before.

She met her future best friend, Judy Lishinsky (later Corman), too. At the time, Judy was a talented young music publicist representing artists such as Miles Davis, John Denver, and Willie Nelson. As Richard Cohen tells it, it wasn't so much that Nora had moved from Wellesley to New York, but that she'd somehow found her "proper place in the city," presiding over the dinner table with her magical, if not often bold, way of being. (Female orgasms, it turns out, weren't off the table for detailed discussion when Nora was around, according to Cohen.)

After all, it was the '60s. Nearly all the rules were being renegotiated. Kids were experimenting with hallucinogenic drugs. The inequities in rights of people of color and women were brimming to the surface. The "Pill," the oral contraceptive, had become legally available. As Nora saw it, it was a time for exploration—professionally and personally.

Her first cookbook crush, *The Gourmet Cookbook*, was quickly giving way to new options, like Julia Child's new tome, *Mastering the Art of French Cooking*, and *Michael Field's Cooking School*.

"If I was home alone at night, I cooked myself an entire meal from one of these cookbooks," Nora later wrote. "Then I sat down in front of the television set and ate it. I felt very brave and plucky as I ate my perfect dinner."

OK, maybe I don't have a date, she thought, *but at least I'm not just at home alone eating yogurt. It might be a meal meant for four, but who cares? At least it was delicious.*

About a month into the strike, Victor called to say he had raised $10,000 to publish parodies of the New York newspapers while they'd gone dark. Would Nora be able to write a parody of Leonard Lyons's famous gossip column?

Of course.

But first, she called Marcia. "What do you know about Leonard Lyons?" she asked.

"His column is a series of short anecdotes," she told her, "with no point whatsoever."

Nora went upstairs to the "morgue" at *Newsweek* where the clippings of old newspapers were held, and started pulling copies of Lyons's columns for research. She wrote her parody version, and the paper, affectionately called the *New York Pest*, made it to the newsstands and into the hands of *New York Post* staffers and its publisher Dorothy Schiff.

The editors weren't impressed; they wanted to sue.

"Don't be ridiculous," Schiff said. "If they can parody the *Post*, they can write for it. Hire them."

And hire them she did. After a two-week tryout, Nora got a job as a staff reporter—and a raise to ninety-eight dollars a week. She covered everything from murders to trials to celebrities. It may not have been glamorous, but it was everything she'd dreamed of. As far as Nora was concerned, she was a real-life Lois Lane. She'd often return to the grimy, smoke-filled newsroom covered in dirt, and she'd race past the copy desk and the noisy telex machines to the first available typewriter to get the story down.

When the Beatles arrived in the United States for the first time on February 7, 1964, at John F. Kennedy International Airport in New York (formerly

Idlewild Airport, until the president's assassination a few months earlier), she was there, covering it for the *Post*. When President Lyndon B. Johnson's daughter, Lynda, got married in 1967, Nora was there—and she concluded her piece with her typical flair for pointing out the absurd: "By the way, there are 1,511 raisins in the wedding cake."

Many of those stories appeared on the front page. She was good—and people had started to take notice. In 1963, Nora quickly became a fixture at Elaine's, the new Upper East Side watering hole where journalists would gather and discuss the news—and the gossip—of the day.

"I loved the city room," she later wrote. "I loved smoking and drinking scotch and playing dollar poker. I didn't know much about anything, and I was in a profession where you didn't have to. I loved the speed. I loved the deadlines. I loved that you wrapped the fish."

Just on the cusp of the mainstream rise in consciousness surrounding women's rights and civil rights, Betty Friedan's book *The Feminine Mystique* was published in 1963. By then, Nora had joined consciousness-raising groups herself and taken up other causes as well.

Still, she remained single. Or at least unattached, until one evening when Victor asked his friend Dan Greenburg to dinner.

"I have someone for you to meet," he told him.

Victor had become a pen pal of sorts with Greenburg, a humor writer who at the time was working in New York and writing for *Playboy* and other publications. Born and raised in Chicago, Greenburg had studied at the University of Illinois before heading to California for graduate school at UCLA.

Once he made it to New York, he made a name for himself both in humor writing and in advertising. One day, when he and a girlfriend were on a date in Times Square about to see a movie, she turned to him and said, "You see that girl right over there? I went to high school with her in Los Angeles; her name is Nora Ephron, and she's really mean."

"I'll remember that," he said.

But back at the Navaskys, Nora turned out not to be so mean—the pair hit it off right away—and after a while, she moved into Greenburg's duplex at Sixty-Seventh Street and Fifth Avenue.

Nora and Dan looking at one another. *Photograph courtesy of Dan Greenburg*

Nora and Dan on a park bench. *Photographs courtesy of Dan Greenburg*

Nora, age twenty-six (around 1967). *Photo by Dan Greenburg / courtesy of the photographer*

Just as Nora was establishing herself as a tenacious cub reporter in New York, Phoebe and Henry's work was being lauded publicly in Hollywood. They were nominated for their first and only Academy Award for Screenwriting (along with Richard L. Breen) in 1963 for *Captain Newman, M.D.* The film was also nominated for Sound and Actor in a Supporting Role for Bobby Darin's portrayal of Corporal Jim Tompkins, and also starred Gregory Peck (whose production company financed the film), Robert Duvall, Tony Curtis, and Angie Dickinson.

The screenwriting award ultimately went to playwright John Osborne for *Tom Jones* that year—one of four wins out of the film's ten nominations, including Best Picture, Best Director, and Best Musical Score.

The film industry was starting to realize it was in crisis. By the early 1960s, nine out of ten households had televisions—around fifty-one million households—and by 1964, color broadcasting had begun during prime time. While there were opportunities to innovate in the new medium, the advent of television and changing tastes meant that the screenwriting work had all but dried up for the older Ephrons at that point—and the cozy, happy home they'd once shared was crumbling. It was a tough pill to swallow, made even tougher by the fact that Henry refused to give up his philandering ways, and Phoebe, privately coping with the grief from the loss of her father and mother in quick succession, was very much alone.

6 | WALLFLOWER

IT WAS A PARTICULARLY COLD, rainy day in New York on October 22, 1962.

Marcia was at work at the UN when she received news that everyone was being sent home early. As she would often do, she called Nora.

"Something's going on," Marcia told her. "It's confidential . . . but I'm scared."

When President Kennedy addressed the nation on television that evening, he explained that Soviet nuclear missile sites had been found on the island of Cuba. For thirteen days, the nation—and the world—hoped for a resolution to what seemed like the verge of nuclear war. It became known as the Cuban Missile Crisis.

As for Nora, she was confronting a crisis of her own: how to emerge from behind the city desk to become the writer she'd always known she could be. By 1966, the New Journalism movement was in full swing, and Nora was ready for a change. As she and Dan Greenburg became engaged to be married, she was eager to make her mark in the magazine world.

At home, in the tradition of Phoebe and Henry, Nora wanted to be—and *was*—the quintessential dinner host. Like her parents, she was invigorated by the idea of vibrant conversation, lively exchange of interesting ideas, and wonderful food, not unlike the famed Algonquin Round Table where Dorothy Parker had once led the sparkling literary discussions in the 1930s. (Parker did later confess, though, that the Algonquin wasn't quite as entertaining as Nora's parties likely were. At least Nora thought so.)

Nora seated strumming Dan's guitar, around 1967. *Photo by Dan Greenburg / courtesy of the photographer*

As Dan remembers it, she'd walk up to famous people at parties, introduce herself, and simply invite them over for dinner.

"Hi, my name is Nora Ephron," she'd say. "Now, I'm having a little dinner, would you come?"

"Not one person said no!" he recalled.

Regular dinner guests included author John Gregory Dunne and his wife Joan Didion—fresh off the 1968 publication of *Slouching Towards Bethlehem*, her iconic collection of essays about 1960s California—gossip columnist Liz Smith, Barbara Walters, and many others who loomed large in the New York literary, film, and theatre communities.

"There would be conversation and there would be laughter," said Barbara Walters.

Nora was in heaven, but Dan, a shy, introverted type, preferred to stay out of the fray.

"I always thought that Nora was like a magnet," friend and fellow writer Ken Auletta recalled. "People were just drawn to her."

By the time Nora was a newlywed, both Henry and Phoebe were in bad shape. The alcoholism and loss of work was catching up with them. They'd both attended Nora and Dan's wedding ceremony at the Rainbow Room at 30 Rockefeller Plaza in New York in 1967, but they weren't quite themselves.

Sometimes Henry would come stay with them for the weekend in their East Hampton house. He would get drunk and bump into things—and some nights, when he became belligerent, Nora would lock the door against him out of fear.

"One night, we heard him bumbling about and getting into his car and driving off," Greenburg remembered. "And we thought, that's the end of him. He somehow managed to drive to New York without killing himself."

The phone calls with him weren't much better.

"Whenever you'd call him, he was on this verbal salami of conversation," Greenburg explained. "He would just cut off a few slices and give them to you, and after you hung up, he'd call someone else and keep on with the slices of salami."

For a while, Nora's youngest sister, little Amy, came to stay with them. Things back home had gotten so frightening. But then again, many things in the mid-to-late 1960s in America were frightening, especially for young people. The Vietnam War was escalating, and multiple assassinations (President Kennedy in 1963, his brother Robert Kennedy in 1968, and Martin Luther King Jr. in 1968) gave way to a youth uprising driven by frustration and impatience with the status quo. For many, chaos and violence seemed to be everywhere during those tumultuous years.

Meanwhile, in 1966, two defining profile pieces of the New Journalism movement were published by Gay Talese: "The Silent Season of a Hero" about Joe DiMaggio and "Frank Sinatra Has a Cold." The idea of using the first person in a news article, and the technique of implementing literary devices typically used for fiction, were considered revolutionary, though early examples of the writing that inspired the movement include James Baldwin, Zora Neale Hurston, and Mark Twain, among others.

Writer Tom Wolfe definitively labeled the movement in his 1972 piece in the *New York Times* and in his 1973 anthology *The New Journalism* (with E. W. Johnson). Most reporters at the time still professed to be objective or at least invisible when it came to reporting the news. But for Nora, she thought the label was a bit over the top; writing had always been personal to her. "Write as if you're sending me a letter," Phoebe had once told her, "then, tear off the salutation."

Mr. and Mrs. Henry Ephron

request the pleasure of your company

at the wedding reception of their daughter

Nora Louise

and

Mr. Daniel Greenburg

on Sunday, the ninth of April

at seven o'clock in the evening

The Rainbow Grill

Thirty Rockefeller Plaza

New York, New York

R.S.V.P.
703 North Linden Drive
Beverly Hills, California 90210

Invitation from Henry and Phoebe Ephron to Nora and Dan Greenburg's wedding, 1967. *Courtesy of Dan Greenburg*

Marcia Burick and Henry Ephron at Nora and Dan Greenburg's wedding at the Rainbow Room, 30 Rockefeller Plaza, New York City, April 9, 1967. *Courtesy of Marcia Burick*

Nora and Henry at her wedding, April 9, 1967. *Photo by Dan Greenburg / courtesy of the photographer*

Nora and Dan (center) cutting their wedding cake with his parents, Leah and Sam (left), and her parents, Henry and Phoebe (right), at the Rainbow Room, 30 Rock, New York, April 9, 1967. *Photos courtesy of Dan Greenburg*

Nora outside Dan Greenburg's East Hampton house around 1968. *Photo by Dan Greenburg / courtesy of the photographer*

In early 1969, Nora and Dan headed to Mexico, where she was on assignment for the *New York Times Magazine*. Her adult son Jacob would one day follow in her footsteps as a staff reporter for the newspaper of record. Both Hollywood and journalism were undergoing major shifts in how their art was being crafted and whose stories were being heard. She would be covering a story on *Catch-22*, a movie being made on location in the desert by filmmaker Mike Nichols, who two years earlier had emerged as a hitmaker with *Who's Afraid of Virginia Woolf?* and the unexpected success of *The Graduate*.

When she arrived, he was desperately trying to remember the words from a memory game he and the crew were playing.

"Bladder. Whimsy. Dailies. Rumble. Barren. Crystal. Pastry," he said.

"No," replied actor and friend Anthony "Tony" Perkins. "Not pastry."

Nora soon fell in love, both with Mike's charm and intelligence, and with being on a movie set. *Note to self*, she thought. *This could be really fun if the whole journalism thing doesn't work out.* For now, though, she genuinely thought she was a rebel by way of becoming a reporter. It was a way of both pleasing her mother—who insisted each of her daughters have careers—and shunning the possibility that she could be anything like her.

Nora and Dan at the premiere of
Dan's play *Arf!*, New York, 1969.
Photograph courtesy of Dan Greenburg

"Whether 'Catch-22' will be a masterpiece, merely a very funny film, or
the first failure for Mike Nichols after two smash hit movies ('The Graduate'
and 'Who's Afraid of Virginia Woolf?') and seven hit plays (among them 'The
Odd Couple,' 'Luv' and 'Plaza Suite') is at this point almost an irrelevant question for the actors in it," Nora wrote. Indeed, at thirty-seven years old, Nichols
was "the most successful director in America and probably the most popular
actors' director in the world," she added.

It wasn't clear, though, if he'd be able to pull off a compelling adaptation
of Joseph Heller's bestselling novel about World War II. To Nichols, *Catch-22*
wasn't about war so much as it was "a picture about dying and a picture about
when you get off and at what point you take control over your own life and
say, 'No, I won't. *I* decide. *I* draw the line,'" he told Nora.

That December 1969, the first military draft lottery of the era was held,
which meant that for the first time since 1950, a man could be sent involun-
tarily to active duty, this time in Vietnam.

While many of Nora's contemporaries received exemptions for being married, or deferments while they were in school, opposition to the war in Vietnam led to widespread protests and demonstrations against the draft. Thousands of men either destroyed their draft cards—some publicly—or left the country to avoid it altogether. (For his part, boxer Muhammad Ali was convicted of draft evasion on June 20, 1967, and sentenced to five years in prison, fined $10,000, and banned from boxing for three years.)

Back home, Phoebe was growing sicker by the day. By 1968, she and Henry had moved back to their beloved New York. They rented a new apartment on Fifty-Seventh Street and worked on new ideas for plays.

But when she was noticeably absent from the Thanksgiving dinner table in 1970, Nora knew she was dying. "My mother loved Thanksgiving almost as much as she loved making a show of normal life," she wrote. Phoebe was in and out of the hospital, and as the months went on, she became thin and weak.

Nora would visit. She'd help feed her by the spoonful. They would talk, at least as best they could, given that the antipsychotic medication Thorazine kept Phoebe "quiet and groggy and hallucinating." Still, she kept up the appearance of normalcy as long as she could. "Nurse," she'd say, "this is my daughter, Mrs. Greenburg," one of the few people who referred to Nora that way.

By the fall, she was moved to a nice corner room up on the sixth floor of Doctors Hospital, where she could see a view of Gracie Mansion and the park's fall leaves turning from green to gold and red. But as time went on, Nora grew angry over the realization that in her final act, Phoebe wasn't going to explain what to do—or how they'd gotten there. Or what it all meant.

"I found it unbearable to be there and unbearable not to be there," Nora wrote. "She would moan with pain, and the nurse would reach under her, move her slightly, and the sheet would fall away and I would catch a glimpse of her legs, her beautiful legs now drained of muscle tone, gone to bones."

Just then, Phoebe came into focus.

"Nora," she said. "You're a reporter. Take notes."

For Delia, the memory of her mother's final days is just as painful, but for a different reason.

"I hope you never tell anyone what happens here," Phoebe said.

To Delia, she was reminding her to keep the family secrets. That a child must keep up appearances on behalf of the family. That being loved depended on it. How confusing and strange it must have been given what she'd told Nora. How could her younger sister account for the discrepancy?

"We're all born into a family at a different time and we relate to our parents differently," Delia later explained. "And anyone who thinks they have the same parent as their sibling—it's really not true, I don't think."

What happened next depends on whom you ask. In Henry's retelling of the story, Nora's call letting him know about her visit with Phoebe had left him in tears. Watching her suffer was excruciating. Phoebe came home, and within a week, she was gone.

"I'm going to give the nurse the night off," he'd told Nora that final evening. "The doctor gave me these in case I was having trouble sleeping," he said, handing her a bottle of sleeping pills he'd taken out of his pocket.

The next morning, he had a different instruction for her: "Flush them down the toilet," he said. Had Phoebe asked for the pills? Or was Henry desperate to take her out of her misery? To Nora and her sisters, it somehow didn't much matter; their beloved, sharp, witty mother had been gone for a long time. Phoebe had truly died the way she lived: mysteriously.

"My mother died of cirrhosis, but the immediate cause of her death was an overdose of sleeping pills administered by my father," Nora wrote later. "At the time, this didn't seem to fall under the rubric of 'everything is copy.'"

On October 13, 1971, Nora delivered her mother's eulogy at her funeral. In her sadness, Nora still managed to be witty, and with her wit, she managed to be poignant. It was a preview of what was to come in her later years as she wrote about loss with even greater life experience and comedic ability to back it up.

Even after all this time, it was hard to describe who Phoebe really was. "She was tough . . . but she was also soft, somewhat mystical, and intensely proud," she told mourners that day. "She could not bear being called a feminist. She merely was, and simply by her example, we all grew up with blind faith in our own abilities and destinies."

A year later, it was 1972, the height of the women's movement, and as Nora tells it, "everyone" was getting a divorce. "My first husband is a perfectly nice person," Nora later wrote, "although he's pathologically attached to his cats."

Still, they'd been planning a photo safari trip to Africa, and Nora felt uneasy about going on the trip if she were to leave the marriage. But Dan reassured her. "Don't be crazy," he told her. "I love you and you love me and we're not getting a divorce, and even if we do, you're the only person I want to go to Africa with."

So off they went. One afternoon in Tanzania, they took a stroll near the hotel—and suddenly, among the tall trees, they saw an elephant's head peeking out. And then stepping out. And walking toward them—rapidly.

"Oh my god, what do we do now?" Nora said.

"Grab my hand—we'll run!" They ran up a hill and the elephant just whizzed by, narrowly missing them. It didn't follow them—it was too much trouble. But it was a moment Dan never forgot.

Hearts racing, they returned to the hotel. "You're not supposed to run from an elephant!" the man at the front desk told them.

By 1974, near-elephant-trampling notwithstanding, she and Dan were separated.

"We just decided that we didn't want to be married anymore, we would just be friends," he said. "But we had the most amicable divorce that I've ever heard anybody have. We used one lawyer between us, we didn't haggle over who got what. We had bought a house in East Hampton, and we immediately came to the settlement on that."

Incidentally, about two years after they got divorced, Nora called him with a request.

"You know, people in my therapy group say that I settled for too little money on the East Hampton house," she said.

"Oh, what did they say you should have gotten?" he replied.

After she shared the figure, Dan says he took out his checkbook and wrote her a check on the spot.

After Nora found her own apartment, they continued to date despite being separated.

"We dated as if we were married," he remembered. "But we really had a real friendship, and when she accepted Carl Bernstein's offer to get married, the three of us went out to dinner together. It was that kind of closeness."

Ever the matchmaker, she even introduced him to his future wife, Suzanne O'Malley, a fellow writer at *Esquire*.

As for how he remembers Nora now, Dan seems to feel reverence more than anything else. "I remember her as a good friend, and a brilliant woman with a great sense of humor," he told me. "I liked her movies a lot, but I thought her essays were just the best essays I've ever read in my life. Truly the most brilliant essays I've ever read. And she knew how to grab the reader by the throat, that's something I learned in advertising, but she knew it."

7 | AFTER WALLFLOWER (WOMEN'S ISSUES)

IT WAS DURING NORA'S FIRST CAREER as a journalist and essayist in the early 1970s that she put her sharp pencil to paper and established her voice as a savvy, sassy, smart, and forward-thinking writer on everything from her candid disdain for the size of her breasts ("A Few Words About Breasts") to the complicated relationships between women and men, work, love, friendship, and family.

"She thought she was the most interesting subject to write about," said the late Richard Reeves, a historian and former colleague of Nora's from her journalism days at *New York* magazine. It became her calling card. She covered "women's issues" in the early 1960s before "women's issues" had become part of a potent movement, and it was her biting prose that earned her a column in *Esquire* in 1972.

It started with a phone call from *Esquire*'s editor, Harold Hayes, who called Nora with the offer: a column about the movies. Nora thought about it—and declined. The thought of writing in the dark during one of her favorite pastimes didn't seem like it would suit her.

"Well, what is it you want to write about?!" he asked in a classic "Harold" moment (as in, *I'm offering you the world . . . so what is it that you want to do?*).

"Women," she replied. "I'd like to write about women."

She realized it about the same time the words left her mouth.

Writing as a woman—about women—in a men's magazine, no less, was not only revolutionary but in 1972 undoubtedly a tall order as well. Nora fulfilled it with vigor, tackling everything from the personal to the political, and often both.

Hayes, though he was on his way out, had by all accounts returned glory to the old gentleman's magazine by emphasizing opportunities for young writers to experiment with a new form of journalism as it was being born. He believed it was a return to the literary journalism of the days of yore, when writers like Ernest Hemingway and Mark Twain used the devices of a novelist to cover nonfiction events. Humor and a strong point of view were vital.

"Postwar affluence and a rapidly developing American culture gave fodder to the medium, more sophisticated than a newspaper, more intimate than the burgeoning medium of television, more satisfying than film," wrote Brian Clarey in 2014. "And *Esquire* was asserting itself as a major player in the game."

Nora and her colleagues were fueled by Hayes's openness to their creativity during a critical moment in history. The long lead times of colorful magazines like *Esquire* at the time meant that experimentation with the form was necessary to create relevant stories months after something radical had happened. The role of the reporter in the story became a critical component—and the publication's bent toward smart and funny satire was right up Nora's alley.

"Ephron, as a columnist charged with expressing her own opinions, managed to strike the right balance between story and self," wrote Jonathan Yardley, the longtime *Washington Post* book critic, in 2004. "That she had a large and devoted readership had much to do with her ability to create a persona (one that presumably was fairly close to reality) with which readers could identify, in large measure because she was self-deprecating and actually seemed to mean it."

A former US Marine and United Press reporter, Hayes had come up under publisher Arnold Gingrich, as did his rival, Clay Felker, who ended up creating the supplement that would later become *New York* magazine. Both are credited with putting the nascent New Journalism movement on the map.

"[Hayes] had the exact thing that all of the great editors and producers and studio heads and politicians have, which is that he absolutely trusted his gut," Nora later recalled. "He knew what he wanted. He acted on it."

Across town, two up-and-coming writers, Gay Talese and his cousin, Nick Pileggi, were rooming together in a small apartment.

Nick fell into journalism almost by accident. He took what he thought was a job at the local A&P grocery store, but it turned out to be a night shift reporting job for the AP, as in the Associated Press. He fell in love and ended up staying with the wire service for fifteen years, starting out as a police reporter telephoning in stories from the field.

"I'd literally check in at a police station to start my working day and I'd spend all day with the detectives," Pileggi told the *Los Angeles Times* in 1991. "I wound up becoming almost a cop. I'd ride in their cars, go to their bars, play cards in their stations. And, of course, I'd get to know not only the officers but the characters that inhabited those places."

Talese got a job as what was then known as a "copy boy"—distributing the carbon copies of reporters' stories to editors at the *New York Times*. (He was in good company; Superman was a copy boy at the *Daily Planet* in the original radio serial, as was Carl Bernstein at the *Washington Star*.)

In 1973, Nora received a call from Sandy Socolow, an executive at CBS News. They'd been friendly throughout her first decade in New York, and he wanted to meet up for lunch to discuss a job opportunity at the network. She'd long admired her friend Barbara Walters's glamorous job in television—and this seemed like it was "as close to it as I was ever going to get," she explained.

She left the lunch wanting the job—a chance to coanchor the morning news program with Hughes Rudd—but she also knew it would mean terrible early morning hours, and it would make writing every day difficult. While she'd no longer have privacy, she thought, her world would in some ways become smaller.

"If you take the job," Greenburg had told her, "the only person in New York you'll be able to have an affair with is Hughes Rudd."

The job ended up going to Sally Quinn, a young blonde reporter from Savannah, Georgia, who at the time was a reporter at the *Washington Post*. When she explained to Nora that "being blonde doesn't hurt," Nora was offended.

"I thought what she was saying was demeaning to the profession and to women in it," Nora explained. "Then I realized that that wasn't really true, that the profession would somehow survive her remarks. My second thought, and this came during a period of what I like to think of as mental health, was that I had been upset because I thought that Sally's remarks were demeaning to herself."

But as it turned out, what hurt her most was that deep down, she knew Sally was right: being blonde and flirtatious *did* help—at least sometimes. As Lillian Hellman had put it, "I had no jealousy of work, no jealousy of money. I was just jealous of women who took advantage of men, because I didn't know how to do it."

Nora was growing—or perhaps outgrowing—*Esquire*, and although she was in charge of editing the July 1973 issue that was entirely about women, it was time for a change. Nora left the magazine and decided to join *New York*. "I figured there are worse things in this world than letting [editor] Clay Felker make you a star," she wrote. "And here I am."

Still, Nora's writing didn't catch on with everyone right away. For some, "she was a bit of an acquired taste at first," said Reeves. "But once she wrote *Wallflower at the Orgy*, people didn't have a choice but to sit up and take notice of her."

Wallflower, which was published three years earlier in 1970, would be the first of three essay collections published within the decade, with *Crazy Salad: Some Things About Women* (1975) and *Scribble Scribble: Notes on the Media* (1978) following behind. With *Wallflower*'s success came more work—first at *Esquire*, then at *New York* and elsewhere, as she took on ambitious long reporting assignments that would take her all over the world as a freelance journalist: from Israel to Paris to Mexico.

One of her most enthusiastic readers was a young Lynda Obst, then a graduate student at Columbia University studying philosophy. She would later become the producer of two of Nora's films, *This Is My Life* and *Sleepless in Seattle*, and a longtime friend.

"She was the first person to write about women," she explained. Before they met and became friends she thought, "I don't have small breasts, but she made me *want* small breasts because they seemed so cool."

As journalist Hadley Freeman said, whether her pieces were written in 1972 or 1996, they are still "so fresh you could smudge the ink," even if the subject matter itself was dated.

But the title of the 1975 collection, *Crazy Salad: Some Things about Women* (featuring essays that were originally published in her *Esquire* magazine column), still seems apropos today: it takes its name from the William Butler Yeats poem written for his daughter in 1919, in which he cautions her that beautiful and successful ("fine") women tend to often marry men (referred to here as the "crazy salad") who—in his opinion—are not "good" enough partners:

> It's certain that fine women eat
> a crazy salad with their meat

It was an observation ripe for Nora's signature sharp pen as the women's movement was taking shape in America.

Her "sympathetic but mischievous and occasionally contrarian look" at the women's movement was what made *Crazy Salad* so fresh at the time it was published, wrote Yardley in 2004, adding that he had included it in his list of best books that year, and that it's "still crisp" nearly thirty years later. "At a moment in its history when that movement was almost aggressively humorless, Ephron wrote about it with irreverence and a merciless eye for hypocrisy and self-satisfaction . . . and the reading public greeted it enthusiastically," he said.

She recognized that the issues facing women were serious, but according to Richard Cohen, "Nora couldn't take a movement without humor." She lived the life of a feminist, he said, but was at heart a journalist, an *observer*, not a joiner.

But the way she lived her life was probably the most powerful and persuasive unwritten statement for today's generation about how feminism is neither about "self-pity" nor "self-importance," nor is it a bad word; it's not about hating men or giving up on the dream of a great partnership. Nora loved men and felt they should be a part of the conversation, but she also fervently believed in individual agency and passion in what you do on behalf of women.

Obst said that while they were in production on *This Is My Life* in Toronto, trying to bring the city of New York to life on the film set, Nora's repeated requests for Dr. Brown's cream soda were ignored by the props department, which kept bringing her generic Canadian cream soda instead. It might seem insignificant to an outside observer, but Nora was frustrated and baffled that her precise instructions as a director were being ignored. She wasn't about to give up on what she wanted—and she knew her male colleagues certainly wouldn't.

"Fight for the cream soda," Obst said with a mischievous smile. "Whatever your sensibility is, fight for it. If anyone on your team is letting you down, don't give up."

In the summer of 1972, Carl Bernstein, a local news reporter at the *Washington Post*, was dating New York–based journalist Marie Brenner.

"I can't come up to see you this weekend," he told her. "I'm working on a big story."

"OK, sure, Carl," Marie said. *The usual excuse*, she thought.

It was June 17, 1972, when five burglars were arrested in the office of the Democratic National Committee, located in the Watergate complex of buildings in Washington, DC. Five Held in Plot to Bug Democratic Offices Here, the front-page headline read in the *Washington Post* the next day. The byline came from two young reporters—Bernstein and his colleague Bob Woodward.

While the Bernstein-Brenner romance didn't last, their friendship did. And just a year later, Marie watched as he struck up a conversation with another bright writer, Nora, at a party at Brenner's Manhattan apartment.

Brenner saw it all unfold: sparks were flying. Carl leaned in and took down Nora's number.

Interesting, Marie thought.

Carl said he'd call in a few days—but he didn't wait. He called her the next day. "I was dazzled," he recalled to his son later. Though he claimed not to have known of her "in terms of her work," it was clear they were in love—and it seemed like everyone in New York, and in Washington, knew it.

Nora was fresh off her divorce from Greenburg, and Carl was fresh off one, too, from fellow *Washington Post* reporter Carol Honsa. A local "district" kid, he'd grown up the son of civil rights activists. Since 1966, he had been covering the usual happenings around Washington at the *Post*, but never before had he—or anyone else, for that matter—covered anything like Watergate.

Breaking arguably the biggest story of not only the decade but of the century made Bernstein a rock star—or at least a "star," Liz Smith said. His intelligence and charisma were palpable, and his brash yin to Woodward's calm and reasoned yang helped them earn credit for essentially taking down a president for the first time in United States history. It was considered "maybe the single greatest reporting effort of all time," according to Gene Roberts.

In 1968, a new Columbia Journalism grad had been assigned a seat behind Bernstein in the *Post*'s newsroom. His name was Richard Cohen. The pair became lifelong friends, and during the ups and downs of divorces, loves, and losses, they'd remained loyal to one another.

One night, Cohen finally got to meet the girl Carl had been raving about: his girlfriend, Nora Ephron. It was actually their second meeting—Cohen knew of her as a subject of an article he'd written about writer couples, and their first meeting a few months earlier at a *Rolling Stone* party hadn't gone well, to say the least.

"She turned on me with a cold fury and to a friend standing nearby spit out every one of my offending words—one after another, precisely as I had typed them," he explained. "I was awestruck, also intimidated."

But Nora saw it as the ultimate real-life meet-cute, drawing on her love of the "I hate you, I hate you, I love you" romantic comedy trope that dates back to Shakespeare.

"Richard, this will be just like the movies," Nora told him. "We started off hating each other and we'll wind up loving each other."

"She extended her hand," Cohen remembered. "I took it and never let it go."

Meanwhile, Nora was ready to make a change. Even though she'd been working for *Esquire* as a columnist, by 1974 she was moonlighting as a freelance reporter for publications such as *New York* magazine and *Rolling Stone*. And soon she was engaged to be married once again.

Bernstein and Woodward were busier than ever. After their coverage of Watergate earned them the Pulitzer Prize for Public Service in 1973 (on behalf of the *Washington Post*), they wrote a book together the following year, *All the President's Men*, which in 1976 became a hit movie starring Dustin Hoffman and Robert Redford. It was nominated for eight Academy Awards, including Best Picture and Best Director for Alan J. Pakula, winning three of them (Best Adapted Screenplay for William Goldman, Best Supporting Actor for Jason Robards, and Best Art Direction for George Jenkins and George Gaines).

And it was Nora's chance to explore something entirely new: screenwriting.

ACT III

BERNSTEIN AND BERNIE (1976–1987)

8 | MS. EPHRON GOES TO WASHINGTON

> She gave me that, too—the instinctive need to pull
> back from sentiment, to cover feeling with self-
> denigration. But I am managing to overcome that
> part of her legacy. So I will tell you one more thing:
> I miss her.
>
> —Nora Ephron on her mother, Phoebe, 1978

JUST AS *CRAZY SALAD* was being published in 1975, Nora's future East
Hampton neighbor Steven Spielberg was finishing up directing a movie called
Jaws. That summer, the blockbuster era, as it came to be known, was born. The
exciting new cultural phenomenon would end up changing how studios and
consumers viewed the experience of going to the movies for decades to come.

As for Nora, she was still immersed in long-form journalism. As a feisty
thirty-four-year-old, she was still a few years away from becoming a mother, so
she was able to take on assignments that sent her all over the world—assignments that nourished her curiosity and passion for learning, particularly as a
former political science major.

The Vietnam War had officially ended in April 1975, but when Nora was
reporting on the war in Israel in 1974, she found herself in an uncomfortable situation—not unlike that of one of her journalistic heroines before her,
Marguerite "Maggie" Higgins, who'd been on the front lines of the Korean
War and would become an inspiration for Nora's beloved but never developed
screenplay *Higgins & Beech*.

Because war correspondents were mostly men, accessible places to relieve oneself weren't easy to come by. In a television interview on WTTW's *Book Beat* with Robert Cromie in 1975, Nora told the story of what it was like reporting on the front lines in the Middle East.

"The men who cover wars have a kind of Hemingway view of war as this great experience in which you see people behaving at their best, which I did not share," she explained. "But also, it is really hard to cover a war when you're a woman."

One night, she and a few other male colleagues left Tel Aviv to go look at the cease-fire line at Kilometer 101 where the Israeli-Egyptian six-point agreement had been made to end the war. They drove all through the night. The men were able to relieve themselves on the side of the road while Nora was trying to find a place that "wasn't in full view of the entire Israeli army" and that also wasn't in a minefield.

She managed to figure it out, but just then, she saw a beautiful sight: about 150 yards down the road was a big tent with three Egyptian officers in front of it, and behind it was a little tent—a latrine.

"Nora, you can't go there," one of the men said. "It's across the cease-fire line."

"Oh, yes, I can," she said.

She used her champion charade skills to get the officers' attention, and learned that an Israeli colonel had negotiated with the UN, which negotiated with the Egyptians to have the latrine put in—and Nora said she became the only reporter to cross the line.

Sometimes when she'd fall asleep at night, she'd toss and turn anxious thoughts over and over in her head. Mostly, though, she wondered what it would be like to get the perfect one-liner off at the perfect time, like her heroine, Dorothy Parker. She'd often wonder, *What should I have said? What, really, should I have said at that moment?* It's a theme that would show up later in *You've Got Mail* as Kathleen Kelly struggles with the same concern. (As Nora explained later, Ambien helped her immensely with this later in life—as did years of psychoanalysis, a.k.a. therapy.)

Meanwhile, the women's movement had grown and changed, and she had too.

She'd met and started working with Mildred Newman and Bernard "Bernie" Berkowitz, psychoanalysts who specialized in helping creative people. They saw clients out of their Greenwich Village home and later their Upper East Side residence. Her friend Mike Nichols, actor Anthony "Tony" Perkins, and many other writers and playwrights relied on Mildred's and Bernie's advice to help them through difficult times. They especially helped Nora understand that being a child of alcoholics didn't have to define who she was.

When their national bestseller, *How to Be Your Own Best Friend*, was published in 1973, Nora provided an enthusiastic blurb on the back cover: "I want to tell you that it's magic, but the whole point of the book is that there is no magic. So instead let me simply say that I can't live without it," she wrote.

———

Actors Robert Redford and Dustin Hoffman graced the cover of *People* magazine the week of May 3, 1976, with the headline REDFORD & HOFFMAN: THE TRIUMPH OF 'PRESIDENT'S MEN' STUNS THEM TOO.

Carl Bernstein and Bob Woodward (center) and their on-screen doppelgängers Dustin Hoffman and Robert Redford at the Washington premiere of the critically acclaimed film (based on Woodward and Bernstein's book), *All the President's Men*, 1976. *The Everett Collection*

Carl was on top of the world. Two years after President Nixon was forced to resign, and in the midst of the success of the film version of *All The President's Men* chronicling their triumphant reporting efforts, he was on a book tour to promote *The Final Days*, his second book with his reporting partner, Bob Woodward, when he and Nora married in April. It was a simple, small ceremony in surrogate Millard L. Midonick's chambers at city hall in New York. Woodward (alongside his wife, Francie Barnard) served as the best man and reported on the event for the *Washington Post*. Also present were Richard Cohen and his wife, Barbara, who was then the national editor of the *Washington Star*.

A chic but sweet black-and-white photo of the newlyweds taken by acclaimed photographer Jill Krementz in *People* shows them smiling and looking adoringly at one another—her in a fab '70s coat with a furry collar, and him with a high-collared shirt and suede jacket.

It is quite literally the image of two people in love. The headline, which simply reads HAPPY in block letters, says it all.

As for the honeymoon, Nora said she'd be taking hers at the Beverly Hills Hotel while Carl and Bob finished their book tour as her colleagues at the *Esquire* offices toasted them with champagne. (By now, she held the title of associate editor.)

"This wedding had to be wedged in between interviews about [Carl's] book," Nora explained, adding, "Nobody's moving to the other person's town." True, she'd been swept up in love, but she wasn't about to give up her home and her life in New York City for a guy—even if he *had* been credited with helping to take down a president.

Nora's dear friend Marcia was hosting her annual Passover seder when she got Nora's call.

"I just married Carl Bernstein at city hall," she said. "And I wanted you to be one of the first to know."

And so it began. It was, by all accounts, a love affair for the ages—a sort of intellectual celebrity coupling akin to a modern-day Noah Baumbach and Greta Gerwig, perhaps.

Traveling back and forth from New York to Adams Morgan in DC on the Eastern Shuttle, where "everybody is nobody," as David Remnick put it in a *Post* column at the time, Nora and Carl found a way to make it work in spite of their busy schedules. In fact, they even worked together on a screenplay called *The Eastern Shuttle*, based on the goings-on on the plane that shuttled businesspeople and politicians alike to their destinations every two hours daily for $29.64—without a reservation.

While the shuttle made an appearance again in *Heartburn* by way of their respective alter egos in Mark's repeated proposals of marriage to Rachel—he told her he'd only ask once on the Eastern Shuttle—the screenplay never made it out of the closet when they broke up.

———————

Meeting and marrying Carl was a profound moment in Nora's story because it happened at a time when gender roles were actively being renegotiated in the wake of the women's movement. It was the most prominent sign, perhaps, that her interests in becoming a devoted wife and mother had changed with time and with age—and with meeting the "right" person at the right time—a concept she apparently loathed just a few years earlier.

As she would later explain in a speech at Wellesley, the five most important things about Nora in 1972 were: journalist, feminist, New Yorker, divorced, funny. (By 1996, her five things were: writer, director, mother, sister, happy.)

Ten years after Nora left Wellesley to forge a path of her own in New York, she returned to the beautiful green campus in the spring to cover the class of '62 reunion for *Esquire*. In her article, "Reunion," published in her column on women in the October 1972 issue, she wrote about her frustration with Wellesley for not taking more of a leadership role in the women's movement—and with her classmates who'd cheerfully chosen motherhood over careers. To be more precise, she labeled "Them"—the term she used to refer to some of the women—as "bland" during what she referred to as a painfully bland time in America.

In truth, *America* might have indeed been bland in 1958—as in, much less diverse and progressive than it became just a few short years (or for some, many decades) later—but a number of Nora's classmates at Wellesley were in fact not only accomplished at work but successful at home as devoted mothers and wives. Some of them were even directly involved in creating change, and specifically in advocating for a new reality for themselves and for future generations of women. Nora allowed that she and a few fellow "troublemakers" were actively trying to make a difference—but often at the expense of those she saw as holding one another back vis-à-vis a life lived quietly and unobtrusively.

"Our class was actually at the edge of change, and even in college we challenged and changed rules," one of her classmates recalled. "We have authors, painters, doctors, lawyers, computer specialists (one of whom is a national specialist on election fraud and electronic voting today), a CIA operative and a CIA analyst (one of whom has just written her first novel), economists, poets, philanthropists, architectural historians, museum curators, peace activists, professors, judges, teachers, publishers, nurses, communicators, and broadcasters."

While Nora's classmates were proud of her and everything she'd accomplished, some of them were hurt by how cavalier (and in some cases downright mean) she was in her article about what some assumed were private conversations. But like most things Nora wrote, her article was multilayered: it was actually about the complicated feelings she was grappling with as a proud alumna rather than simply a hit piece. She wrote about how she was genuinely concerned about Wellesley's role in pushing the women's movement forward. And she cared. She may not have wanted to care, but she did. Like it or not, she was one of "Them," and she knew it.

"I can pretend that I have come back to Wellesley only because I want to write about it, but I am really here because I still care," she wrote. "I still care about this Mickey Mouse institution. I am foolish enough to think that someday it will do something important in the women's movement."

Marcia Burick, one of her closest friends from Wellesley, could see how some of their other classmates were both in awe of and jealous of Nora too. Some were wary of her sharp pen and acutely sensitive eyes and ears that saw everything and missed nothing. Nora was always taking notes.

"Are you still covering that frothy pop culture stuff?" someone asked.

"Well, somebody has to do it," Nora replied, proudly.

In what would later be called a "remarkable chapter in diplomatic history," Marcia was at the time in the prestigious position of serving as press officer for the US Ping-Pong team as they traveled to Hong Kong and China when she received a letter—and a copy of the *Esquire* article—from Nora. *Oh, God*, she thought, after giving it a read.

"It really attacked our classmates," Marcia told me. "I think all these years later, almost fifty years later, they're still referring to it. She attacked people in our class by name about what they said, and somebody said, 'Shakespeare will have to wait until my children are grown.' They were conversations we had with people coming into our room, and nobody had any idea she was writing about it. It hurt a lot of people."

She sent a letter back to Nora and said, "You can't do this."

"Too late," Nora replied. "It's coming out next week."

The piece—complete with her complaints, would-be private disclosures, and her call to action—caught the attention of the Wellesley College leadership at the time. After a fact-checker from the magazine called to verify information for the piece, a series of internal memos and letters considered what the appropriate official response should be. Should Nora be invited back to Wellesley to see the college with students around on campus to see how much it had changed and grown? Would it be best to send a letter to the editor signed by fellow alumni, students, or the administration?

After the article was published, a letter from a fellow 1962 alumna, Betty Diener (a Harvard Business School grad who later became the first female dean of Old Dominion University), to Mrs. Gordon (director of information services at Wellesley) recommended seeing Nora as a "potential resource for Wellesley rather than a threat": "I believe Nora's interests in the education of women are both sincere and articulate," she wrote, adding, "My guess would be that Nora could be tremendously supportive of any genuine attempts by Wellesley, through its new leadership, to redefine the objectives and strategies of a woman's college."

Indeed, when Nora was invited to speak at commencement seven years later in 1979, she told the new graduates to "make trouble," in a preview of the speech she delivered when she returned to her alma mater again in 1996. She realized Wellesley had indeed changed, but not enough, she said, to make the kind of "troublemakers" needed to create real change in the supposed real world.

"We were born into a society that expected us to be good girls . . . we were sent off into a college environment that expected us to grow up to be soothing women," she explained, adding, "above all . . . find out who you are, what you think, what you want out of life."

But as her romance with Carl blossomed, she found herself a mother-to-be in 1978, and in an article for the New York Times published just before her first baby's birth, she considered and reconsidered how her new softer identity might fit in with who she'd always been: a fierce feminist. Her mother's daughter. A woman who refused to believe that women can't have, and do, it all.

"I am bulging, laden, sloggy, logy, sway-backed, winded; the soles of my feet are numb from the extra weight," she wrote. "My idea of heaven, at this point, would be a night spent sleeping on my stomach."

As if the physical and emotional toll of pregnancy wasn't hard enough, there were also worries about feeling sexually attractive again. (Carl, as ever, was reassuring . . .)

"How do you feel about your wife's body?" he was asked one evening in Lamaze class.

"I like it," he said, "but I won't be sorry when she gets her old one back."

These were the days of Lamaze, of no-drugs-or-you're-a-bad-woman-and-even-worse-mother labor and deliveries. Nora thought about her choices in the context of the abortion rights that had been hard won just a few years earlier.

At that time, she and fifty-two other famous women signed their names in a manifesto in the new (and first of its kind) feminist magazine *Ms.* in the spring 1972 issue.

In 1971, the French philosopher Simone de Beauvoir wrote the "Manifesto of the 343," a document signed by 343 women who told their abortion stories as an explicitly political act. Beauvoir signed it herself along with actress Catherine Deneuve, French playwright Françoise Sagan, and "all of philosopher Jean-Paul Sartre's lovers." It appeared in the prominent French magazine *Le Nouvel Observateur* (now *L'Obs*) on April 5, 1971.

"Free abortion on demand is not the ultimate goal of women's plight," Beauvoir wrote. "On the contrary, it is but the most basic necessity, without which the political fight cannot even begin." *Charlie Hebdo* called the signers the "343 *salopes*," which roughly translates to "sluts." Their courageous act helped get abortion legalized in France in 1975.

Inspired by the 343, the *Ms.* manifesto included a cutout coupon for readers to write in as well. Titled "We Had Abortions," it was signed by women such as Patricia Bosworth, Susan Sontag, Grace Paley, Anaïs Nin, and Billie Jean King, all of whom acknowledged that they had gone through abortions. A fierce but unconventional feminist, Nora agreed to list her name with the other women. Just one year later, a Supreme Court case known as *Roe v. Wade* made abortion legal in every state in the United States.

Still, as Nora excitedly (and painfully) awaited Jacob's birth, she naturally wrote about it. Having had the requisite amniocentesis at Mount Sinai Hospital a few months earlier, she and Carl knew they were expecting a boy. Nora was thirty-seven years old, and Carl was thirty-four. Even at six months pregnant, Nora was out on tour promoting her latest essay collection, *Scribble, Scribble: Notes on the Media.*

"Why are you having a baby *now*?" some of the attendees would ask. Nora felt the question essentially implied that she'd decided not to have a baby in the past because of her feminist politics.

"I'm not making a political statement," she finally replied, exasperated. "I'm just having a baby."

But this was 1978, and only a few short years after *Roe v. Wade.* The truth was that having a baby after thirty-five (or not having one) *was* a sort of political statement, whether Nora wanted it to be or not. (Of course, Carl was not asked in his press interviews why he'd waited to become a father.)

"I had not wanted a child until recently for one reason: It had always seemed important to me to have one with a man who wanted children very much," she wrote. "And so, in some sense, I got lucky: I had 15 years between graduating from college and becoming pregnant, 15 years to work at my career and live my life without the responsibilities of motherhood."

"It seems to be currently trendy to say that it is the last revolutionary act, that it is the only worthwhile thing to do, that it is an uncommonly brave move in this age of divorce and an uncommonly unselfish one in this age of narcissism," she continued. "I don't know about any of that. What I know is that we wanted a baby."

Being pregnant also made her miss her mother, Phoebe, more than ever. "I have thought of [my mother] often in these past months," she wrote. "The baby kicks, or turns over, and I think of my odd, complicated mother, choosing to have a child, choosing to have me. For many years, it has been hard for me to remember what she was like before she became sick. It is still hard to remember, but for the first time in a long time, I feel connected to her. More than that: I feel grateful."

9 | WHEN NORA MET JACOB . . .

ON AUGUST 22, 1978, Nora's first son Jacob was born. After delivering him via cesarean section at Mount Sinai Hospital in New York, Nora instantly fell in love. Having her little baby, she said, was the accomplishment of which she was most proud.

"Jacob is like a dish of ice cream," she wrote in a sweet letter to her friend and fellow journalist Marie Brenner. "I just stare at him all day."

Nora, the ambitious, sophisticated Manhattanite who moved in elite literary and media circles had become swept away by the magic of motherhood.

She and Carl made their home in Washington in a four-bedroom apartment in the Ontario, a grand Beaux-Arts building that had become a co-op in the 1950s. In the summers, they'd relax on the porch or have dinner with friends—often fellow writers—at their big white house in Bridgehampton. The Cohens, Richard and Barbara, and the Reeves, Richard and Catherine, made regular appearances, as did Ken Auletta and his wife, Amanda "Binky" Urban.

"Any apartment she lived in, she was in charge," Reeves told me. "There was only one way to do things: Nora's way."

Many smart, talented men like Reeves relied on Nora for counsel on almost everything. She was their very own sharp-tongued "Dear Abby," he explained: "She planned everyone's life. People would go to her for advice, but it was like, 'Don't be an *idiot*.'"

Though she wasn't a fan of Washington (to put it mildly), she started to settle in as she and Carl carefully renovated the house to match their tastes.

For her, that meant everything painted white. For him, that meant a sort of shabby chic, Americana design aesthetic. She wasn't traditional in almost any way, but when it came to motherhood, she was by all accounts a traditional, doting Jewish mother.

At the end of his 1977 memoir a year earlier, *We Thought We Could Do Anything*, it was clear that Henry Ephron was immensely proud of Nora and of all his daughters as they'd grown up, married, and started families of their own. He remarried in 1978 to the actress June Gale, the mother of Nora's childhood friend Marcia Levant. By early the following year, Nora had news of her own: she was pregnant again.

It was wonderful news, but the pain of the loss of her mother at such a young age was still palpable. Nora was only thirty years old when Phoebe died of cirrhosis at fifty-seven. In letters and phone calls with friends, she revealed some of her most vulnerable moments as she transitioned from Nora the woman to Nora the mother. It was a role with a number of layers given her complicated relationship with her own mother's influence in life and death. She wanted to do it well, and if possible, avoid the mistakes of her parents. Or, as she put it, at least make different ones.

"The women's movement didn't prepare us for our children, who really are the loves of our lives," she said in a 1992 interview that echoes the Carly Simon lyric featured in *This Is My Life*. "But the question is how to handle both responsibilities well."

While there had been rumors of an affair—it was an open secret that Carl hadn't exactly changed his ways during their courtship—Ken Auletta remembered how happy he and Nora seemed together as a married couple. The petite seven-months-pregnant Nora had "waddled" down for dinner one night with Carl by her side just before Max was born. "Boy, are they happy," Ken said to his wife.

But the very next day, it was announced that they were divorcing.

Nora asked her friend Liz Smith to run the item in her gossip column. "Writing this scoop makes me feel sick," Smith said, adding that two weeks earlier, she'd confronted Nora about rumors that he had "resumed swinging."

For Nora, it was as if the words themselves would somehow make the pain of the shock and heartbreak become just another news story to be forgotten the next day. And once it was out there, there was no going back. There was no taking *him* back.

Nora was distraught. She went into early labor with Max Ephron Bernstein on November 16, 1979. Because he was two months premature, he had to stay for more than five weeks in the neonatal intensive care unit (NICU) at Mount Sinai Hospital and was finally able to go home around the first of the year.

Over Christmas, Nora, Ken, and Binky went down to visit him as the lights twinkled all around them. Carl, on the other hand, would stop by Elaine's after visiting to gloat about his new son, joking they'd thought of naming him "Early."

"Nora could forgive him," a friend told *People* at the time. "But she is down and broken up by it. She went a little crazy over the whole thing."

The other woman was Margaret Jay, a tall, blonde thirty-nine-year-old former BBC producer who'd become a consultant for National Public Radio (she's the daughter of former British prime minister James Callaghan). *Your basic nightmare*, as Nora might have put it.

In the (slightly) fictionalized version of how Nora found out, it was a "disgusting inscription" in a book of children's songs that gave the affair away. (In real life, it was said that Jay apparently circled the line about her "big feet" in the copy of the book *Heartburn* that remained at the Bridgehampton house—and drew a line with a note in the margin: "not true!")

In a January 1980 gossip column in *People* magazine, friends of the couple weighed in on what might happen next after the news of their split had spread far and wide. After Carl had spent five years being faithful, some thought it was just a matter of time before he would return to his "skirt-chasing" ways.

In the summer of 1979, Nora asked Carl about his friendship with Jay, but he downplayed it. But there had been the infamous photograph taken by the didn't-miss-anything New York photographer Ron Galella at the Amnesty International benefit in November 1977. The black-and-white photo shows Carl and Nora sitting together at a table at the elegant Tavern on the Green restaurant in Central Park—she in her beautiful silk dress and he in a suit holding a glass of wine—with a "guest" (as she's known in the official caption of the photo) on his lap. The woman is looking at Nora as she, hand to her head, looks utterly mortified. They're not even trying to hide it; the joke, it seemed, was on Nora. It's a rare vision of her so completely vulnerable.

"She isn't trying to play it off like she's in on the joke and she hasn't yet turned the situation into a funny story," Michelle Markowitz wrote in *New York* magazine's *The Cut* in 2018. "She's just frozen in time in that moment feeling exactly what she's feeling."

Still, "no one is betting against a Bernstein-Ephron reconciliation," the authors of the *People* column wrote at the time.

But Nora knew better. Just before Christmas of 1979, she packed up her books and bags, bundled up little one-year-old Jacob and newborn Max, stormed out of their condo, and got the *hell* out of Washington, DC, for good. Destination: home. New York. She initially moved in with her father, but then for six months, Nora and the boys stayed with her editor and friend Robert Gottlieb and his wife Maria Tucci. Between screenwriting assignments, she worked on the manuscript for what would become the novel *Heartburn*.

But Nora—the clever shape-shifter—refused to play the victim in the version of the story she was writing. "Like a cat, in mid-jump, she changed direction," Mike Nichols said. "She moved to the Gottliebs' house, and cried for six months, and wrote it funny. And in writing it funny, she won. And betrayed women all over the world knew it . . . and cheered."

Her novel *Heartburn* became a bestseller, and Nichols directed the film version, starring Meryl Streep, just a few years later. Nichols became and remained a critical ally both in Nora's personal life post-Bernstein and in her professional life as she transitioned from journalist to screenwriter and one day, to film director.

In truth, her transition to working on screenplays was partially out of pragmatism. "The real reason was that, with young children, I could not imagine going off to do the kinds of reporting things that I had done—and loved doing—as a magazine writer," she explained later. "Suddenly, I had two little babies and no husband and no money, and I was in a complete financial panic. I was saved by the movie business."

Privately, she cried. She was heartbroken. She was embarrassed.

In these moments, was she really Phoebe's daughter—a fearless woman refusing to allow a sad story to be the last word? Or was she Phoebe's daughter—a woman so wounded that comedy was the only way to safely hide the pain?

Three legends gone too soon: Carrie Fisher, Mike Nichols, and Nora at the Mike Nichols Tribute at the Film Society of Lincoln Center, May 3, 1999. *Stephanie Berger, © 2020. Copyright belongs to Stephanie Berger. All rights reserved*

As with all things difficult and complex, perhaps the answer is both. Of course, the writing of *Heartburn* was a means of both survival and control, two things Phoebe, sadly, couldn't keep hold of, and a chance at vindication for her grandmother, Kate, since neither Kate nor Phoebe had had the strength to leave their husbands.

Nora may not have had any money, but she had friends, and she had connections. Most importantly, she had guts. And ambition.

She ended up sharing custody of the boys with Carl, and, despite their flaws together and apart, he later said how great they were at parenting.

"What Nora and I did right was that we managed to stay focused on our sons," he said. "Even after the divorce, we collaborated on every aspect as parents. We were pretty good at communicating for the kids. One thing I am forever grateful to Nora for is that we got two wonderful sons."

It was hard to pull a fast one on Nora. She was always taking note, and had even discovered the real identity of confidential Watergate informant "Deep Throat" decades before it was revealed to the world.

"M.F.?" she said. "Mark Felt?"

"No," Carl replied, "it stands for My Friend."

But at her friend Arianna Huffington's request, she wrote about it for her first blog piece for the new publication, the *Huffington Post*, in 2005:

"For many years, I have lived with the secret of Deep Throat's identity," she later explained. "It has been hell, and I have dealt with the situation by telling pretty much anyone who asked me, including total strangers, who Deep Throat was. Not for nothing is indiscretion my middle name."

As it turned out, Carl wasn't a very good liar about the affair or the identity of Woodward's secret source. But something good did come out of the whole ordeal, aside from the fact that Carl and Nora now had two beautiful, healthy baby boys: their short-lived rewrite of the *All The President's Men* script led to more screenwriting work for Nora.

Apparently, Robert Redford, Carl, and Bob weren't happy with the initial draft they received from screenwriter William Goldman. Nora and Carl thought they'd take a stab at it. After all, she'd grown up reading scripts as if they were the daily newspaper.

"It was a great way to learn, because Goldman was such a great screenwriter that just typing his stage directions taught me a huge amount," she later explained, but Goldman wasn't amused. The Oscar-winning scribe thought it was a "gutless betrayal" that Redford would allow them to mess with his screenplay.

The Ephron-Bernstein script wasn't ultimately used for the film, save for one scene: when a charming Bernstein sneaks past a secretary by fibbing about who he is (this was supposedly fictional). But someone in Hollywood gave it a read and thought there might be a future for Nora in pictures.

Meanwhile, after leaving the *Post* a few years earlier in 1977, Carl was hard at work on a memoir about his parents (it ended up being published in 1989 under the title *Loyalties: A Son's Memoir*, in which he revealed they'd been members of the Communist Party, as had been alleged over the years). In 1980, he became the DC bureau chief for ABC News. The University of Maryland dropout had done well for himself: his confident, sharp writing and reporting skills continued to create new opportunities.

As for Nora, she wrote screenplay after screenplay in order to finance her work on *Heartburn*. She would work on the novel for a few months, then go back to screenwriting.

She'd finished the screenplay for Susan Isaacs's 1978 bestseller, *Compromising Positions*, for Warner Bros. while going through the horrific loss of her marriage—though she never received a credit for her draft after the project was turned back over to Isaacs to complete in advance of the film's 1985 release. But she did receive her first writing credits for *Perfect Gentlemen*, which starred Lauren Bacall, and for *Cookie*, which she cowrote with her friend and fellow journalist Alice Arlen. She later referred to it as "a horrible television movie. But it was the beginning of my being paid as a screenwriter."

By 1983, *Heartburn* was finally complete, and Nora received a reported $341,000 for the manuscript from Knopf, the book's publisher.

———————

Meanwhile, Nora was ready to take on the dating scene again. And her list of potential prospects was, like most of her lists, specific and well defined based on research. (The tidy list of eligible bachelors was not unlike the Rolodex Marie, played by Carrie Fisher, keeps in *When Harry Met Sally...*)

She went out a lot. To some, it seemed like almost everyone had two dates with Nora. But some men couldn't shake the feeling that *Heartburn* could happen to them—you could tell a woman (or in this case, you could tell Nora herself) all your secrets, and she could turn around and tell them to the world.

But Nora's first opportunity to fall in love again came in the form of a building: the Apthorp, which she moved into with giddy delight in February 1980. "I honestly believed that at the lowest moment in my adult life I'd been rescued by a building," she wrote of her post-Bernstein-split abode. For her, moving into the historic "stone pile" at Broadway and Seventy-Eighth Street in her beloved Manhattan was just what she needed after the humiliation and heartbreak she endured at the end of her marriage.

For $1,500 a month, the large, bright apartment featured five bedrooms, sky-high ceilings, and a view from the fifth floor. It was a sign: she could—and would—start over again. A new dream could be dreamt. All was not lost.

"One afternoon I walked just ten steps into an apartment on the Upper West Side of Manhattan and my heart stood still," she wrote in "Moving On, a Love Story" for the *New Yorker* in 2006. "This was it. At first sight. Eureka."

10 | RESCUED BY A BUILDING

ONE DAY IN 1982, Nora received a call from her agent Sam Cohn.

"Would you like to meet Meryl Streep?" he asked.

Having read Nora's recent script for *Compromising Positions*, Cohn's girlfriend, fellow ICM agent Arlene Donovan, suggested Nora for a project that Streep was interested in: the life of Karen Silkwood, an ordinary woman turned power plant whistleblower who died mysteriously in 1974.

Naturally, Nora answered the only way a person could—yes!—and the meeting went well. While Streep's star was still rising, her critically acclaimed roles in *The Deer Hunter* (1978) and *Kramer vs. Kramer* (1979) had already established that she was a force to be reckoned with (the latter earned her the first Academy Award win of her career, for Best Supporting Actress). But the executives at ABC Motion Pictures who owned the Silkwood project thought Nora could do only comedy—a far cry from how they envisioned the Silkwood story playing out on screen. Streep and Cohn both fought for Nora to get the gig—and they won.

Streep was born in Summit, New Jersey, in 1949. Her theater experience began when she played the lead in a Vassar College stage production of *Miss Julie*, which led to opportunities to perform in the prestigious honors exchange program at Dartmouth and the Yale School of Drama before transitioning to film work with her debut in *Julia* in 1977. Though she was eight years Nora's junior, she had a son, Henry, who was Max's age, and she and Nora grew close over the years—connecting on their mutual affection for food, family, theater, and sharp humor.

85

Upon learning that the Silkwood script was hers to write, Nora called Alice Arlen, who had a contact in the Silkwood case and had followed it closely as a reporter. "The original impulse was she was going to help," Nora later recalled to author Rachel Abramowitz. "She'd go out to Oklahoma and do all this research, but as it turned out, it was a completely equal collaboration."

Alice Reeve Albright (later Arlen)—whose last name at least partially inspired the name of Meg Ryan's iconic character in *When Harry Met Sally . . .*)—came from a family with a strong journalism pedigree. Her grandfather, Joseph Medill Patterson, founded and published the *Daily News* in New York; her great-aunt, Eleanor Medill Patterson, owned and published the *Washington Times-Herald*; and her aunt, Alicia Patterson, founded and edited the Long Island newspaper *Newsday*. Her mother, Josephine Patterson Albright, was a crime reporter for the *Chicago Daily News* in the 1930s. (Arlen's brother was the husband of Madeleine Albright, a fellow Wellesley grad who became the first woman to be named secretary of state under President Bill Clinton.)

A journalist and cultural critic in her own right, Alice was "a rebel and a writer by nature" who was passionate about telling stories of injustice. Working in New York in the 1960s, she and Nora struck up a friendship and a genuine mutual respect for one another's work.

By the time the Silkwood project came up, Alice was at Columbia University working on postgraduate studies in film. When Nora called and asked her to help, she immediately said yes.

"What was great is that we worked together and had a huge amount of fun doing it," Nora said of their collaboration. "She's very brilliant at screenplays and its structure."

The pair worked closely with director Mike Nichols to conceptualize what the story was really about—and who Karen Silkwood really was.

"You're always looking for a moment when you can connect to somebody," Nora explained, clapping her hands for emphasis to say, "Oh, *that's* who it was." For Karen, Nora found her essence in the pages of a long interview transcript Drew Stephens, her boyfriend, had given to a producer. "Be careful," he'd told Karen as she veered further into dangerous whistleblower territory. Her response? A flash of her breast.

"I knew exactly who she was at that moment," Nora said.

Streep, meanwhile, was filming Alan J. Pakula's epic *Sophie's Choice*. For her harrowing Academy Award–winning role, she learned to speak Polish, lost weight, and traveled to Yugoslavia to finish filming on June 1, 1982, just two months before filming began on *Silkwood*.

Nichols related to Silkwood's story on a deeply personal level. He'd been battling depression, and to him, this movie was about waking up, Nora said. She was having her own awakening as well. She was riveted by the process of filmmaking—and in Nichols, she found a more-than-willing mentor to show her the ropes.

"I love that movies have a way of being autobiographical for all of us even though they aren't at all autobiographical," she said.

If everything was narrative, and the line between nonfiction and fiction had been blurred all along, how different was filmmaking from reporting, anyway? Was her allegiance to the truth or to the story? To the audience or to the powers that be?

The links and clues were all there; *Silkwood*'s preproduction was full of hurdles, and during the process, a new precedent was set for producers in Hollywood that awarded them the same protection journalists have in keeping their sources confidential. Before Nora typed one word of the screenplay, the story of the making of the movie had Nora written all over it, incorporating important notions of activism and truth-telling in defiance of the powers that be.

It all began back in 1974, when two young producers, Buzz Hirsch and Larry Cano, read about Karen Silkwood's ominous and untimely demise in the *New York Times* (the whistleblower and union activist was in a mysterious car crash on her way to meet a reporter at that paper). Two years later, in 1976, Hirsch, Cano, and Carlos Anderson met at a summer film production workshop at UCLA. Hirsch and Cano had already started working on developing the Silkwood story for film, and Anderson was eager to "get into the movies."

Hirsch and Cano, who ended up serving as executive producers on the film, spent seven years investigating and researching Karen's real-life story in order to get the movie made and to ensure that her portrayal and the events surrounding her activism were presented as accurately as possible.

They arranged for financing and met with Karen's father, Bill, in Nederland, Texas, to get his permission to make a deal with the Silkwood estate. That meant securing interview releases from Stephens, Karen's boyfriend (played by Kurt Russell in the movie), and others who knew her. Slowly, they began to put together a massive library of information about Karen's life and death: reports, transcripts of hearings, taped interviews.

Meanwhile, the Silkwood estate had filed a federal lawsuit against her former employer, Kerr-McGee Chemical Corporation, and Hirsch was subpoenaed to appear as a witness in an Oklahoma court. He was ordered to turn over all his research materials to Kerr-McGee, an order he refused to comply with.

The young budding filmmakers said their investigative rights were protected under the United States Constitution, but the judge disagreed, and they were threatened with jail time.

That's when director Robert Wise brought together some of Hollywood's greatest activists—Norman Lear, Neil Simon, Jane Fonda (who'd also been interested in the Silkwood story but was unable to secure the life rights; she ended up making *The China Syndrome* with Michael Douglas in 1979 instead), Paddy Chayefsky, and others—to show their support and raise funds for the legal costs Hirsch and Cano were facing. The Bill of Rights Foundation, the Motion Picture Association of America (MPAA), the Writers Guild, and the Reporters' Committee for Freedom of the Press in Washington, DC, all got involved in the case.

Finally, the US Court of Appeals in Denver, Colorado, ruled in Hirsch's favor. The landmark decision ended up granting the same First Amendment rights to filmmakers as print journalists have to protect sensitive sources and materials.

After attending the three-month *Silkwood v. Kerr-McGee Corp.* trial in 1979, the producers were finally ready to present a draft of the script to Streep.

Back in New York, Nora would soon face her own legal battles.

After the 1983 publication of *Heartburn*, the divorce proceedings between Nora and Carl went from bad to ugly. In a 1989 profile in the magazine *Fame*, Charles Mann noted that "he began to play hardball, demanding that Ephron give him certain rights over the [*Heartburn*] movie script."

Coming down from the glory of Watergate and a crumbling marriage at the same time was difficult, to say the least. Suing on behalf of his children, as he put it, perhaps gave a sense of control over an increasingly painful period in Carl's life.

"I'd just come out of this experience of breaking the biggest story in history, and now I'm in a cottage in Bridgehampton looking at my navel at the age of 33," he said. "I hated it. Nora had a vision of the two of us being this gentrified literary couple up there in the Hamptons, walking around our lands and writing our books, and I sort of hated the idea, too. It all made me nuts."

Down in Oklahoma, the real-life legal drama surrounding the death of Karen Silkwood continued for several more years. In the civil suit the family filed against Kerr-McGee, they alleged that Karen had been contaminated with plutonium while working at the Cimarron Fuel Fabrication Site either "negligently or purposefully." Judge Frank Theis reportedly told the jury, "If you find that the damage to the person or property of Karen Silkwood resulted from the operation of this plant, Kerr-McGee is liable."

By 1986, the original judgment rendered by the jury in 1979 ($10 million in punitive damages) had been reduced and then restored by the US Supreme Court, and then was on its way to a retrial when Kerr-McGee decided to settle out of court for $1.38 million in 1986. The company admitted no liability.

Further, the company's lawyers threatened to sue—and to "tie the entire thing up in litigation unless they took certain things out of the movie," said Daniel Sheehan, the principal lawyer for the Karen Silkwood Fund in 1984. (Upon the movie's release, Kerr-McGee officials said it was "a highly fictionalized Hollywood dramatization," despite sworn testimony to the contrary.)

But despite all the setbacks, the producers struck a deal with ABC Motion Pictures in spring 1980. Production began on September 7, 1982, and ended in November just after Thanksgiving in New York. Principal photography took place on location in Albuquerque and Los Alamos in New Mexico; Dallas, Howe, Texas City, and Tom Bean in Texas; and in Washington, DC.

As Nora observed Mike in action, she was herself on her way to becoming a director because "she was out and out studying it," he later recalled. As for Nora, she was "riveted."

"One of the things Mike teaches you is constantly asking, what is this story about, what is this scene about, what is this section of the movie about?" Nora later recalled about attending the "Nichols film school" of her dreams by way of observing him on set.

Mike was going through his own personal struggles and found himself relating more to Karen than Drew. He felt Jay Presson Allen, the screenwriter and longtime friend, had betrayed him while they prepared to work together on *La Cage aux Folles*, and this was a chance to work through his pain by telling Karen's story. It also marked an important, triumphant return for him to film after an eight-year hiatus.

In Meryl's first partnership with costume designer Ann Roth, the actress impressed everyone when she came to set in a short denim skirt, a denim jacket, and cowboy boots—and brown hair. "You don't see [Meryl]," Roth said. "You see the character."

The pair later reteamed for a number of other Nora projects—*Heartburn*, *Julie & Julia*—and on *The Post* (which was directed by Steven Spielberg but dedicated to Nora).

"I looked at photographs of Karen Silkwood in Tulsa in the '70s," Roth recalled. "[Director] Mike Nichols wanted Cher [who plays Karen's coworker and roommate] and Meryl to be Snow White and Rose Red. He wanted Meryl to be beautiful and blond and Cher to be the exotic brunette. Meryl and I met in Manhattan, and we had photos of Karen Silkwood, and she had brown hair and a little bit of a shag."

The Nichols and Nora collab was likewise coming into its own. "They both had that ability to live in several different spheres of influence at once," Nichols's biographer, Mark Harris, told me. "Nora Ephron wasn't just a screenwriter or just an essayist or just a journalist. She lived in a lot of worlds and kind of mastered them all. And I think Mike was very much the same but also appreciated that in her."

Nichols, one half of the legendary improv duo Nichols and May, was born in Berlin in 1931. He escaped Nazi Germany and settled in New York at the age of seven. After pursuing his education at the University of Chicago, he and Elaine May, along with Paul Sills, Alan Arkin, and Barbara Harris, formed an improv group called the Compass Players, which would later come to be known as Second City. He'd turned to Broadway in 1963 with his debut as the director of Neil Simon's *Barefoot in the Park* with a young actor he'd seen on television named Robert Redford, and actress Elizabeth Ashley (who a year earlier had starred as Nora's alter ego Mollie in Nora's parents' play *Take Her, She's Mine*, for which Ashley earned a Tony Award).

After directing the critically acclaimed 1966 film *Who's Afraid of Virginia Woolf?* and his Oscar-winning landmark comedy drama *The Graduate* in 1967, Nichols went on to direct *Catch-22*, where he first met Nora, and then *Carnal Knowledge*, while producing the hit musical *Annie* on Broadway in his spare time. But after the commercial and critical failure of *The Fortune* in 1975, he took a nearly eight-year hiatus from the movies.

"Even when he leaves movies for eight years," Harris said, "it wasn't because he was sick of the process. It was because he knew that he wasn't living up to his own standards in a way and he needed to stop and not start again until he really felt reconnected to that original feeling that it was something he wanted to do forever."

Nichols also seemed to appreciate Nora's disposition in terms of material. It seemed as if they both tended to fall in love with things. The word they used was "love": it could be a hot dog, it could be a book—whatever the thing was, they were both so passionate about it.

"For me, that's one of the things that distinguishes Mike's career," Harris added. "Starting with *Silkwood* in a way is when he really starts to think of his work less in terms of, 'I can do something with this,' when he's trying to decide what to direct, and more in terms of 'I love this,' . . . 'I love this writer,' or 'I love this actor,' and really going with his heart."

He was in love with the process of making things, too, and like Nora, he loved the idea of revision—that you could create, write, or edit yourself out of trouble if you just kept working at it.

11 | WHEN NICK MET NORA . . .

IT WAS 1983 WHEN Nick officially met Nora. She'd just published *Heartburn*, the novel, and her first screenplay for *Silkwood* (cowritten with Alice Arlen) had just been nominated for an Academy Award. Nick had been working the crime beat for the Associated Press and *New York* magazine—and was well known in his own right.

They'd exchanged glances over the years through the cigarette smoke that lingered in the air at Elaine's—the legendary local watering hole for writers on the Upper East Side—but they'd never spoken, until this particular night. He was out with a fellow single pal, while Nora was dining with Arlen and her husband.

In Nora's real-life meet-cute, the sparks were palpable. There was no question about it. They made a date: drinks with friends (writer Ken Auletta and literary agent Amanda "Binky" Urban, and the then president of CBS News, Howard Stringer, and his wife, Jennifer) the following night. But drinks became dinner—and that dinner became a lifetime of dinners with friends, trips all over the world, and tiny moments that simply meant, for better or worse—in sickness, and in health—that they belonged together.

Nora liked to say that the secret of life could be summed in three words: "marry an Italian." On the third try, she'd finally gotten it right. There really wasn't a "worse" for more than twenty years—after a brief courtship, Nick moved into her place at the Apthorp and finally stopped "living out of a Chinese takeout container," as she put it. She loved to cook for him, and he seemed to bring out her more tender side at home.

Then, in March of 1987, Richard Cohen got a call. It was Nora.

"Richard," she said. "You must come to my dinner party in New York on the 28th."

In typical Nora fashion, she wasn't really asking so much as telling him. A beat.

"I'm sorry, I can't," he told her, adding that *Meet the Press*, which aired on Sunday mornings, would make travel by plane or train difficult for him and Barbara, who was the executive producer for the popular news program at the time.

"Nick and I are getting married," she said. "It's a surprise. You two are the only ones who know."

"Of course we will be there," he told her.

When the Cohens arrived, little Jacob and Max excitedly greeted them at the door. "They're getting married!" they said.

Nora wore a black-and-white polka-dot dress—and she cooked a delicious wedding meal for the guests.

Nick was dapper—and calm—as usual, dazzling in a crisp suit and a smile.

The Honorable Richard A. Brown, prior to becoming district attorney for Queens County, was on hand to make it official, just as he had for Ken and Binky a few years earlier.

As she reflected back later, Nora revealed that her romance with Nick had not only partially inspired the story of *When Harry Met Sally . . .* but also the hit *Sleepless in Seattle* a few years later.

"It was one of those things," she told the *Boston Herald* in 1993. "We'd known each other for years and years and years. If I hadn't gone to that restaurant with Michael and Alice, and he hadn't gone with Bradley and come over to my table to say hello, where would we be? We'd be two much less happy people now and I wouldn't have made *Sleepless in Seattle*. Everything would have been different, I know it."

The Oscars were held on a Monday evening in April 1984—and the stars sparkled as they waltzed into the Dorothy Chandler Pavilion in downtown Los Angeles. The late-night comedian (and subject of Nora's 1968 biography) Johnny Carson hosted.

It was a typically cool, breezy evening when Nora arrived in glorious 1980s fashion, though her classic, crisp Armani suit may, in retrospect, have had "too much padding in the shoulders," as Jacob remembers it.

Nora and Alice were thrilled to be nominated for an Oscar for Best Screenplay, twenty-one years after Phoebe and Henry had been recognized by the Academy for their writing. *Silkwood* earned four other nominations, including Best Actress for Meryl Streep, Best Supporting Actress for Cher, Best Film Editing for Sam O'Steen, and Best Director for Mike Nichols.

But James L. Brooks's iconic mother-daughter tearjerker *Terms of Endearment* swept the awards—winning five of its eleven nominations—with Jack Nicholson taking home the statue for his role in the film alongside Debra Winger and Shirley MacLaine. (Nicholson and MacLaine would later collaborate with Nora—as would fellow winner Sven Nykvist, who won for Best Cinematography for Ingmar Berman's *Fanny & Alexander* that year.)

Meanwhile, Mike was looking for a new project—and any possible way to collaborate with Meryl and Nora again. He'd been reinvigorated by their creative collaboration together on *Silkwood*. Knopf had just published the first edition of Nora's first novel *Heartburn*, and while critics at the time were harsh, the book became a bestseller and the publisher sold the film rights to Nichols before it was even released. The book, complete with Nora's own recipes—such as her famous vinaigrette salad dressing, key lime pie, and mashed potatoes—has endured and perhaps become even more meaningful as new generations of women (and men) discover it and decide for themselves what to make of it.

"A by-the-book feminist interpretation of her decision to broadcast the story of her leave-taking of her high-profile marriage to a faithless man in the best-selling 1983 roman à clef *Heartburn* might go something like this," writes Nell Beram in a 2013 piece for *Salon*: "She was showing the world that women should not put up with shabby treatment from their partners, that a woman was better off with no man than with a bad one. A quieter but no less feminist interpretation is that with *Heartburn*, Nora was speaking for less than an entire movement but for more than just herself: She was speaking, and writing, for two."

The two Beram mentioned? Nora and Phoebe. It wasn't just that Carl had betrayed Nora; it was a betrayal of how hard she'd worked to escape becoming her mother and even her mother's mother—both of whom hadn't been able or willing to leave their husbands after their affairs.

But to some critics—many of them men—the novel wasn't viewed as the work of a clever creative but of an "effective self-publicizer."

At the time, placing something so painful in the hands of even a trusted friend felt scary.

"Giving Nichols *Heartburn*—her own story, less raw than it had been a few years earlier but still the expression and repository of a great deal of hurt—was an act of faith," Nichols biographer Mark Harris later wrote.

"He was moved by the way Ephron had turned a crushing emotional blow into a statement of survival," Harris added. "He initially saw it as a movie about 'a woman doomed to be right, and therefore alone.'"

Carl met Mike at the Russian Tea Room to discuss the potential project over drinks. He was furious.

"I can't believe you're going to do this," Carl told him, "particularly since, more than anybody I know, you're a person who cherishes his privacy and that of your children."

"Somebody is going to make this movie," Mike replied, "and you're much better off if I make it because I'm your friend."

In September of 1984, the first 118-page draft of the *Heartburn* screenplay was submitted to Jeffrey Katzenberg, who was then a young executive at Paramount. He'd been an assistant to Nora's high school classmate and lifelong friend, Barry Diller (then chairman and CEO of the studio), and had worked his way up to president of production when the script analysis for *Heartburn* came across his desk from analyst Dan Bronson.

"Much better than the book!" Bronson wrote. "The screenplay is together, more carefully constructed than the novel, and its protagonist is more sympathetic and appealing, less cynical and brittle."

This version of Nora's novel, he thought, was like a "woman's *Annie Hall*," and while it was well put together, he also thought that the inevitable comparisons might prove to be a negative since Woody Allen's 1977 film had been—and would always be—the original.

Still, with a bit of tightening up on the more verbose sections of the dialogue and the addition of some warmth, it seemed to be on its way to becoming a successful movie.

By the time the shooting script was submitted in March of 1985, Diller protégé Dawn Steel had taken over Katzenberg's role after he left for the

Walt Disney Company and following her support of the megahit *Flashdance* in 1983.

The kids were changed from boys to girls, and analyst Donna Goodman brought up a number of points that likely mystified Nora in real life as well, such as: what was lacking in their marriage that drove him to cheat?

In June, Carl was still fighting with Nora, Nichols, and Paramount over the final details, but ultimately seemed to be willing to let the project move forward despite his objections. Carl insisted that the movie portrayal of him always show him as the good father he was in real life, and he requested a sign-off on the final script. As part of their divorce settlement, he was also given the right to review and approve any rewrites, and to view a first cut of the film and submit any complaints.

Initially, Kevin Kline was cast to play Mark, the fictional version of Carl, but the role eventually went to an up-and-coming Mandy Patinkin.

Following two weeks of rehearsals, production for the movie version of *Heartburn* began on July 19, 1985. Streep and Patinkin, another fellow Sam Cohn client, seemed to work well together in the lead roles. But after just five days of shooting, something seemed off.

"This is not happening," Mike told his producer, Robert Greenhut. "I think we should try to replace Mandy."

Nora was displeased. As Mike negotiated to bring in his longtime friend Jack Nicholson, the two "Nicks," as they called themselves (Nichols and Nicholson), seemingly rebalanced the entire production. Nicholson was a bona fide movie star, and suddenly Nora's story of resilience seemed to be subjugated to that of the cheating husband begging for forgiveness.

Meryl remembered that when Mike mentioned to Nora on the set of *Heartburn* that Nicholson's character needed more development, "steam came out of her ears. I said to Mike, 'I think this is a movie about the person who got hit by the bus. It's not about the bus.'"

But like *Silkwood* a few years earlier, *Heartburn* was also a set full of talented women working both above and below the line in key roles. Costume designer Ann Roth, musician Carly Simon, Streep, and of course, Nora, were all there—bringing much-needed balance to the production.

"Nora was always there," Meryl remembered. "[Mike] and she always had that confab. They were the Gang of Two. And often they didn't even have to say much—there was so much between them that was understood."

Simon worked closely with Mike and Nora as she wrote the lyrics for the film's main theme, "Coming Around Again." She recalled how Nora had helped her with certain lines from the hit song, and later with "Love of My Life" from *This Is My Life*.

"She would get inside of the head of the character and do some channeling, and I would add some rhythm and this and that," Simon remembered. "She had a gift for the specific, and could hone in on a character by giving me (in this case the songwriter) a word like 'souffle' and I added the verb 'burn' as in 'burn the souffle,' and it says a whole lot more than what I could have cooked up alone for Meryl's character to be feeling through song."

Indeed, one of the most poignant and excruciating lines from the film's screenplay and novel is when the fictional Nora, Rachel, explains why she can't stay with Mark, in spite of how much she loves him and the dream of the life they almost had together: "And then the dreams break into a million tiny pieces," she says in the novel. "The dream dies. Which leaves you with a choice: you can settle for reality, or you can go off, like a fool, and dream another dream." In the movie, Rachel takes her beautiful key lime pie (Nora's recipe) and shoves it into Mark's face. In real life, it was a bottle of red wine that she poured slowly over Carl's head.

Heartburn opened at No. 2 on July 25, 1986, one week after James Cameron's *Aliens* had swept the summer box office on its way to becoming one of the highest-grossing films worldwide that year. Nora confided in her friend Carrie Fisher that she'd been displeased with the film version of *Heartburn*, especially after Nicholson had been brought on.

"I guess it was the restrictions imposed by her ex-husband [prior to the movie]," Fisher explained. "His character couldn't scream, 'You know why I fucked someone when you were pregnant? I was terrified!' A lot of men do that. She married a man not known for his fidelity. A known hound. She was thirty-nine. She needed to have children. Nora never copped to that. It was implicit."

But a lunch date with her friend Rob Reiner at the Russian Tea Room in Midtown for lunch would soon change everything. "I have an idea for a movie," he told her as they slid into a booth.

ACT IV

NORA THE FILMMAKER (1989–2000s)

12 | WHAT NORA'S HAVING

IT WAS OCTOBER 1984 when Nora turned down Rob's idea before they even placed their lunch orders. Coming off the success of *This Is Spinal Tap*, Rob and his producing partner, Andy Scheinman, requested a lunch meeting to go over a script idea they had for a movie about a lawyer.

"No," Nora said. "Sorry, I'm not interested."

"I should've at least waited until we ate a little bit and were having our coffee," Rob said later of his embarrassment.

But as the men shared the goings-on of their respective love lives as single guys on the dating scene, Nora became intrigued. And disgusted. *This is really what men think?*

Scheinman and Reiner regaled her with real-life tales from bachelorhood. It wasn't so much that the things flying out of their mouths were shocking but that they were, as Nora put it, a woman's worst nightmare of what a typical heterosexual guy might put her through out of a seemingly instinctual fear of commitment. Rob, who'd been out of the game for ten years while he was married to director Penny Marshall, suddenly found himself right back in it after his divorce in 1981. It was rough, to say the least.

Some months passed before Nora and Rob met up again, but this time, he presented Nora with an idea she could get behind: it was the story of two friends who, at the end of the first major relationship in each of their lives, decide not to have sex because it will ruin the friendship—and then they have sex and it ruins the friendship.

Nora immediately began to visualize how the script would come together. On her cab ride home, she could see that there was a clear beginning, middle, and end, and that "it started before it really started."

"It would be a couple that kept bumping into each other at all the wrong moments," she explained.

As ever, Nora took notes. From her notebook on February 5, 1985: "This is a talk piece," Rob said. "There are no chase scenes. No food fights. This is walks, apartments, phones, restaurants, movies . . . we're talking about a movie about two people who get each other from the breakup of the first big relationship in their lives to the beginning of the second."

Nora modeled Harry after Rob, who was "funny but extremely depressed," and made Sally a sort of sunnier (and blonder) version of herself. Rather than use the trope commonly associated with the "Christian" version of romantic comedy, in which there's an obstacle that keeps the couple apart, Nora settled on leaning into the neurosis of the male character like Woody Allen in *Annie Hall* a decade earlier.

When Nora met up with Rob and Andy for lunch for the fifth day in a row, she ordered the way she always did.

"I'll have the avocado and bacon sandwich with sprouts, please," she said. "But I'd like the mayonnaise on the side, the bread toasted and slightly burnt, and the bacon crisp."

The two men looked at each other.

"What?" she said. "I just like it the way I like it."

It was written into the movie.

Once when Nora was on an airplane home from Europe, she provided her precise order instructions in her trademark unique way. The flight attendant was reminded of Sally and asked, "Have you ever seen the movie *When Harry Met Sally . . .*?"

———————————————

In the years that passed, Rob went off to make two cult-classics: *Stand by Me* (1986) and *The Princess Bride* (1987).

Nora worked with Nichols on making *Heartburn* the movie in 1986.

For Rob and Nora, it was a lot of hurry up and wait for a number of years. Like their protagonists, getting the timing right was key.

Just as Nichols had done, Rob invited Nora to be a part of the production process. Casting was difficult. In the beginning, she recalled, Sally was to be Jewish and Harry was to be Gentile, but then "Rob fell in love with [pre-*Downton Abbey* Elizabeth McGovern] so Elizabeth McGovern was going to play it," Nora said. That's when they switched the characters' last names and made him Jewish and her Gentile instead.

As for Harry, a long line of popular young actors at the time turned down the role, including Tom Hanks, Albert Brooks, Michael Keaton, and most painfully, Richard Dreyfuss.

Hanks felt he couldn't relate to the character's suffering after his marriage ended. In real life, Nora realized he'd actually been happy when his first marriage ended. "I don't think Tom ever regretted not doing it, because he just never knew how to play it," she said. "That part really was very much out of Rob's own kind of Jewish self-obsessed thing that I don't think Tom has a clue about."

As for Dreyfuss, Nora was there when he said to Rob, "God, it's too bad you don't want to direct the movie I really want to do—*Let It Ride*. It's the opposite of this situation. That [film] has a great script and no director."

Reiner dismissed the actor's comments, and they moved forward without him.

In the first draft of the script, Harry and Sally weren't meant to end up together, but rather they'd "nurse each other through breakups of their first big relationships to the beginnings of their second."

Back at lunch, Rob was interested in what Nora could tell him about women.

"We've told you all this stuff about guys, why don't you tell us something we don't know about women?" he said, almost daring her to say something shocking. The implication was, *there's no way we don't already know everything.*

Nora took a beat.

"Women fake orgasms," she said.

"Not with me," Rob and Andy both said.

"Yes, with you," she said.

"No, no, no," they said.

Rob was flabbergasted. He stormed out into the Castle Rock bullpen and corralled all the women into the conference room.

"Is this *true*?" he asked, demanding an answer.

"Well . . ." the women each replied, slowly, ". . . yes."

They added it to the script.

When Rob returned from making *Stand by Me*, he and Nora decided the pair would have to end up together. They'd come to new conclusions about Harry and Sally's fate with time and life experiences.

Nora had married the greatest love of her life, Nick Pileggi, in 1987, and Rob had met his future wife, photographer Michele Singer, whom he married in 1989. They were both changed, and the ending of the movie reflected that.

Nora wrote a second draft, and Rob directed *The Princess Bride*. Together, they worked on five more drafts.

From Nichols, she had learned that the words in a screenplay are sacred—a theater director would never change a word of a play; rather, "we honor the script and we rehearse the script," Nora explained.

But with Rob, it was a whole new world. He'd come from television, where the script is always changing and evolving as actors try new lines in real time during filming, often with a live audience. Playing Michael "Meathead" Stivic from 1971 to 1976 on the most watched television series of the time, Norman Lear's *All in the Family*, Rob followed in the footsteps of his comedian-actor-producer father Carl Reiner and actress-singer mother, Estelle. (Aside from his directing and producing credits, Nora would later convince him to appear as Tom Hanks's friend in *Sleepless in Seattle* in 1993 and in a small role in *Mixed Nuts*, and he eventually had a recurring role in Liz Meriweather's Fox television series *New Girl*.)

"The director is constantly trying to screw the writer out of the things that mean the most," Nora said later. "Every script I've done, my favorite scene was on the floor, except of course the ones that I have directed . . . there is the pretense that there is collaboration, but the truth is the director has all the power and you have none."

But this project was different. Nora owned Sally, and Rob owned Harry, and that meant they could both be invested in their story. "It was as much fun as I've ever had," Nora said. "Rob's so funny. He's also very combative. We fought bitterly about lots of stuff that's in the movie, and, as a result, the fights are in the scenes."

The New Year's Eve finale is perhaps the most visible example. "We had a huge battle," she said. "Rob wanted him to basically say, 'I've been thinking it over and I love you.' I wanted him to talk about her."

"This guy has been a narcissist for the entire movie," Nora told him. "It's time for him to talk about what it is about her that's important."

The result? The iconic final scene that has both.

Another point of contention was the title. Rob loved *When Harry Met Sally . . .*, but Nora didn't. (He was especially passionate about the three-dot ellipsis.)

But by 1988, the script was finally ready, and shooting began in August in New York—nearly four years after that first lunch meeting.

Billy Crystal signed on to play Rob's alter ego, Harry. Meg Ryan, who'd been chosen to play Sally, was fearless in her approach to the role. She suggested that rather than just talk about it, she should actually act out the fake orgasm—while Rob thought it should occur somewhere surprising, like at a deli. At first, Meg was timid and unsure of how to do it. But after Rob showed her how it was done (literally, with his fists pounding on the table), she got into the rhythm and ended up having to do it over and over and over again all day through multiple takes.

Billy suggested that a patron at the next table should say, "I'll have what she's having."

Rob said, "And I know just who to ask to say the line: my mother, Estelle Reiner."

Still, they didn't know if the scene would work. If it didn't, Rob wasn't sure if he'd be able to keep the line in the final cut.

"It's OK," Estelle told him. "At least I got to spend the day with you—and I can get a hot dog at Katz's while I'm there."

Cut to a couple of decades later: "It ended up being the funniest line in the movie and the funniest line in any movie I've done," Rob said. The line is part of the American Film Institute's list of the 100 top 100 film quotes, and in Estelle's *New York Times* obituary, she was referred to as the woman "who delivered one of the most memorably funny lines in movie history."

In early previews, the women in the audience were laughing so loud that the song in the next scene could barely be heard. The men were silent.

"It's hard to imagine that that was a genuine secret from half the population," Nora said later. "But it was."

One of those women giggling was the late Princess Diana at the London premiere of the movie. She leaned over to Billy Crystal, who was seated next to her in the theater.

"I would be laughing a lot more, but I know people are looking at me," she whispered. Later, she asked to have the film shown at Buckingham Palace with her girlfriends so she could fully enjoy it.

As he does with all his films, Rob had the cast rehearse for two weeks so they could get to know their characters. With his production company Castle Rock financing the movie, they could afford to take a little extra time—and they set their expectations low in terms of the box office. Two huge blockbusters, *Indiana Jones and the Last Crusade* and *Batman*, were set to be released around the same time.

It was a beautiful spring afternoon the day Rob shot the scene in Cafe Luxembourg in which Harry sets up Sally with his friend Jess (Bruno Kirby), and Sally sets up Harry with Marie (Carrie Fisher). Nora realized they had something really special. Between Kirby's improvs, Carrie's delivery, and Billy's and Meg's talent for timing, it just kept getting funnier. As she walked home she thought, *This movie is going to be so fabulous.*

She revealed how personal the screenplay actually was when she gave a candid interview to Terry Lawson, the film critic at the *Dayton Daily News*, in 1989 when the film premiered that summer.

"I'm a fixer," Nora said. "I want everything to be all right for everyone."

Nora was also a prudent recycler of material, and, as she liked to call herself, a "squirrel" when it came to hoarding her words. Some leftovers from *Silkwood* (days of the week underwear) and *Heartburn* proved useful for the *Sally* script, as did some of her witty essays from a decade or two earlier.

When Meg is at the mailbox checking that each letter falls into the bin one by one, it's a tiny moment, but it's very Nora, as is this hilarious bit of dialogue:

"And I'm gonna be *forty*!" Sally says to Harry upon learning of her ex's upcoming nuptials.

"When?" he replies.

"Someday!"

Nora wasn't afraid to borrow the best story lines from her real-life best friends either. The giant wagon-wheel coffee table that causes the fictional fight between Marie and Jess in the movie? It actually exists at the Bridgehampton home of Ken Auletta and Amanda "Binky" Urban. ("What could I do? Once she put it in the movie, I couldn't throw it out," Binky said.)

And the line about how Sally is the worst kind of high-maintenance woman because she thinks she's low maintenance? That's actually courtesy of Nick, though he undoubtedly said it to Nora with love.

Over the years, she became a skilled acrobat when it came to the questions she wanted to answer and those she didn't, but she admitted that Sally's "verbal denial of pain when the physical signs are apparent, that 'I'm fine, I'm fine, don't worry about me,'" was in fact very much her modus operandi. And while she was (sometimes) willing to admit that she was a child of alcoholics, she was not willing to admit that this in any way impacted or informed her way of life or her way of being, nor was she ever able to admit that there was more to the story—that there might have been abuse, that there was certain darkness, and pain, and perhaps overwhelming feelings of shame and sadness.

That was just not her way.

13 | *MY BLUE HEAVEN*

NORA OFTEN SAID that *When Harry Met Sally...* changed her life, and the movie's success likewise impacted the lives of almost everyone who made it for the better. It's widely considered the greatest romantic comedy of all time.

But it wasn't always so. At the time of the film's release in July 1989, it garnered nearly $93 million (on a $14.5 million production budget) at the box office—and was a huge sleeper hit by the end of the summer—but some critics thought of it as slightly above average (Roger Ebert, for his part, picked up on its brilliance right away).

Nora's second collaboration with Alice Arlen, *Cookie*, was scheduled for wide release on September 15, 1989, but her future in the movies was still coming together as the cultural impact of *When Harry Met Sally...* was slowly being understood. America was in transition from the conservative Reagan-era 1980s into the 1990s, when alternative modes of media (music, film, art) started to become more popular. As was typical of her work, Nora was a bit ahead of her time.

Her name will likely always be associated with the iconic line "I'll have what she's having," and the scene with Sally's fake orgasm is the one that most people remember from *When Harry Met Sally...* (and the one that gave the film its R rating by the MPAA).

But there's another deli scene from the movie that's actually the *most* Nora:

                    SALLY
I'd like the chef salad, please, with the
oil and vinegar on the side. And the apple
pie a la mode.

                    WAITRESS
        (writing)
Chef and apple a la mode.

                    SALLY
But I'd like the pie heated, and I don't
want the ice cream on top, I want it on the
side. And I'd like strawberry instead of
vanilla if you have it. If not, then no ice
cream, just whipped cream, but only if it's
real. If it's out of a can, then nothing.

                    WAITRESS
Not even the pie?

                    SALLY
No, just the pie. But then not heated.

There were other moments that were highly personal, if not autobiographical, too. Like Sally, Nora drove to New York the day after she graduated from college, wondering if anything would ever happen to her. One of the vignettes of the older couples telling "how we met" stories actually featured the beloved story of how Phoebe and Henry Ephron met when they were both camp counselors.

Nora said she wanted to include Christmas and New Year's Eve in the movie to show the gravity of the emotions of the characters, but the holidays were so important to her that she included them in nearly every movie she made as a recurring motif—a time every year when, like at Tiffany's, nothing bad could happen, perhaps.

Meg said she was at times as perplexed as anyone else by Nora's interest in having her play a Gentile interpretation of Nora's classic Jewish New York heroine. "At times we would look at each other like, *Hmm*," Meg recalled in

2019. "But I was so interested in her. She wasn't like anybody. She was different. On the sets with her, it wasn't just about being directed. It was like, 'How *do* you give a dinner party?' and 'What *do* you cook?' and 'What *about* a seating chart?' You were invited into her life, and it was so charming. I'm grateful we found each other. I also always appreciated that on a movie set she led with her intellect."

For Nora, auteur theory can be summed up in her own foodie-based philosophy about how movies get made like pizzas after a screenplay gets developed and ultimately made into a movie:

> When you write a script, it's like delivering a great big beautiful plain pizza, the one with only cheese and tomatoes. And then you give it to the director, and the director says, 'I love this pizza. I am willing to commit to this pizza. But I really think this pizza should have mushrooms on it' . . . and then someone else comes along and says, 'I love this pizza, too, but it really needs green peppers' . . . and when you get done, what you have is a pizza with everything. Sometimes it's wonderful. And sometimes you look at it and you think, I knew we shouldn't have put the green peppers onto it. Why didn't I say so at the time?

But Nora was thrilled to learn how a collaboration with such talented comedic actors and producers could help take something from good to great. Nora later explained, for example, how some tiny moments, like "I need a Kleenex," can jump off the page when said by the right actor, in this case Meg Ryan as she is being consoled by Harry. Likewise, the line "Thin. Pretty. Big tits. Your basic nightmare," as delivered by the late Carrie Fisher, is now a classic.

"If you want to know how we got from *Annie Hall* to *Knocked Up*, there's only one route, and it's through this movie," Mark Harris deftly explained in *Grantland* in 2014. "*When Harry Met Sally . . .* is a milestone in the shape of a happy collaboration between three distinct Jewish comedy sensibilities—those of director Reiner (menschy and sentimental), screenwriter Nora Ephron (romantic but also tough-minded and feminist), and costar Billy Crystal (blunt, jabby, wisecracking)—that together became more than the sum of their parts."

Over the decades, the screenplay and the characters became so ingrained in culture it can be a challenge to parse out the film's influence in a singular fashion. It's inspired new generations of writers and directors, from actress-writer-producer Mindy Kaling, to Meriweather, to Amy Sherman-Palladino (*Gilmore Girls, The Marvelous Mrs. Maisel*), to many others.

Kaling, for example, was unabashed in her homage to Nora throughout her hit series *The Mindy Project*—and in her approach to life. (She'd even once blogged under the name "Mindy Ephron.") Among her numerous references to Nora's works in the series, an especially hilarious Nora-esque moment is when Danny (Chris Messina) wears a jacket like Harry's as he runs to meet Mindy at the top of the Empire State Building—getting hit by, and rolling atop, a New York City taxicab along the way. She's also producing an adaptation of the novel *Hana Khan Carries On* as a film, putting a "modern Muslim spin" on *The Shop Around the Corner*, the same Lubitsch classic Nora adapted as *You've Got Mail*.

It isn't just women who've been taking notes. Both comedian Chris Rock and actor-writer Seth Rogen count Nora's work as inspiration for their humor. But for writer-director Nick Stoller (*Forgetting Sarah Marshall, The Five-Year Engagement*), it was Nora's bold refusal to fully remove the darkness from the supposed lightest of genres that has stuck with him.

"*When Harry Met Sally* is kind of a dark movie," Stoller told the *Huffington Post*. "It's sweet and it ends beautifully and romantic, but those are two pretty messed up characters. They're pretty flawed. They do pretty nasty things to each other. It goes to a dark, pretty real place between them. That's why it's a classic. Nora Ephron does not pull her punches in that movie."

Mostly, what resonates today for viewers and filmmakers alike is that we hope beyond all hope that, flaws and all, we'll eventually find a way to be someone's person—and someone will want to be ours. And in the movie of our lives, maybe we can manage to have just a smidge of the courage Harry and Sally (Rob and Nora) had to go on in spite of it all. It's true that Sally wants to be understood by someone, but men, like Harry, want to be gotten too.

"When each character hits rock bottom, they're with each other, and we're with them," Harris concluded. "The sad/scary undertow of every romantic comedy is 'What if I'm not in a romantic comedy but a melodrama? What if it never works out for me?' By letting them—and all of us—feel that tug, the movie finds its stakes, and it also finds the punch line that has really made it last: At Harry's and Sally's lowest moments, we want what they're wanting."

Two years earlier, in 1987, New York City was experiencing an unusually hot summer. Temperatures were hovering above ninety degrees—nearly ten degrees higher than normal—and Nora, Nick, and her boys were eager to leave town to get a break from the heat. The kids were off to stay with their father, Carl Bernstein, and Nora and Nick—still relative newlyweds—were getting ready to head to London.

Jacob, her oldest, was about to turn nine years old on August 22, and Max was still a few months shy of eight. The Ephron-Pileggi household was busy, happy, and cozy. On this particular day, the large, shabby chic flat at the historic Apthorp building was lovingly lived in: dishes were being rinsed in the sink, wet clothes hung from the shower curtain rod in the bathroom, and Nick and Nora's bedsheets were still tousled from the morning's rush to move from coffee and newspapers to the typewriter.

Through mutual friend Pat Conroy, author Michael Mewshaw found himself a guest in their home while they traveled. Out of money and stranded with nowhere to stay (his publicity tour for his book, *Money to Burn*, had been unexpectedly cut short), Nora suggested that he simply crash at her place.

"Nora, how could I ever thank you for this kindness?" he asked before she left.

"Take me down to the deli and buy me a Popsicle," she replied. (He chose lemon-lime; she chose a red cherry one.)

Soon after they left, there was a call. It was Carl.

"Hey, who the hell is this?" Bernstein said.

"This is Michael. Michael Mewshaw . . . I'm house-sitting here . . ."

"Nora didn't tell me anything about this," Bernstein said. "How do I know you're not a burglar?"

"Call Nora in London," Mewshaw replied as he recited the phone number she left.

"If you're bullshitting me," Bernstein said, "the cops'll knock down the door in five minutes."

Nora was able to calm him down, but soon there was another call: it was Henry Ephron. In fact, each morning he would call, ready to perform his comedy routine for an audience.

"I depended on those calls to get my day off to a rollicking start," Mewshaw remembered in his 2019 memoir *The Lost Prince: A Search for Pat Conroy*. "And as my time at the Apthorp wound down, I told Henry I would miss him."

"Well, if you're ever on the West Coast," Henry said, "gimme a ring and I'll buy you a drink."

The ailing screenwriter asked what Mewshaw planned to get Nick and Nora as a thank-you gift.

"What do you suggest?" Mewshaw asked.

"Wine," Henry replied. "Not a bottle, a box."

Often drunk and with a dwindling memory, Henry was experiencing declining health. As seen in the lightly fictionalized version of the Ephron patriarch portrayed in Delia's bestselling novel and movie *Hanging Up*, he'd developed a case of "the dwindles," as she called them. He struggled with his aggression and with staying sober. The diagnosis at the time was manic depression—what we would today call bipolar disorder.

Eventually, he would need around-the-clock care as his condition worsened, and he became an inpatient at the Motion Picture and Television Fund Hospital in Woodland Hills, California, where he lived out his final days in the residential retirement community alongside some of his contemporaries.

———————

Back at the Dorothy Chandler Pavilion in downtown Los Angeles, Nora was thrilled to be nominated for an Oscar for a second time—and this time, the nomination was all hers. Billy Crystal, also hot off the success of *When Harry Met Sally...*, was selected to host the Oscars ceremony for the first time in March 1990. (He ended up hosting a record nine times, the second most of any host, after Bob Hope.)

Even Nora, the only female scribe nominated that year, conceded that she wouldn't have voted for herself in what was tough competition in the Original Screenplay category: she was nominated alongside Woody Allen for *Crimes and Misdemeanors* (in which Nora had a walk-on role); Spike Lee for *Do the Right Thing*; Steven Soderbergh for *Sex, Lies, and Videotape*; and winner Tom Schulman for *Dead Poets Society*. Many of the films honored that year, including the Best Picture winner *Driving Miss Daisy*, have gone on to become classics in the modern American film canon.

When Nick and Nora got to attend the Oscars a year later, this time for his nomination for the screenplay for *Goodfellas*, they arrived in style.

Nick was nominated alongside director and friend Martin "Marty" Scorsese for Best Writing, Screenplay Based on Material from Another Medium.

When Harry Met Sally . . . marked an important transition in Nora's work and life from a cynic to a romantic, allowing her to explore other complex material in the years to come. Most importantly, the film is a love letter of sorts to Nick—and the long lead-up to their lasting love affair. Best of all, the experience of making *Sally* provided a renewed joie de vivre vis-à-vis a new raison d'être.

And while getting the proverbial screenwriting pizza remade over and over somehow still ended up being delicious on that film, her experience working with director Herbert Ross on her next film wasn't so.

"Herb Ross could turn any screenwriter into a director," she said a few years later. "In some ways, I'm very grateful to him."

For *My Blue Heaven*, the story of a mafioso (Steve Martin) who gets a new identity courtesy of the FBI's witness protection program, Nora had envisioned Goldie Hawn (who executive produced alongside Nora and Andrew Stone) for the part of the district attorney. The role ended up being played by Joan Cusack after Hawn had to drop out for family reasons.

With her boys now ten (Max) and eleven (Jacob), Nora understood the importance of family herself. She'd started to consider the idea of directing while revising the Korean War love story *Higgins & Beech*, presumed to be her next project.

On the weekends, Max and Jacob would play Super Mario Brothers or catch a baseball game. Of their taste in television, Nora proudly shared that they had "very good taste"—*Seinfeld, Little House on the Prairie*, and *Roseanne* were some of their favorites, which she loved, too. Max, who'd been a hard-core Mets fan, soon turned from baseball to wrestling and then heavy metal. Nora did her best to keep up—she even asked to go to Shea Stadium for Mother's Day. Her devotion to learning such things she might never have considered before shows up in the script and in Cusack's character as an exhausted but ultimately proud single mother.

The boys were truly shocked when Nora left to film *This Is My Life* later that year. She'd always been there every day after school. She'd make dinner, she'd make Halloween costumes, she'd try her best to show the genuine, unconditional positive regard and empathy she'd missed growing up.

Given her unconventional upbringing, Nora sometimes took inspiration from unlikely places, and for *Heaven* it was not only mobster Henry Hill but the infamous gangster John Gotti, whose photo above her desk helped her get through difficult times in the movie business.

"It was a picture of him walking out of the federal courthouse while he was on trial," she said. ". . . But Gotti looked like he didn't have a care in the world. I can't tell you what an inspiration it was to me, to look at that picture when little things went wrong in my life. To remember you can just sort of button your jacket, and no one will know."

Still, the early 1990s were, by all accounts, the time of Nick's and Nora's lives. When asked once about the happiest time in her life, she cited the summer of 1993 in East Hampton.

But at forty-nine, the "slender and spirited" Nora said in later interviews that it continued to frustrate her that movies about supposed "women's issues" were so challenging to get made.

"It's unbelievably hard to get studios to make a script about women," she said. "If I went to a studio with a script about a 32-year-old man with a hang-nail, they'd make it. *Silkwood* was made over their [the studios'] dead bodies."

As far as Nora was concerned, Hollywood wasn't the place to look for "real" creativity; it was one of the reasons she was proud to point out that she didn't *really* live there (she and Nick maintained a home in Beverly Hills for the times they had to be in L.A. for work). To her, it was a place to make a comfort food equivalent of a movie—not that there's anything wrong with that. After all, comfort food is delicious. And it can still be complex, interesting, and something we go back to often for a reason.

But she still knew how to sneak in what she wanted to say, and there was an economic payoff to playing the game too: she reportedly commanded more than $1 million for a script by 1990.

As scholar Liz Dance points out, *Cookie*, *My Blue Heaven*, and *Mixed Nuts* are three of Nora's "most interesting and revealing films" because they show her "affection for the quirky and absurd."

But none of them were a commercial or critical success. While Dance calls them "overwhelmingly complex," critics at the time weren't so convinced.

Before Nora's *My Blue Heaven* was released in August 1990, she and Nick had both been working from the same source material: the life of Henry Hill, a real-life gangster turned informant who went into the witness protection program in 1980. Nick reportedly even lent Hill money and took his phone calls from secret FBI locations to get the story.

Soon after Nick's book about Hill, *Wiseguy: Life in a Mafia Family*, was published in 1985, Nick started to receive messages that there was interest from Hollywood. "Call Martin Scorsese," the pink slips of paper would say, but he assumed it was a joke and ignored them—until Nora stepped in.

"Martin Scorsese is trying to reach you—and you won't call him back!" she said. "You need to call him!"

And thus began Nick and Scorsese's collaboration on what would become *Goodfellas*. The adapted screenplay (with Scorsese) and the film itself were among the six Oscar nominations it received, with Joe Pesci winning Best Actor in a Supporting Role for his iconic portrayal of mobster Tommy DeVito. The screenplay won the Chicago Film Critics Association Award and the BAFTA Award for best adapted screenplay the following year.

They later worked together on a number of other critically acclaimed films, including *Casino* (1995) and *The Irishman* (2019).

While Nick's take on Hill's story was authentic and gritty—drawing on his training as a crime reporter for two decades—Nora's was, unsurprisingly, a humorous one based on an outsider's observations of a seemingly absurd and ironic situation: a government-sanctioned program that allows former criminals to live freely.

"When I was working for *New York* magazine in the '60s there was a story from the FBI that the mob had infiltrated conventional businesses in New York for the first time," Nick told the *Guardian* in 2013. "I already knew of 500 businesses [that had been infiltrated], so I just typed up what I knew. I had a big scoop, everyone went crazy."

Nora, naturally, thought the whole thing was hilarious. Well, maybe not the whole thing.

"The idea, of course, that you could set these people down in, say, Wichita, and expect them to be model citizens, is ludicrous," she says in the production notes for *My Blue Heaven*. "And there they are, suddenly in pineapple-and-cottage-cheese-land. It seemed like a funny idea to explore."

When Steve Martin first read the script for *My Blue Heaven*, he was sure he wanted to be part of the film; he just wasn't sure that the lead role was the right part for him. He'd already worked with costar Rick Moranis on Ron

Howard's *Parenthood* (1989) and in the film version of the off-Broadway hit musical *Little Shop of Horrors* (1986).

"It was interesting watching Steve [Martin] find his way gradually into the character of Vinnie after some of his early doubts," Nora said, noting that his use of a shiny silk gray jacket seemed to help him get into the role.

The role was based on Henry Hill, yes, but also on Nick himself, friends said. The moment in the film when Martin tries to tip the FBI agent (played by Moranis, also of *Ghostbusters* fame) who is assigned to keep track of him? Classic Nick.

"He even tried to tip me," Nora's son Jacob shared in his 2015 documentary, *Everything Is Copy*. It was all part of his charm. Nick was the "yin to Nora's yang," as mutual friend and journalist Richard Reeves put it.

But despite the talent and charm of all involved in *My Blue Heaven*, they ultimately weren't enough to save the film from itself. One critic said that Martin's talent was "tossed away on this sketchy outline of a howlingly funny idea," while another said his "nutball idiosyncrasies almost manage to transcend the film's spread-all-over focus." (Martin also couldn't seem to save the next Nora-scripted attempt at a layered comedy about misfits working at a crisis hotline in the 1994 flop *Mixed Nuts*.)

Nora was devastated. She was frustrated that getting someone to sign on to make a movie about the kind of female-centric stories she wanted to make was difficult even with a *good* track record at the box office. She knew it was time to commit to directing. And to go Hollywood as her parents had done decades earlier.

14 | *THIS IS MY LIFE*

> It's hard to know the truth about a movie you're working on. You basically fall in love with it in some very damaging way.
>
> —Nora Ephron

WHILE NORA HAD DECIDED she'd become a journalist at the tender age of thirteen, it wasn't until she was nearly fifty that she realized that she'd like to become a film director. Not that anyone was surprised—least of all pal and executive producer Lynda Obst, who'd always known Nora could direct based on how she ordered a sandwich.

One day in the late 1980s, Nora got a call from the venerable Dawn Steel—who at the time was an executive at Paramount—and one of only a few women headed for the top in Hollywood. With the nickname "Steelie Dawn," it was possible that she was even more bossy than—and just as tough as—Nora was.

Nora's star was rising—and the time to strike a deal with the budding filmmaker was now.

"Lynda says we should meet," Steel said. "How about lunch?"

It was just a month after Meg Ryan's talent (and fabulous hair), Billy Crystal's charm, and Nora's sparkling screenplay had rocked the summer box office and delighted audiences in July of 1989 with the smash hit release of *When Harry Met Sally . . .* when Steel called again. She was now the president of Columbia Pictures, and as the distributor of *Sally*, she could see the potential for greatness in front of her.

"Nora, I told you I wanted you to direct a movie, and I want you to do it," she said. "I put Lynda in charge of finding you something to direct."

"Terrific," Nora replied.

Just three days later, Lynda called: she'd found the perfect project: *New York Times* bestselling author Meg Wolitzer's 1988 novel *This Is Your Life*. Obst, who'd met Nora years earlier when they both worked at *New York* magazine through her then husband David Obst (he was Bob Woodward and Carl Bernstein's literary agent), was coming off back-to-back producing successes in *Adventures in Babysitting* (1987) and *Heartbreak Hotel* (1988). She could already visualize the novel becoming the inspiration for a comedy drama of the same name about a mother who used material from her family's life to help in her work as a stand-up comedian. The story line's resemblance to the real-life Ephron family lore was uncanny, "where everything is copy, where the lives of the children become the subject matter of the work of their parents," Obst noted in 1989 when the project was first announced.

Columbia Pictures picked it up as part of a first-look development deal that was to include two motion pictures, the second of which would be Steel's choice (alongside Nora's and Lynda's) based on either an Ephron original or possibly another book adaptation, Obst said.

Over the years, Nora's vibrant, creative spirit would attract a number of other like-minded women to her projects. One of those women, Patricia (Patty) K. Meyer was just twenty-nine years old when she first crossed paths with the emerging film director.

Meyer was herself a screenwriter and an up-and-coming independent producer who was "sick of working for the man" when she came across Wolitzer's novel and optioned the rights for its film adaptation along with her producing partner Carole Isenberg. "You've got such great taste in material," Carole told her, "I'll split it with you."

The producing duo were in postproduction on the groundbreaking NAACP Image Award–winning and Emmy Award–nominated miniseries *The Women of Brewster Place* when they got word that Nora and Lynda were interested in Wolitzer's witty novel too.

"Could we take a meeting?" Obst asked.

The first project to be produced by Oprah Winfrey's Harpo Studios, *Brewster* featured an acclaimed African American ensemble cast of Winfrey, the late Cicely Tyson, and the late Olivia Cole, and gave American TV viewers its first Black lesbian couple. Meyer had spotted the critically acclaimed novel of the same name (by first-time author Gloria Naylor, for which she won the National Book Award) at Penguin and borrowed money for the rights to it while Winfrey remained on a waiting list. In fact, Winfrey came to her to make a deal—and Meyer ended up serving as producer on *Brewster* alongside executive producers Winfrey and Isenberg.

Somehow, though, Meyer felt this might be different. Obst had a reputation for being difficult, and she worried that she and Isenberg wouldn't be welcome to be involved in the process as much as they had been on *Brewster*. Still, Meyer was thrilled, because "tonally, there was no other filmmaker or writer in Hollywood that could capture this book like Nora Ephron."

When they met at Columbia Studios to discuss the project, Meyer remembers that she'd got an inkling that her instincts might be right. "Nora, Dawn, and I are girls that go shopping for shoes together," Obst had told her. "We really, really love each other, we're such great friends, and we can't wait to make this movie."

Meyer's attorney advised her not to take the deal they were being offered by Columbia, so she called Nora to see if there might be anything she could do.

"Look, Nora, I know you don't know me from Adam, you don't know my skills, but we've been offered a really raw deal by Columbia," Meyer explained. "Would you be willing to take this project elsewhere?"

"Honestly, Patty, I appreciate your position, but my heart belongs to Lynda," Nora replied. "And my loyalty is to Dawn and Lynda, so I really can't help you."

The deal was made—and while Nora was still glowing from the invigorating experience she'd had working with Rob Reiner on *Sally*, she was still nervous. How would she possibly do this with her two boys at home? What if, for the first time, she wasn't successful at trying something new? What if she got it wrong and was laughed out of town forever?

She called for reinforcements.

"Del, will you come help me write this screenplay?"

Delia was Nora's source of truth—and that mattered on the film set just as much, if not more, than it did in life. Nora thought she might struggle with directing and writing at the same time, and she knew she could count on Delia to do the on-set rewrites in her stead.

"Everybody comes at everything from their own point of view, from their own craziness, and you're always trying to find the person whose craziness meshes with yours, so if they say that scene isn't working right, it's true, and you've got to deal with it. Delia is that person for me. She's very tough."

Truth mattered to Nora as a journalist, and it mattered in her conceptualization of the fictional worlds she created on film sets, too, because she wanted things to be right. She wanted them to be real. Writing about sisters dealing with a working mother they admired, but who ultimately couldn't be physically or emotionally present, felt particularly raw—even almost twenty years after the loss of their mother too soon. Nora saw script revisions and feedback for what they really were: an opportunity to create a different reality. In a way, the daughters of two alcoholic screenwriters were finally free by getting closer to the painful material—the truth—rather than running away. A happy ending in a movie was a chance to rewrite history.

By the time the sisters turned in a draft of the script in September 1989, producers Peter Guber and Jon Peters had become cochairmen for what would become Sony Pictures Entertainment and had replaced Steel on the project. Sony acquired Columbia Pictures Entertainment from the Coca-Cola Company, the owner at the time, and by November, the transaction was complete. Steel was out entirely by the following January. But love and friendship from the Steel and Obst–led girls club notwithstanding, what was to become of Nora's directorial debut that had been so carefully shepherded along by Dawn and Lynda's don't-take-shit-from-anyone approach?

Peters, the prolific producer behind such hits as the 1976 version of *A Star Is Born*, *Flashdance*, and *Rain Man*, had begun his career in Hollywood as an extra on Cecil B. DeMille's landmark 1956 film *The Ten Commandments*. At the time of that film's production, Nora's mother, Phoebe, was in her office at Paramount and told Nora in one of her letters, "The Red Sea was made of blue Jell-o."

A conversation with him one afternoon in Manhattan gave Nora some indication of where her film was headed now that Dawn was literally out of the picture.

As Nora remembers it, she learned a lot about Peters during that meeting. He was joined by his Norwegian Swedish supermodel girlfriend, the tall, blonde Vendela Kirsebom, and Amy Pascal, a young studio executive. He said he had a therapist who was helping him "get in touch with his inner child" and he gossiped about his producing partner's marriage. After a few minutes, they turned to business.

"What exactly is your movie about, Nora?" he asked.

"Well," she replied, "have you read the script yet?"

"Look, I've made sixty-eight movies," he said, "and I've never read a script, and I don't need to read a script."

Nora was flabbergasted. She took a deep breath. "OK," she told him. "Here's what it's about . . ."

Within a few moments, Peters and Kirsebom were both giving their thoughts about working mothers. Nora tried to force a smile, but all she could think was, *It can't get any worse than this.*

Almost an entire year went by with no progress on the project, and Nora became depressed by the whole thing. "Columbia was horrible," she remembered. "They weren't going to make it. They didn't know what it was. They didn't care about me. They just weren't going to put it into turnaround."

That's when her clever, if a bit offbeat, agent, Sam Cohn, snuck a copy of the script over to Joe Roth, who was then chairman at Twentieth Century Fox, and with some back-and-forth, Columbia let it go. Finally, the movie might have a chance of being made, but there was still the matter of proving Nora was a suitable director and securing a strong cast.

Soon after Fox took over, a classic Sally-like lunch-ordering scene at the Russian Tea Room in Manhattan sealed the directing deal for Nora. If there was one skill she'd been honing for decades, it was how to make sure that she and everyone around her got the best life had to offer. And she delivered her recommendations with confidence, grace, and ease.

"You should try the chicken Kiev," Nora told Roth. "And Roger [Roth's assistant], you should have the beef Stroganoff. I'm going to order the chicken salad but without the mayonnaise."

Roth sat back in awe, looked at Obst, and just said, "I know I have a director!"

As for the movie's casting, Fox wanted a star—someone like Cher or Michelle Pfeiffer—in the lead role as the Jewish up-and-coming comedian from Queens. A news item in *Screen International* said Tracey Ullman was attached. Bette Midler was interested, but she was stuck in a contract for a movie with the working title *Disney's Halloween House* at Walt Disney Pictures. (That movie was, of course, later renamed *Hocus Pocus*, which became a cult classic with record-breaking annual showings on television, spawning rides, festivals, books, and a forthcoming sequel with Midler and the other original stars set to begin filming in fall 2021.)

"I think the movie would have done better if Bette had been in it," Nora said later in an interview with the Academy of Achievement. "I love Julie Kavner in it, but I begged [Disney Chairman] Jeffrey Katzenberg to let her out of her contract or for him to make it, and he simply had no interest in the subject matter of that movie and told me so. He had no interest in what it was about, which was balancing a career and work. It was about a woman stand-up comic who had two children."

For Nora, his decision felt personal. Just as he'd approached *Heartburn* years earlier, she felt he didn't understand or appreciate the value of telling the story of a divorced, independent woman on-screen. "It was a very funny script and a good script," she added, "and Jeffrey isn't really interested in women—his wife is a housewife, he just wasn't there. It was heartbreaking to me."

But back at Fox, Roth and Obst were still on board the Nora train and eager to see it arrive at its destination, as were Isenberg and Meyer. Nora got Roth's go-ahead to hire Kavner, who at the time had been voicing the character of Marge Simpson on a popular new animated show called *The Simpsons*—and was mostly known to television audiences as Brenda, the younger sister to Valerie Harper's Rhoda in the popular *Mary Tyler Moore Show* spin-off, for which she'd won an Emmy Award in 1978 for Outstanding Supporting Actress. She'd also made appearances in several Woody Allen films and had a supporting role as a nurse in Penny Marshall's *Awakenings* in 1990. But on the shoestring $10 million production budget, would someone like Kavner agree to come on board?

"I said, 'Julie' [Kavner], Joe said, 'Great,' and everyone went into complete shock," Ephron said. Suddenly, it seemed, they finally had a movie. The comedic actress agreed to take the lead role of Dottie Ingels in what was a fascinating departure for Kavner from her more typical role of the empathetic underdog. She embraced the idea that she could play someone as unlikeable and "selfish" as the single mother who leaves her two daughters behind as her career takes off. Still, costume designer and friend Jeffrey Kurland said at the time, "Julie is not like the characters she plays. She honestly doesn't believe that anybody would be interested in her private life."

Nora's directorial debut: on the set of *This Is My Life* with Julie Kavner, 1992. *™ & copyright © 20th Century Fox Film Corp. All rights reserved / The Everett Collection*

Director Nora (front) on the set of *This Is My Life*, 1992. *™ & copyright © 20th Century Fox Film Corp. All rights reserved / The Everett Collection*

But Kavner threw herself into research for the role of the self-absorbed star, just as she always did. While she'd initially been envisioned for the role of Claudia (which ended up being played by Carrie Fisher), the assistant to a not-so-different-from-real-life agent Sam Cohn (played by Dan Aykroyd), the part of Dottie thrilled her. Before shooting began, she visited comedy clubs and studied the tapes of comedians such as Totie Fields, Joy Behar (who makes a cameo in the film as a makeup consultant), and Rosie O'Donnell, as well as the legendary George Carlin. She practiced and perfected her own improv performance during the three weeks of rehearsals, and said she figured out how to play "a person who is very selfish, very on."

Wolitzer joined Nora at her apartment at the Apthorp for casting sessions with casting director Juliet Taylor, who'd worked with Nora previously on *Heartburn*. They found gems in young actresses Gaby Hoffmann and Samantha Mathis to play the roles of Opal and Erica Ingels, respectively. With the key players in place, Nora was relieved, excited, and nervous. Before she left for Toronto for the ten-week shoot, she sought the advice of her friends who happened to be award-winning directors.

"What if you give someone a note and it makes the performance worse?" she asked Mike Nichols, to which he replied, simply, "you just walk up to them and say, 'ignore everything I just said to you.'" She and Reiner met for lunch and spent an afternoon going through the script. He gave her a piece of advice that she took to heart to the *n*th degree: "He said that making a movie was like having a party," she remembered. "And that he was the host of the party, and he had invited all these people to come to the party, and it was up to him to make sure they had a good time."

Now that, she thought, she could do.

15 | *SLEEPLESS*

> You gotta learn to laugh. It's the way to true love.
> —*Michael*

THE YEAR WAS 1992. Nora, at fifty-one, had just finished the final edit on her directorial debut in *This Is My Life* and was ready for her next adventure. While that film had been deeply personal, it also had a relatively small budget (a reported $10 million) and—thanks in part to a limited release—fared modestly at the box office, bringing in only $2.9 million.

```
FADE IN ON:


A ROOMFUL OF MEN


Men at desks. Men as far as the eye can see. We're in:


INT: CITY ROOM OF THE NEW YORK HERALD-TRIBUNE-DAY


It's 1950. We hear the rattling of Underwoods, like a forest full
of mechanical cricks. We track through the city ... and finally we
come to rest on:


THE ONLY WOMAN IN THE ROOM.
```

That's the beginning of a script Nora was also particularly excited about working on with her *Silkwood* cowriter Alice Arlen and thus "dusting off her skills as a reporter" following the success of *When Harry Met Sally . . .* in 1989, a few years earlier. The story focused on Pulitzer Prize–winning Korean War correspondent Marguerite Higgins. It would be several years and several revisions later before the film would ultimately be put on hold. But what if it hadn't been?

Nora could have conceivably stuck to directing smaller, more personal directorial projects. But if she were to make the directing thing a full-time gig, she'd need a hit.

In the meantime, there were lots of opportunities for rewrites on scripts that needed her sharp pen. "I was dying to work with Adrian Lyne," Nora told *Rolling Stone*. "I had made the mistake of foolishly turning down a rewrite on *Fatal Attraction*." That film, of course, went on to become not only a box office megahit (bringing in more than $156 million domestically) but a cult classic that catapulted actress Glenn Close to fame.

In addition to another fruitful creative collaboration, Nora was seeking a cash infusion. She applied for but ultimately didn't get the job to rewrite Lyne's *Indecent Proposal* (1993). That's when a script came across her desk that seemed to fit like a glove. It was David S. Ward's second draft of a screenplay called *Sleepless in Seattle*.

"It had all these weird, wonderful ideas to play with, including this stuff about what the movies do to your brain and how so many of our notions about romance are based on the movies that we've seen," she said.

There was Nora, a child of the movies, a child of screenwriters, and a fierce (albeit funny) feminist. She could both understand and appreciate the nostalgia for old films—but with her trademark gimlet eye.

For her, falling in love at the movies was personal. As far as she could remember, it all started when her mother, Phoebe, took her to a screening of *An Affair to Remember* in Westwood, California, in 1957. After the movie ended, Nora stood up to leave. But Phoebe took her hand. She wanted her to meet the star of the film, Mr. Cary Grant himself.

"Nora, say hello to Mr. Grant."

"There I was, a hopeless teenage girl awash in salt water," she later recalled. "I now look at this movie 'What was I thinking?' but I could play the last ten minutes of that movie for you now, and we'd be crying."

Of course, meeting Grant after seeing him on-screen was more than just a romantic experience. The notion of mixing the imagined with the real was powerful—and it informed much of Nora's work for decades to come, says Ephron scholar Liz Dance.

Indeed, she inherited an ardent commitment to narrative and a blurring of the lines between fiction and nonfiction from her dramatically inclined screenwriter parents, Henry and Phoebe, at an early age. Remember: she was named after a character in an Ibsen play, and was no more than three years old before she first saw her own life up on the silver screen in *Three Is a Family* (1944). Referring to life as a movie and the movies as life was as common as peaches and milk in the Ephron household.

"Henry described moments of his life in terms of cinematic references, as did Nora," Dance adds. "Their lives were peopled, and for Nora continued to be peopled, by both the real and the imagined—and both had influence."

The cultural significance of that influence was first put on display in her parents' screenplay *Always Together* (1947). In that film, a marriage is tested and ultimately saved by virtue of the main characters watching and digesting another film about marriage. Nora said she wanted to use that same plot device more overtly in *Sleepless in Seattle* in order to "make a movie about how movies screw up your brain about love," adding that "if we did a good job, we would become one of the movies that would screw up people's brains about love forever."

But before anyone's brains could—or, arguably, would—be screwed up forever as Nora gleefully predicted, she'd need a leading lady and a leading man to star in the film. Before she signed on, director Garry Marshall and the newly minted romantic comedy star Julia Roberts had been attached to the project—coming off the major box office success *Pretty Woman* (1990). That film had grossed more than $178 million domestically and more than $463 million worldwide.

Still, it would be what producer Gary Foster called "a bumpy two-year stretch" just to get *Sleepless* made. Believe it or not, we technically have Tony Robbins to thank for what would become Nora's highest-grossing (and arguably her most beloved) film of all time. A writer named Jeff Arch was so inspired by Robbins that he flew out from his hometown in Virginia to attend one of the self-help guru's talks in La Jolla, California, in 1990. The thirty-five-year-old English teacher returned home and sat down to write a romantic drama about two star-crossed lovers (originally known as Tom Baldwin, later renamed Sam, and Annie Reed) brought together by a nationally syndicated radio show host and a hopeful little boy (Jonah, Tom's son).

"I was looking for a happy ending for me," Arch said. "I was all three of those characters. I didn't know it."

———————

If the development process had been challenging for Foster, it wasn't about to get any easier for Nora. In January 1992, while the rest of America was entranced by the skating phenom Kristi Yamaguchi's win at the US Figure Skating Championships—or perhaps, then presidential candidate Bill Clinton's real-life drama with Gennifer Flowers—Nora had work to do. The *Sleepless* script had already been through revisions with playwright Larry Atlas that Arch deemed "terrible," and Ward had been brought on in 1991 to add much-needed humor to tone down some of the earnestness of the original. TriStar Pictures studio head Mike Medavoy was into the idea of hiring Dennis Quaid and Meg Ryan—who at the time were married in real life—to star together, and Nick Castle was to direct as a consolation prize for being replaced by Steven Spielberg on *Hook* the year prior. "I didn't have my choice of scripts," he said. "'You want to do this, we'll make you the director.' I read it and really liked it."

Meanwhile, *This Is My Life* was having its world premiere at the Sundance Film Festival. In fact, the small but mighty film opened the prestigious Robert Redford–founded annual film event. Noted *Rolling Stone* critic Peter Travers at the time, "*This Is My Life* also marks Nora Ephron's first crack at directing, and she makes a cleanly executed and pungently comic job of it. . . . As always, she uses her ironic edge to cut to the nerve. It's an auspicious debut; you sense Ephron is just starting to stretch her muscles as a director and is eyeing other moldy rules in need of breaking."

Still, audiences may not have been ready yet for such fresh storytelling, executive producer Lynda Obst later explained. "[*This Is My Life*] was made in a time when movies weren't made about women," she said in 2015. "It was ahead of its time. A movie about a single mother? Now there's *Boyhood*. Now we're ready for movies about single mothers."

Back on *Sleepless*, Nora had submitted her rewrites, and her first order of business was getting Ryan (whom she had collaborated with on *When Harry Met Sally* . . . in 1989) and budding young movie star Tom Hanks to sign on. Tom was on the verge of making movie history by winning back-to-back

Best Actor Academy Awards in 1994 and 1995 for his unforgettable dramatic performances in *Philadelphia* and *Forrest Gump*, respectively (he's one of only two actors to do this, the other being Spencer Tracy).

But in early 1992, he may have looked more like a washed-up baseball player than a critically acclaimed actor. That's because he'd just finished filming Penny Marshall's *A League of Their Own* and had put on twenty pounds for the role of Jimmy Dugan, the tough but ultimately beloved manager of the fictional Rockford Peaches all-female baseball team.

Nora and Tom met at the famed Beverly Hills Hotel for lunch to talk about *Sleepless*. He and his wife Rita Wilson had seen *This Is My Life*. They could see what was in front of them: a talented new film auteur. In one particular scene in the film, Tom was impressed by how Nora chose to capture Julie Kavner's character and her two daughters as they moved from Queens to Manhattan. "It was a geographically accurate movie montage," he told longtime mutual friend Richard Cohen. "They got on the 59th Street Bridge and they drove up First Avenue. They went across the Park at 79th Street or whatever it was. That always knocked me out."

But Tom still wasn't quite convinced this was the right project—or, for that matter, that Nora was the right person to lead it. He described himself as "persnickety" in their first meeting, and sometimes the meetings grew contentious. "I thought I was a hotshot and I was supposed to have opinions and supposed to carry weight," he added. "I didn't want the kid to have better lines than me. I didn't want to play the pussy." The pair worked together on casting and dialogue, and Nora later credited Tom with his "wonderful work" on the script, adding that there had been "trillions of drafts of this movie in a short period of time . . . and [sister] Delia and I just kept pushing and pushing."

Back at the studio, a proverbial bomb had gone off: Castle was suddenly—and quite literally—out of the picture. With Ephron's smart rewrites, the project had become hot, and everyone from Julia Roberts to Kim Basinger to Sharon Stone, and even Madonna, was interested in playing the part of Annie Reed. But would the film ever get made?

"Hello, Nora?"

"Yes?"

"I'm flying you to L.A. to meet with Medavoy, Snider, and Platt. You must present your ideas to them because you *must* direct this movie."

Gary Foster was convinced that in the hands of anyone else, the now-sharp *Sleepless* script would become too sweet—but first, he'd need to convince the powers that be that the novice film director was up to the task. It was to be a production with a budget of $25 million—could a *woman* handle that? Especially one with virtually no experience? Medavoy consulted with his colleagues Stacey Snider and Marc Platt.

"This is the woman who understands the genre better than anyone else," Foster told Medavoy. "This is the woman who took this script from being a solid B to an A. And she just had experience, so you should at least meet with her."

Nora was also a woman who knew how to make incredible connections. It was as an extra on the set of Woody Allen's *Crimes and Misdemeanors* that she'd had the good fortune of meeting the legendary cinematographer Sven Nykvist.

"Go out and hire the greatest cinematographer you can find," Medavoy had told her as *Sleepless* was being developed. "Because this movie has to look gorgeous."

Two days later, Nora called to share the good news. "I did it!" she told him. "I hired the *greatest* cinematographer in the *world*, not the greatest one I could find."

Not only did Nora dazzle them in the conference room, Lynda said a key factor in making the directing decision for *Sleepless* was based on—get this— how a person orders lunch in a restaurant. It was in the bag. "Nora was the greatest food orderer that ever lived," Lynda recalled. "She *was* Sally." Nora's clarity in everything from the lunch menu to the best doctor/hairdresser/florist in town was a sign she'd make a great film director.

And at long last, she won the directing gig for *Sleepless*, but she quickly brought on her trusted advisers: Lynda as executive producer, and sister Delia to help with more rewrites in preparation for filming.

It was a Wednesday in mid-July 1992 when filming began on *Sleepless in Seattle*, and as longtime friend Richard Cohen put it, "When Nora showed up in Seattle, all eyes were on her." It's hard to imagine now, but yes, the novice film director was still trying to prove that she was "tough enough" for the job. Nick joined her for the summer, and she considered their apartment overlooking the famed Pike Place Market "heaven." During the day, he'd write and visit the local Italian deli, often bringing home jars of his favorite olives while he waited for her to finish long days of shooting.

It took only a few days before Nora had the chance to make a lasting impression—for better or worse, depending on whom you ask. She saw the dailies—that is, the raw footage shot each day during production on a film—and made a call to her trusted friend and executive producer, Lynda Obst. "Lynda," she said, "we must replace the kid."

Shock waves reverberated through the set.

"She was protecting the movie," Cohen later wrote. What was at stake if the film failed to be a success? Only her entire career. But members of the cast— including Tom's wife, Rita—were nonetheless terrified. She was friendly with Nora, but she'd still auditioned for and ultimately won the part of Tom's sister in *Sleepless* as well as a role in *Mixed Nuts*. "I kept thinking I was going to get fired," she told Cohen. "I was shocked that I made it through the whole thing."

The young boy's mother, Linda Watt, and his agent, Iris Burton, were confused and devastated. They couldn't understand how a fellow mother could be so cold. When Nathan Watt was later cast in a Diane Keaton film, Linda

Nora enjoying a hot dog on the set of *Sleepless* while Rob Reiner (background left) looks on. *Photo by Elizabeth Segal / courtesy of the photographer*

hoped she'd finally get the acknowledgment she'd been looking for from Nora at the New York premiere—but it wasn't to be. "I remember it being outside, and I look up at Nora with her coat flowing behind her and her entourage behind her," Linda recalled. To Nora, it was as if she didn't exist.

This is part of the paradox of Nora Ephron the person and artist that's both fascinating and frustrating in the context of gender politics in Hollywood. Perhaps she could still hear her mother's voice: "Nora, you are sixteen years old, and if I haven't raised you to make your own decisions, it won't do [you] any good to tell you what I think." Nora could be tough. She could be ruthless. She could be bored with incompetence.

In some ways, she *was* her mother's daughter.

Ironically, for someone who made such seemingly tender romantic films, Lynda says Nora "loathed" sentiment but that she knew how to capture the crazy idea that men have feelings too in the minutiae of her flawed characters and clever dialogue ("Did you see *Fatal Attraction*? Well I did, and it scared the *shit* out of me!" Tom Hanks says in *Sleepless*). If men and women are to come together in any kind of lasting union—be it friendship, romance, marriage, creative collaboration, or otherwise—it's not about making a "woman's movie," in Hollywood or in life, and Nora's films seem to speak to that sensibility. It's part of what makes them classics—and it's part of why her voice endures.

"Tom [Hanks] made it a 'man's' movie," Lynda later said of *Sleepless*. "So many people say it's a 'woman's movie,' but it's really about a man's romantic struggle."

Instead of force-feeding audiences with implausible gag-worthy story lines that are overly sentimental, she said it was always about authenticity with Ephron. "It was like the scene with peeling the apple in *Sleepless*. . . . What's the detail you remember about someone who leaves?" Lynda asked. "It's the touching detail that you'll never see again—it is touching, but it has no sentiment. It has uniqueness, texture, smell."

Actress Caroline Aaron (*The Marvelous Mrs. Maisel*), who starred in a number of Nora's films (among a hundred film performances for other famed directors, such as Mike Nichols and Woody Allen) and her play *Love, Loss, and What I Wore* (cowritten with Delia), also recalled Nora's uniqueness—and how real she wanted everything to look, feel, and sound. "She wanted it to be so authentic that she had me in a soundproof booth as I voiced Dr. Marcia

Fieldstone," she told me. "She felt that Dr. Marcia was sort of moving the story forward."

An important role indeed—one that tied together the idea of a "global village" since the film's protagonists were thousands of miles apart until the last moments of the film. Nora seemingly anticipated the detachment we would face as the Internet took hold in the early 2000s. "We live in a place called the United States of America. We all watch the same television. We all turn on the president at the same moment, or fall in love with the first lady at the same moment, or start drinking Snapple or whatever it is," she said in 1992.

What she may not have anticipated is just how fragmented and divisive sections of America would become (much of it rooted in the inequity and violence that's always been here)—is that part of what makes her particular brand of optimism so appealing in this current moment? Possibly. But that doesn't mean Nora the person, and indeed, Nora the filmmaker, were not without critics then and now.

Some of the harshest, in fact, came from inside her own family.

16 | AFTER *SLEEPLESS*

You could see the bright side of the plague.

—*Mixed Nuts*

WHEN DELIA EPHRON WAS first brought home from L.A.'s Good Samaritan Hospital in 1944, her precocious big sister, Nora, would sneak upstairs to pinch her whenever her parents weren't looking. From her bassinet, she'd stare up at Nora with a pair of big brown eyes and curly brown hair, perhaps already realizing this would be the perfect metaphor for life with Nora: fun, yes, but painful at times too.

"My first memory of Nora is that she bit a tomato so perfectly as to squirt juice into my eyes," Delia said. "I was an opportunity."

Henry Ephron later wrote that in Phoebe's postdelivery haze she thought about calling their new daughter Veneer, but thankfully, she was instead named Delia, after the Greek island. Her name means "peace."

Over the years, the sisters shared everything—food in the refrigerator, screenplays, great one-liners—and to say that closeness helped save them during difficult times would be an understatement. Delia's gentleness seemed to serve her well when it came to disagreements.

Still, when Henry grew more and more ill and eventually passed away in September 1992, it was Delia—not Nora—whom he called. And called. And called.

"My father had died, and Nora was shooting, I think, *Sleepless*," Delia recalled. "The problems of his death really were Amy's and mine. Nora wasn't there. I had resentment for that."

Delia's 1995 novel, *Hanging Up*, was—in the Ephron family tradition—partly autobiographical, Delia said at the time, and the sisters seemed friendly enough about the portrayal of the fictional quarreling sisters in media interviews. But when it came time to develop the book into a movie, the real-life similarities hit far too close to home, and Nora and Delia didn't speak for at least a month.

"I'm sure she thinks I was mean about it. I think she was mean about it," Delia lamented. "And we made up. But it was horrible, actually, for each of us. I mean, we'd been together our whole lives, and then we weren't speaking over a piece of material. In retrospect, how stupid is that?"

Delia left it out of *Hanging Up* that Nora hadn't gone to Henry's funeral. Had the tables been turned, would Nora have done the same? Would she later come to regret the decision not to go? We can guess, but no one really knows for sure—except Nora and perhaps Delia. Nora spoke a lot about regrets in life and love and the "mashed potatoes that went with them," but never about regrets over her father.

But that didn't preclude her from wishful thinking.

"You always think that a bolt of lightning is going to strike and your parents will magically change into the people you wish they were or back into the people they used to be," she later wrote. "But they're never going to. And even though you know they're never going to, you still hope they will."

For now, the sisters had work to do. Family drama would have to wait—though almost any sibling can likely attest to the fact that sooner or later those pains from the past would need to be dealt with, or they'd bubble up to the surface at an inopportune moment.

But they knew the drill. Bury the pain and write. And write it funny. Or at least write something good. This was the deeper, darker undercurrent informing the lovely "everything is copy" maxim they'd heard growing up over and over again from Phoebe.

If the pain gets too severe, perhaps a witty one-liner might be just as effective as a shot of whiskey. Naturally, they obliged, but the result shows how difficult all of that can be when the material is both too personal and not personal enough.

On a crisp October day in the fall of 1993, Nora met with film scholar Marsha McCreadie to help with her book about women screenwriters. Poised and put together, she sat in her bright Upper West Side apartment in her slacks and silky wrap layers. Having recently been cornered by the author in the ladies' room at the Loews 84th Street Movie Complex, Nora graciously agreed to the interview even though she was busy casting for her next film, *Mixed Nuts*.

At fifty-two, she was as attractive and funny as ever. Nora was also in control—always.

"She spontaneously broke in and broke up (laughing) at times, as one thought would lead to another, and she would refocus the topic and the conversation," McCreadie wrote. "And when that happened her hands would fly into descriptive images—running quickly with her thoughts—almost as if they had their own will and life away from a very collected posture."

"It is the writer's job to get screwed," Nora had quipped. "Writers are the women of the movie business." But with her back in the director's chair, and with a healthy production budget somewhere between $20 and $29 million, principal photography on *Mixed Nuts* started on Valentine's Day in 1994 after a brief delay. Given the hype around what was considered Nora's "highly anticipated follow-up" to *Sleepless*, beginning on that special holiday somehow now seems fitting. Meg Ryan and Tom Hanks, staring into one another's eyes, hand in hand on top of the Empire State Building on Valentine's Day? That's a tough act to follow.

Not that *Mixed Nuts* was necessarily meant to be a love story. Actually, quite the opposite. The quirky comedy was based on a French play and subsequent film, *Le Père Noël est une ordure*, or *Santa Claus Is a Stinker*.

"The last thing I wanted to do was a love story about two people who think they're destined for one another," Nora told the *Los Angeles Daily News* in 1994. "I loved this and Delia loved it because the premise just killed us: people at the suicide hot line who were more neurotic than the people calling."

In fact the film, formerly known as both *Lifesavers* and *The Night Before Christmas*, had been in development since long before *Sleepless*. Never one to shy away from a fun double entendre, Nora allowed a focus group to choose the new name, *Mixed Nuts*, which also happened to be one of her favorite snacks to serve during dinner parties.

Getting an all-star cast to sign on started with Steve Martin, even after the disappointment of *My Blue Heaven* just a few years earlier. "It started with Nora," he told the *Daily News*, "then the cast and the script; plus, it's a place to call home for three months."

"I just trust Nora, and I know that when we get there on the set, it's going to end up funny somehow," he added. Rita Wilson, the late Madeline Kahn, Juliette Lewis, and Anthony LaPaglia starred, while Liev Schreiber (fresh out of the Yale School of Drama), Robert Klein, the late Garry Shandling, and then *SNL* comedian Adam Sandler rounded out the cast of misfits. Parker Posey and (pre-*Daily Show*) Jon Stewart made cameos as the uppity Rollerblading couple.

Nerves over potential craftworker strikes at the time prevented production from taking place in Venice Beach, so a number of key moments were actually filmed in New York. Once cameras started rolling (with the elegant and Oscar-winning Sven Nykvist helming once again), Sandler was responsible for keeping the laughs going on long nights of shooting. "[He] kept us in stitches during six weeks of night shoots with his catalogue of filthy, hilarious jokes," Rita recalled on Facebook. "And, I got to go to work every day and see my friend Nora Ephron. I'm so glad this film has somehow endured and people have found it."

Nora would be glad too.

"I love having a group of people that I get to work with, so you have this little company and every 18 months or so, you all spend three months together and eat in restaurants in cities where you don't live," she said at the time of the film's release. "But mostly I want to make funny movies."

Director Nora and her director of photography, the legendary Sven Nykvist (right) on the set of *Mixed Nuts*, 1994. © *TriStar Pictures / The Everett Collection*

This time around, Nora and her collaborators had a chance to eat in her favorite city, New York, as a competitive bid from Kaufman Astoria Studios provided the would-be Venice Beach backdrop for seven weeks of filming. Daytime and nighttime cycloramas depicting Venice were created as well as a four-story replica of Venice's Waldorf Hotel—made of wood, glass, plaster, and steel. The price tag: $630,000. A replica (empty) elevator shaft was built alongside a working one so that difficult camera angles could be achieved.

Four weeks of exteriors were actually filmed in Venice Beach, beginning in April. Nora had fallen in love with the artwork of Laura Levine in the *Utne Reader*, an alternative weekly aggregator, and commissioned her to paint a thirty-foot mural and a thrift store façade shown in the film to be attributed to LaPaglia's artistic but suicidal character Felix. Levine and two assistants spent a month painting the mural on Pacific Avenue in Venice. A girl after Nora's own heart, Levine was New York born and raised and unafraid to break boundaries: she recalled talking her way into a Patti Smith and Paul Simon shoot at Central Park at age sixteen by printing a fake press pass—launching her multidisciplinary artistic career that has included photographing musicians from the Ramones to Madonna.

Adam Sandler (left), kept everyone laughing while shooting *Mixed Nuts*, including director Nora (center, standing), Steve Martin (right of center), and Rita Wilson (front), 1994. © TriStar Pictures / The Everett Collection

Nora chose the British composer George Fenton for the music for *Mixed Nuts* after being introduced to him a year earlier by mutual producer pal Lynda Obst. "She was amazing," he recalled of working with Nora on the soundstage in New York. "I mean the things that she used to dislike and the grounds on which she disliked them seemed so eccentric. That she would rule out using a song because of one lyric line. And I used to think, 'I don't think anyone would even notice that line,' but she was really forensic about it. She had this incredible memory for lyrics and knew hundreds of lyrics, the details of songs." In addition to his original theme, "Mixed Notes," the final soundtrack includes such eclectic choices as Sandler's "Grape Jelly," and Carly Simon's "The Night Before Christmas" (from *This Is My Life*) along with Christmas classics from Eartha Kitt and the Drifters.

Meanwhile, after shooting for *Mixed Nuts* wrapped, Nora was honored at the Women in Film Crystal Awards Luncheon at the Beverly Hilton in June, where she was chosen for the Crystal Award for her achievements in film, alongside Polly Platt, Joan Plowright, and Susan Sarandon. First presented in 1977 by what is now the Los Angeles chapter of the Women in Film global organization, the Women in Film Crystal + Lucy Awards are presented to honor "outstanding women who, through their endurance and the excellence of their work, have helped to expand the role of women within the entertainment industry."

Still, a great deal was on the line when *Mixed Nuts* hit theaters just before Christmas that year. Most studio heads were already reluctant to put a woman in charge on a film set—and naturally any evidence that proved them right just raised the bar even higher. But even though *Mixed Nuts* failed to impress critics and fans at the time, there are moments of pure comedic genius throughout—the kind only Nora and Delia could write together. In one particularly hilarious scene, the grumpy Mrs. Munchnik (Kahn) is answering the phone at the suicide hotline office in Venice Beach. It's the night before Christmas, and all through the house—er, building—she can be heard schooling Catherine (Wilson) re: men. Hair pulled back in a bun and neatly dressed, Mrs. Munchnik doesn't have time for shenanigans.

"Men are not true to *anything*," she tells Catherine. "They will have sex with a tree."

Perhaps she's a stand-in for what it was like getting advice from Phoebe growing up? Or what might have happened to *Heartburn*'s Rachel Samstat had she not gone off to "dream another dream"?

Later, when Philip (Martin) tries to call the *Los Angeles Times*, we get to hear Nora's voice on the other end of the line doing a classic bit we can probably all relate to: a long, confusing automated message that makes it impossible for him to get to an actual live person. It must have cracked her up. Serious about her work and responsible with time and budgets, she, for one, still enjoyed a clever shenanigan every now and again. One of her favorite lines, which Nora said wasn't autobiographical but could have been, was from a caller to the hotline who feared she'd always be in the "ten items or less" line—alone—at Zabar's.

As for Kahn, it would be one of her last film roles before her untimely death from ovarian cancer at the age of fifty-seven in 1999. Like Nora, she kept her condition a secret from most people for almost a year.

Asked how much improvisation was permitted during filming, Kahn explained that Nora told her she would just keep the camera rolling while she sat in the broken elevator and to do whatever occurred to her with the toys and gifts. "That part was spontaneous," she said.

As for Wilson, she knew from working with Nora on *Sleepless* that Nora was never afraid of a note or clever idea from a cast or crew member she trusted. Of course, if it was a terrible idea, she would also let you know. That was Nora: brutally honest and unafraid.

When Rita's character, Catherine, was brooding in the bathtub—fully clothed and talking to herself—Nora went so far as to move a wall so that the camera angle for the scene could be changed based on Rita's suggestion. It worked.

One might imagine that Nora's voice could be felt most in Catherine's character, but certainly Delia's was too. Catherine is earnest in her desire for true love—and authentic, and perhaps realistic, by way of her participation in Adult Children of Alcoholics meetings. Several of Kahn's lines came straight out of Nora's essays, and Rob Reiner's cameo as the neurotic veterinarian, Dr. Kinsky, had the trademark "have you ever noticed . . . ?" shtick that made some of her most famous columns so memorable and relatable. (Reiner's Kinsky, in this case, was lamenting the fact that women like to have so many pillows on the bed only to take them off and then put them back on again. Every. Single. Day.)

"My real occupation is essayist," Nora said. "Just the way that *When Harry Met Sally . . .* is an essay about friendship and love, this is an essay about Christmas. It's the sort of thing Delia and I love to do: Say, 'what is it about this subject?' then figure out what it is and then figure out how we can make it dramatically work for a movie."

Sadly, it largely didn't work. At least not at the time. Fans and critics alike had eagerly awaited her follow-up to the beloved—and Oscar-nominated—*Sleepless in Seattle*. That film had struck box office gold. *Mixed Nuts*, not so much. It earned only $6.8 million at the domestic box office. "I may satirize things to a great degree as I go along, but in the end, I say, 'We believe in love. We believe in the Christmas spirit.' That's what it says at the end of all of my movies. That's true. I think," Nora said.

But in the end, the Christmas miracle she needed in real life just didn't come to pass. Reviews were harsh, and the studio lost money. "Nora Ephron, on the basis of her journalism, is a lot sharper than the director who made the gooey, coercively insipid 'Sleepless in Seattle.' 'Mixed Nuts' is even more insipid than that film," wrote Peter Rainer in the *Los Angeles Times*, adding, "Why start out to make a black comedy and then dump in all that whitener?"

Nora was devastated and was placed firmly in movie jail. She wasn't sure if she would ever direct another film again. She tossed and turned in bed.

What could I have done differently? she wondered. As the film's director, the onus was on her, she thought. And yet, how could she not have known it wouldn't be a hit? How could she have missed the signs? She later explained:

> Two or three hundred people have followed you into the wilderness; they've committed six months or a year of their lives to an endeavor you've made them believe in. . . . You've fought hard to improve the on-set catering. You've flown in the frozen custard from Wisconsin. And everyone is having the most wonderful time.

Even though Nora's confidence often seemed impenetrable, those who knew her best got to see a more vulnerable side of her that was sometimes hidden from the public—one that proved she was, after all, human. "She read the reviews. And she cared about them," longtime assistant, writer/producer, and friend J. J. Sacha recalls. "And she certainly cared about what people thought."

But Nora was right back to work. After all, as Martin's Philip said, "In every pothole you can find the word HOPE." A film that had long been in development since *Sleepless* was back on her radar. "I hope to make eight or nine movies before I'm done," she said at the time. (She ended up making six more films and wrote three plays, usually collaborating with her sister, Delia.)

Meanwhile, her prized screenplay for *Higgins & Beech* was still in flux. After she spent eight years working on multiple drafts with her *Silkwood* writing partner, Alice Arlen, the script was with 20th Century Fox when, in 1993, the studio granted United Artists a one-year option for $100,000. At the time, Michelle Pfeiffer and Richard Gere were attached to star in the lead roles, coming off successes in powerful period dramas, *The Age of Innocence* and *Sommersby*, respectively. Jon Amiel, who'd just worked with Gere, would direct *Higgins*. Pfeiffer, for her part, had been the 1993 recipient of the Crystal Award.

But with a budget escalating quickly to $43 million, UA chose not to renew in March the following year, giving the newly formed New Line Cinema a chance to step in. Negotiations took place, and the budget was trimmed to $35 million. Script changes were made. That's when Fox decided it wanted to keep it. The saga continued.

Important changes were happening for women in Hollywood nonetheless—at least in front of the camera. New Line agreed to a deal that would pay $12 million to Julia Roberts and $8 million to Meg Ryan to star in a remake of George Cukor's 1939 comedy *The Women*. It was the most they'd earned thus far in their careers and led to a shift toward pay parity with their male counterparts.

As for Nora and that Christmas miracle she'd hoped for? It was just around the corner in the form of a smoking, drinking, swearing, country-line-dancing angel named Michael.

17 | *MICHAEL*

MICHAEL: Remember what John and Paul said.
HUEY: The Apostles?
MICHAEL: No, the Beatles. "All you need is love."
—Michael

ON THE HOT, FAST-PACED desert location shoot of *Broken Arrow*—John Woo's action thriller that preceded his megahit *Face/Off* the following year—actor John Travolta gave the latest draft of the script for a film called *Michael* a read. It was late spring 1995. He'd just starred in Quentin Tarantino's mid-1990s neo-noir hit *Pulp Fiction* and was about to hit the silver screen in the mobster comedy thriller *Get Shorty*—two roles that revived his career after a slump during the 1980s.

Needless to say, the tall, dark, and handsome New Jersey–born star was into it. "I saw this angel with extremely contradictory qualities, an angel that drank, smoked, womanized, and I felt that I could make it funny," he said. "I mean, he has two missions: one is to give Quinlan and Dorothy their hearts back, which is what he really came to do. But while he's here, he is also planning to enjoy himself. And he likes to get into fights like any good archangel would."

Nora and Delia—who'd signed on to rewrite the script—were thrilled. They'd envisioned him for the role since the beginning of their work on the project.

"John has that amazing ability to be both completely innocent and deliciously sexy at the same time," Nora said. "There are very few actors who have that combination. We were very lucky to get him."

The genesis for what would become *Michael* was indeed based on the famous archangel—one of the world's great warriors of the same name from the Bible—but with a twist. This angel, as the theatrical release posters promised, was no saint. "Every chance he has, he gets into trouble," Delia said. "He is also irresistible to women, so every waitress he meets falls into his lap. He turns out to be quite a handful."

Nora's interest in the material began before production on *Sleepless* started in 1992. "I always saw it as a story that is really about modern love," she said. "That's what angels are about, that's what romantic comedy is about. It's all about seeking love." As she finished postproduction on the box office misfire *Mixed Nuts*, she followed up with her agent again about the status of what was then a script cowritten by *National Enquirer* veteran Jim Quinlan and award-winning journalist and novelist Pete Dexter.

"I asked Universal to wait until I was finished with *Sleepless*, but they gave it to another filmmaker to develop," she recalled to *Variety* before *Michael* was released in 1996.

The concept of bringing Heaven's most famous warrior, Michael, to life as a modern flaws-and-all character in the flesh piqued the sisters' interest as writers. But even once Nora and Delia became attached to rewrite the script, they'd still have to handle some tough negotiations over Travolta's reported $8 million salary with the help of his manager Jonathan Krane and producers Sean Daniel and Jim Jacks. (That number *would* be a bit of a small bump from the reported $150,000 salary he'd accepted for the indie *Pulp Fiction*.)

Failing to come to an agreement, Nora's agent Jim Wiatt stepped in to help set up the project (with Nora directing) at the newly formed Turner Pictures, which had beat out at least two other studios that were interested. As fate would have it, Amy Pascal was at the helm as president of production—and she was a huge fan of the budding filmmaker after having worked with her on Nora's directorial debut, *This Is My Life*, as a young production executive at Columbia Pictures.

"It's been great to work with Nora again," Pascal told *Variety*. "She has a very unique perspective on the world that is truly her own. She has her own voice."

Pascal had already made a name for herself, too, as an ardent supporter of female-led content and female directors by developing such game-changing projects as Penny Marshall's critically acclaimed *Awakenings* and *A League of Their Own*, as well as the 1994 version of *Little Women* while at Columbia (she'd later be nominated for an Academy Award for Best Picture for producing the 2019 remake scripted and directed by Greta Gerwig). She also knew *Michael* was in good hands with Nora running the show. At least she hoped so: it was her first project to greenlight at Turner—and with a production budget rounding out around $30 million, her reputation as a savvy development executive and Nora's future as a bankable director were both on the line.

But there was reason to have faith.

"Nora is smart, articulate and responsible in terms of budget and time," Travolta's manager Krane noted. "She knows how to handle actors of different temperament. She also has an appreciation for music and editing."

As for Travolta, Pascal bumped him up to a reported $11 million salary—and suddenly, the little movie that could seemed to finally be on its way to becoming a success. "It became a magical project that everyone wanted to be associated with," she added.

The esteemed composer Randy Newman signed on to provide the folksy, Americana-themed music (another big get for Nora, who'd been wanting to collaborate with him for years), and actors Andie MacDowell (for a reported $2 million with a "lucrative" back end) and William Hurt agreed to star as the "angel expert" and cynical reporter, respectively, who ultimately find love with Michael's unorthodox assistance.

MacDowell was coming off the success of the beloved 1993 comedy classic *Groundhog Day* (with Bill Murray) and the 1994 hit British rom-com *Four Weddings and a Funeral* (with Hugh Grant), while Hurt hadn't starred in a mainstream comedy since the iconic James L. Brooks satire *Broadcast News*, for which he earned an Academy Award nomination (as did costar Holly Hunter) for Best Actor in 1988.

"When Andie came in to read, we knew she was this character," Nora said. "She's so real and true as a human being and is so natural as an actress and a comedian."

For both MacDowell and Hurt, the Ephron sisters' revised script is what ultimately drew them in. "This was one of the best scripts I'd ever read," MacDowell said, adding that it was "clever, original and a lot of fun." And Hurt likened it to his experience on *Broadcast News*: "I love being around Nora Ephron," he said. "She's very, very bright. She values words. Jim Brooks went all out with *Broadcast News* and Nora did the same with this film."

Meanwhile, an admiration for words was exactly what was inspiring Nora and Delia to remake one of their favorite films: Ernst Lubitsch's *The Shop Around the Corner*. It was writer-producer Julie Durk—who was then working for Lauren Shuler Donner at her production company—who thought the Jimmy Stewart–Margaret Sullavan 1940 classic needed an update. And Shuler Donner—who'd just come off back-to-back box office hits in *Dave* and *Free Willy* in 1993—knew just how to do it.

"This is [1994], I had just gotten online, and I was on AOL," she said. The only question was, who could write and direct a deftly crafted, '90s-era version of the romantic comedy classic based on falling in love through letters? She knew Turner's Pascal would know.

"I have an idea who could do this," Pascal said. "Nora. Nora Ephron."

Back on the set of *Michael*, rehearsals began around the beginning of 1996, and principal photography took place in the winter and spring in Austin, Texas, and in Chicago.

Cinematographer John Lindley and production designer Dan Davis worked with Nora to create an enchanting look for the film with "a dash of unexpected magic."

"I very much wanted to work with John because he did *Field of Dreams*," Nora explained at the time. "And what we wanted to have happen in this movie was the same thing, where you were absolutely in reality and then in the next minute you weren't."

It was a feeling she could certainly relate to as the daughter of screenwriters who often borrowed material from real life for their scripts—but in this case, those blurred lines were being used for good.

"What she cared about more than anything was telling the story," Lindley told me. "So if I could figure out a way to help her tell the story with a shot, that's what she was happy about."

Nora had scouted some locations in Austin for a scene where Travolta's Michael would find himself in a battle with a bull. She and Lindley hopped in the car so she could show him a few of her favorite places, and after a while, they came upon an open field.

"What is it you like about this place?'" he asked her.

"Well, what is it you *don't* like about it?" she replied.

"If the story of *Michael* is heaven meets earth, let's see if we can find a hillside where the hill goes right up to the sky. Then we can have John running one direction against the sky, and the bull running the other direction against the sky," he explained. "Then we're kind of telling the story of the movie."

The sisters had already developed a rhythm that worked when it came to developing existing material. They'd previously partnered on *Sleepless*, *This Is My Life*, and *Mixed Nuts*—and Nora trusted her younger sister implicitly with dialogue and with the movie's careful construction. Plus, Delia had moved into the Apthorp after *Sleepless*, so she only had to walk across the courtyard to meet with Nora to go over script outlines and to work on drafts together. Once they were on the set, they'd go to dailies together. Two peas, one funny, witty pod.

They seemed to speak in their "own language," Lindley explained. "They always knew what the other was thinking . . . they were like people who had spent their lives in jail together."

Nora directing John Travolta while filming on location for *Michael*, 1996. © *New Line Cinema / The Everett Collection*

Yes, they shared the same parents, the same sense of humor, and often, the same sense of meaning-making when it came to material. Fast forward a few years to when *Hanging Up* was being developed, and the sisters decided Diane Keaton would direct because the material was too close to them both. But when it came to *Michael,* the notion of questioning what's possible with a little magic was most compelling because believing in what's possible also means disbelieving in giving up hope.

"The powerful thing about believing in angels is that there is a sense that things can change in your favor at any moment," Delia said. "For instance, the most terrible thing about being single is the dreaded feeling it could go on forever. In this story, you have two people who have really given up on love, who are stuck in a rut, but the adventure of finding an angel opens them up and changes their lives."

And though it wasn't their material originally, there was plenty for Nora and Delia to build on—especially when it came to how two writers relate to one another in matters of life, love, and perhaps even the afterlife.

Or—at least how they relate over pie:

```
                MICHAEL
        What is it about pie?


                DOROTHY
        It's pretty, you know. There's nothing
        prettier than pie. The scalloped edges
        around the sides and the slits on the
        top so the heat can escape.


                QUINLAN
        Pie gives you the sense that you're a four-
        square person living in a four-square
        country.


                BRIDE
        Well, pie says home.
```

It's a scene that takes place halfway through the film, but for *Vogue* journalist Willow Lindley, it reflects one of her earliest memories of Nora in real life. She was just six years old at the time of production on *Michael,* but her father's friendship and ongoing collaboration with the director meant that by extension, she was part of the family too.

"One of my first memories of Nora was about chocolate cream pie," she told me. "I don't think I'd ever had a cream pie, only fruit pies, and I remember thinking, *Holy moly, this is quite something*. And just tasting a million pies with her. She was in true heaven."

The atmosphere on the Austin set of *Michael* was pure joy, she explained, but Dianne Dreyer, the film's script supervisor and Nora's longtime friend, shared how her ethos on a film set was unique: she balanced joy with hard work in a perfectly organized and feminine way. "Nora had an approach to filmmaking that you wished more people had," she said. "That this work is hard, it's concentrated, and you have to achieve a lot in a finite period of time. You only get one chance to do it right. No one's ever going to make it again. This is your shot, so two things should be true: everybody should bring their A game, and it should be fun. If it's not fun, it's torture."

Some of the film's best—and therefore, most fun—moments are in the one-liners delivered through the film's quirky characters. It's no accident that they seem to draw on Nora's maxims of wisdom or life philosophies revealed both in earlier and later works, such as: "When something isn't going well, it's best just to start over," or "You gotta learn to laugh. That's the way to true love."

One of Nora's favorite moments while filming? When Travolta took to the dance floor, of course. "Everyone who was there, every single man and woman there, wanted to dance with John Travolta," she said. "And the truth is, I think everyone could have. He has this ability to convince you that you could dance with him very easily. It's only a question of him holding out his hand in some magical way and you would be in the movie, dancing with one of the greatest dancers."

Nora, as usual, was right. This wasn't the first time he'd dazzled a clever, powerful woman—or that he'd convinced one to have a dance. In 1985, on a visit to the White House, it was a dance with the late Princess Diana, the Princess of Wales, that led to an iconic moment.

Nancy Reagan, the First Lady at the time, arranged for a dance between the pair, unbeknownst to Travolta. "I didn't know until I got there that I was supposed to dance with her," the actor later recalled. "[Princess Diana] kept that a secret when she met me. She didn't know that Nancy Reagan hadn't told me yet that this was the plan—that I was the Prince Charming of the evening."

Prince Charming—and bona fide movie star or not—he found himself awestruck when it came to sweeping the stunning blonde royal off her feet as they glided around the entrance hall to music from *Saturday Night Fever*. The moment was captured by photographers around the world, and Diana's gorgeous midnight blue, off-the-shoulder velvet gown (designed by Victor Edelstein) became known as the "Travolta dress"—and reportedly became one of her favorites. As for Travolta, he calls it a "highlight of his life." The dress is now on display at Kensington Palace. "It fit her beautifully," Travolta recalled. "I could probably sketch it in my mind because it was so specific."

Travolta's slovenly yet devilishly handsome Michael explains that although he can't solve the problems of the world, he can perform "small miracles." For example, he smells like cookies, he invented standing in line, and he even did some writing of his own (namely, Psalm 85, "but it wasn't called that then") before coming back to earth to help two cynics find love with his magic touch. To Dreyer, that's what Nora did too. "I know she didn't believe in an afterlife, and I know she wasn't a religious person, but she certainly believed in magic," she told me. "She certainly believed that one of the greatest pleasures you can have in life is doing something special for someone else."

But there was something special about the way magic played a role in *Michael*—and it's because it was deeply personal. It was the personal that made all her films special, even though some achieved box office success or critical acclaim while others did not. When Nora talked about time travel through cooking (*Heartburn*), or her love of twinkle lights (pretty much always, but definitely in *You've Got Mail*), or pie, what she was really talking about was Phoebe. What she was really talking about was a mother's love gone too soon—and a love given in a way that was both painful and cold, and wonderful and warm at the same time. For her, the smells, the sounds, the tastes—they all reminded her of home. The one that was safe and loud and full of laughter. The one with all the stories. The one before the drinking.

Nora had once admitted that *The Wizard of Oz* had influenced "every one of her movies" from *Heartburn* to *Bewitched*. "I see it everywhere," she said. Indeed, the "no place like home" motif plays out throughout *Michael* (the main character is even named Dorothy), and there's another layer to the *Wizard of Oz* motif as well: L. Frank Baum's Oz books were among her favorites growing up. Phoebe had purchased the series at a used bookstore and inscribed her name on the front page in block letters: Phoebe Wolkind Ephron. Nora cherished them, and they remained on her bookshelf well into adulthood and motherhood.

Opening on Christmas Day in 1996, *Michael* was a box office success, grossing more than $95 million domestically and nearly $120 million worldwide. Perhaps surprisingly, in the Nora Ephron film canon, it's one of her highest-grossing pictures, ranking third just below *Sleepless* (1993) and *You've Got Mail* (1998) and just above *Julie & Julia* (2009) in both domestic and worldwide ticket sales. The film even beat out the would-be cult classic *Jerry Maguire* (costarring Travolta's late wife Kelly Preston alongside Tom Cruise, Cuba Gooding Jr., and Renée Zellweger) in its premiere weekend and held strong the following weekend too.

But the critics, for the most part, were not fans. While a number of them complained of the film's one-dimensional characters, calling it a "winsome, wafer-thin comedy," and "insipid and flavorless," the *Los Angeles Times* review by Kevin Thomas stood out by calling it a "beguiling, joyous holiday comedy" and noting that "early on Michael explains that he can't change the nature of the world, that he can only perform 'small miracles.' *Michael*, which could so easily have been too silly or too sugary, is itself a small miracle."

Somehow, upon viewing it years later in perhaps an even more cynical and physically and socially distanced world, the fact that *Michael* resonated with audiences in the mid-'90s makes it all the more special now. For the younger Lindley, it's a bittersweet reminder of what Nora left behind: her warmth, her writing, her food, and her obsession with finding love for the ones she loved most. "My boyfriend and I watched it and he hadn't seen it," she said. "He loved it. He's heard me talk about Nora quite a bit. We were supposed to get married this summer but then Covid . . . and those are the moments you think, 'I really wish Nora could meet this person.'"

18 | *MAIL*

Above all, be the heroine of your life, not the victim.
—Nora Ephron, Wellesley speech, 1996

AS KATHLEEN KELLY CLOSES UP her beloved bookshop for the very last time, she stops at the door. She turns around to take one last look. Slowly, as she scans every inch of the Shop Around the Corner—its tall, elegant shelves now empty—she has a vision: it's her as a little girl with her mother. And together, they're twirling.

For cinematographer John Lindley, it's one of the powerful scenes from *You've Got Mail* that he's particularly proud of because the imagery speaks volumes without any dialogue. "We shot that [sequence] separately," he remembered, "but I couldn't have been happier with the final product when the two shots got cut together."*

As composer George Fenton added the music to match the imagery, it became the epitome of movie magic:

> I think the alchemy of film is something that is so elusive . . . there's this knot you've reached where all the ends have tied together, that's what it's about—the story, the characters, the director, the camera-man, the producer—the whole thing. It was all about this moment. Whenever it happens, and you're there and you're conducting the orchestra and they're playing, you just know in a nanosecond whether all those things have come together in the right way. And in that film, they had all come together in the right way.

Nora joined him at the scoring stage as they were nearing the end of their recording sessions for the film. By now, Fenton had grown accustomed to her highly specific and somewhat quirky (if not pedantic) way of looking at film music. But this moment, both in the scene of the movie and in real life, felt different.

"We had quite a big orchestra playing at that point, so they kind of swept off into this waltz version of the theme," he remembered. "And I think it's the only time I saw her not at a loss for words—but she just said, '*George!*' That's what she said. It was so lovely and she was so touched by it."

Nearly a decade after her death, it's the sequence that always makes him well up about her, he says. Indeed, it's emblematic of many of the things that were important to Nora—and perhaps of what the movie was really about: to embrace change, to believe in love, and to treasure how the written word connects us to both our past and to our future.

"She was smart—very, very smart. She was kind to people. She went to endless trouble for her godchildren and people that she would help," Fenton explained, adding that it was a given that there'd always be a "pickle in the sandwich"—a.k.a. a caustic line, or at least a funny one. "At the same time, she could be so insightful about things, but it was always delivered in a way that she could say terrible things to people and they'd completely forgive her. There aren't many people who can do that."

In fact, even Oscar-winning songwriters were willing to do almost anything if Nora asked. When she asked her friend and brilliant lyricist Carole Bayer Sager (who'd earned an Academy Award and Golden Globe for "Arthur's Theme (Best That You Can Do)" in 1981) to write a song for *Mail*, Bayer Sager was thrilled at the prospect of working with one of her songwriting idols, Carole King. David Foster joined the duo and wrote the ballad "It Could Have Been Anyone," with King performing it.

"Carole was one of my inspirations," Bayer Sager told me. "It was a great opportunity Nora gave us."

The collaboration had been nearly three decades in the making. Just as thousands of other baby boomers were playing King's iconic *Tapestry* album on repeat in 1971, so, too, was Bayer Sager. Back then, she had the chance to meet King backstage and asked if they could work on a song together, but it never happened. At the time, King was collaborating only with her then husband Gerry Goffin—and Bayer Sager went on to have fruitful collaborations with

Burt Bacharach, David Foster, Michael Jackson, Kenneth "Babyface" Edmonds, and others who have cowritten many of the top pop hits of the past forty years. But Nora was tough. When they played "It Could Have Been Anyone" for her the first time, "she took an instant dislike to it," Bayer Sager told me. She and King went back to the drawing board and completely rewrote it—and came up with the original song "Anyone At All," which ended up on the beloved film's soundtrack. (King, for her part, kept "It Could Have Been Anyone" for her 2001 studio album *Love Makes the World*).

———————

As rehearsals began on *You've Got Mail*, Nora was always ready with her sharpened pencil. Ever the journalist and keen observer of human behavior, she would "jot down ideas as actors talked and joked"—and would ask them to expand on anything she found to be amusing.

Taking a cue from her mentor Mike Nichols and from her family's theater roots, she believed wholeheartedly in the value of rehearsals. They provided a fruitful foundation for improvisation—and the ultimate in collaboration with the actors and the real world they inhabited. "She'd work in a story of her own life, or something she saw that morning," actor Greg Kinnear said. "It was out of the importance of finding real voices in the people who are populating her movies."

After turning down a role in the Oscar-winning 1994 drama *Forrest Gump* starring Tom Hanks, an up-and-coming young comedian named Dave Chappelle was eager to work alongside him in *Mail*. Hanks would play big-box bookstore owner Joe Fox (named after one of Nora's former beaus, an editor at Random House), and Chappelle would play Fox's business partner and confidant, Kevin. Recognizing an improv genius when she saw one, Nora gave Chappelle the freedom to improvise his lines. "He proved to be a delight and everything she thought he was," Dreyer later recalled. Legend has it that between filming scenes at Cafe Lalo in Manhattan, Hanks and Chappelle would sneak into a nearby bar to watch the series finale of *Seinfeld*. Game, recognize iconic comedy game.

Though they weren't exactly "discovered" by Nora, Adam Sandler (who's gone on to become a bankable star with more than $2 billion in combined box office earnings to date), the often-controversial Chappelle (whose Nora-esque observational comedic writing has been called "poetically unfiltered and socio-politically introspective"), and later Will Ferrell (who's gone on to star in or produce projects ranging from *Vice* to *Dead to Me* to the HBO megahit *Succession*) all benefited from their early creative collaborations with the sharp-tongued writer-director—and vice versa.

Operating on a healthy $65 million budget—the highest of her career—Nora wanted to be sure she was professional, organized, and prepared to stay on time and on budget. She also wanted to be sure the crew had enough ice cream and Popsicles. (And only the best ones.)

"It was a cultivated but casual affair" is how Meg Ryan (who starred as Kelly) put it.

That's how friends and colleagues Dianne Dreyer and Don Lee remember it too.

"Something I think was great about her was that she was completely democratic in terms of the crew and the cast," Lee, who served as coproducer and unit production manager on *Mail*, told me. "And I think that's why you see a lot of success in her films because we always worked hard to try to have a happy set. There's always issues that come up, but overall, we tried to have fun while we made movies, which is increasingly difficult to do."

Nora in her element on the set of *You've Got Mail*, 1998.
© Warner Bros. / The Everett Collection

Dreyer agrees, adding that "it's very unusual for you to work on a movie crew and make the kind of friendships that last a lifetime—the kind of friendships that you've had since primary school or college. With Nora, there are no fewer than a dozen people I met through working with her that I would be so sad if I ever lost them. The people who wanted to be around her, and who would jump through hoops to make it work, was a long list of people."

Still, not on that list then or now are some of her college classmates who hadn't forgiven her for the scathing 1972 *Esquire* piece she'd written about them in her column on women, and who were also not amused by her 1996 commencement speech given at Wellesley twenty-four years later as she prepped for *Mail*.

As Nora sat down at her desk to write the speech, she reflected on how much had changed for women—and how much hadn't. Typing on a personal computer next to a fancy-for-the-time touch-tone phone with an answering machine (not everyone had one just yet), a Rolodex, and a stack of several CDs, she took a sip of tea from her bottle of Snapple and began to reflect on the state of women's rights in America (noting that the Wonderbra was, in fact, "not a step forward"):

> One of the things people always say to you if you get upset is, don't take it personally, but listen hard to what's going on and, please, I beg you, take it personally.

It's a similar sentiment reflected in *Mail* as Kathleen Kelly admonishes the detached Joe Fox for quoting Michael Corleone from *The Godfather*, claiming that anything painful "isn't personal, it's just business." After his new Fox Books megastore leads to the demise of her charming independent bookstore, Shop Around the Corner, he stops by for an unannounced visit bearing flowers. Not just any flowers: daisies, her favorite. A sweet gesture, perhaps, if they came from anyone other than the man who just single-handedly put you out of business.

But unbeknownst to her at the time, Fox is also the person on the other end of the e-mail exchanges she's been beaming about for months. And now he wants to know if she'll forgive him.

                    JOE
But you'll never forgive me. Like
Elizabeth.

                    KATHLEEN
Who?

                    JOE
Elizabeth Bennet in Pride and Prejudice.
She was too proud –

                    KATHLEEN
I thought you hated Pride and Prejudice.

                    JOE
-- or was she too prejudiced and Mr. Darcy
was too proud? I can never remember.
        (beat)
It wasn't personal –

                    KATHLEEN
-- It was business. What is that supposed
to mean? I am so sick of that. All it means
is it's not personal to you, but it's
personal to me, it's personal to a lot of
people.

Most of all, the film—and its message—was personal to Nora.

"When you see *You've Got Mail*, you're seeing Nora," said Lindley. "It's not just in the dialogue or the wit. It's not just that Roald Dahl was her favorite children's author, or that daisies were her favorite flower; what you're seeing is her outlook on life, which is to be happy and embrace change."

And while some fans and critics have never forgiven her for the problematic aspects of the film's main plot and what some have understood as a "dark commentary on capitalism," others remain loyal to the film despite its flawed premise.

"Did 'You've Got Mail,' in fact, predict the rise of Amazon, which has demolished bookstores and then sadistically replaced them with its own algorithm-curated brick-and-mortar shops?" Amanda Hess wrote in a *New York Times* piece reflecting on the film twenty years later. "All I know is this: 'You've Got Mail' is a secret tragedy, too."

But for others, Nora's take on the Lubitsch classic was about both looking forward *and* looking back.

"Ephron's work hearkens back to an era of romance, and evokes feelings of nostalgia for the past," says Dr. Alison Trope, professor of communication studies and director of the Critical Media Project at USC. One of the ways Nora did this is, once again, with music. While her moviemaking mentor Mike Nichols had innovated the use of a contemporary, pop rock soundtrack for his 1967 classic, *The Graduate*, Nora preferred standards from the *Great American Songbook* as a way of connecting with times gone by. With *Mail*, producers convinced her to try something new to open the film: a modern song from the Irish alt-rock band the Cranberries called "Dreams." It worked—and the theme informed the rest of the soundtrack's song choices.

Of course, for her, those memories of times gone by—and the sights, sounds, and smells that accompanied them—were deeply personal and incredibly specific. In closing the film with the *Wizard of Oz* classic "Over the Rainbow," she paid tribute not only to the golden era of Hollywood but also to her Jewish heritage, and to her mother's love of the Oz series.

Nora and Delia were both eager to maintain the connection to Lubitsch's masterpiece *The Shop Around the Corner* as they wrote—and in doing so, to their parents, in more ways than one. First of all, Delia had the clever idea to change the shop from a perfume store in the original film to a children's bookstore, which gave them both an instant connection to it. The shelves, naturally, were populated with many of the books the sisters enjoyed as little girls while Phoebe was healthy and vibrant and interested in helping them develop into the thoughtful women they became.

And, as a second-generation screenwriting duo, they'd developed a rhythm while working together that was not only successful but also fun. Because Delia was also living in the Apthorp, she only had to cross the courtyard to meet with Nora for writing sessions just as they'd done for their work together on *Michael*. Sometimes Nora would sit at the computer to type, and Delia would sit in the chair providing ideas. Other times, Delia would be at the computer typing while Nora was in the chair. The result was a great deal of outlining. And revising. Always outlining—and always revising.

Film scholar Liz Dance points out that with *You've Got Mail*, Nora has "taken bits and pieces, recipes from other people's work and made them her own" just as her fictional counterpart, Rachel Samstat, said she did in *Heartburn*. Still, Nora's personal connection to each and every detail in her unique remix makes the film what Dance calls a "work that is idiosyncratic and recognizable as belonging to her."

This was one of the tension points both for Nora and for feminist fans and scholars alike: the limits of the notion of the female film auteur and the supposed contradiction between what is commercially viable and what is deeply personal and authentic. Was Nora "selling out" by making a film with a happy ending? Could she really lay claim to a film that was a remake of a romantic comedy classic—and still maintain her edge as the wise, wicked New York writer her older fans once knew and loved?

"When these romantic movies showed up that were boy-meets-girl, people expected something bad to happen, and they didn't know what to do with her in a way," longtime agent and friend Bryan Lourd explained. "How dare she not continue this persona."

As friend Richard Cohen points out, it was the "sheer force of her personality" that made a film uniquely Nora's own. The tiny details that made it hers, from her insistence on twinkle lights to the little ruby slipper ornament Kathleen Kelly unwraps and hangs on the Christmas tree in the shop window: this is her homage to Phoebe—and a way to hold on to the past.

But she was also greatly in tune with the future. Anticipating what would come to be with the advent of social media, Hanks says Nora's fictional stories, to him, were always "ripped right out of society."

"Nora was A REPORTER ('everything is copy,' eh?) and the movies I did with her were all based on nonfiction," Hanks told me. "*Sleepless* was about the anonymous voices we hear yearning for the same things we yearn for. . . . She said we had to make *You've Got Mail* before AOL changed and became something else."

Of course, embracing change is actually at the heart of the beloved romantic comedy. Nora couldn't have known at the time that in just eight years she'd face her own changes and be forced to move from a place of anger to one of acceptance. The Upper West Side was changing right before her very eyes, and her beloved Apthorp building was no longer to be home. Worst of all, her own body was beginning to betray her, despite a lifelong dedication to good health.

She couldn't have known that New York would be forced to live without her just fourteen years later.

Then again, maybe she did know. Nora did have an uncanny sense of all-knowing power in weird and wonderful ways. Sometimes, she was able to key into this ability when choosing film projects. Other times, not so much.

You've Got Mail opened at No. 1 at the box office just a week before Christmas on December 18, 1998, edging out DreamWorks' *The Prince of Egypt* and Disney's *A Bug's Life*—ultimately bringing in nearly $116 million domestically and nearly $251 million worldwide in overall box office receipts. "Remember this moment," Nora told her assistant J. J. Sacha upon the film's successful release, "because it's a hit—and they don't come along very often."

It remains one of the highest-grossing films directed by a woman, and even though Nora would bristle at that qualifier, the path to that kind of success has in many ways become even more challenging. Only fifty-seven women—including Nora—directed the 1,300 top-grossing films from 2007 to 2019, according to a September 2020 report by the Annenberg Inclusion Initiative at USC. The all-time high for women behind the camera? Just over 10 percent in 2019, with little progress made in terms of inclusion for women of color (of the 112 directors across all 2019 movies, a full 80.4 percent were White and 19.6 percent were from underrepresented racial/ethnic groups, according to the report).

Clearly, more work remains to be done, and it may be no surprise that it's streaming services rather than most of the legacy studios that seem to be leading the charge in changing hiring practices to be more inclusive.

As *Mail* struck box office gold, Nora and Delia had already begun work on the adaptation of Delia's 1995 book *Hanging Up*. It became clear rather quickly that this was no movie about "love in the movies"—this was as real as any fictional dramedy could be.

They'd decided to bring in a director (instead of Nora) to minimize conflict given how raw the material (and the emotions) was. The sisters stayed on as writers and producers while Diane Keaton took the helm as both director and actor playing the fictional version of Nora (Georgia) with Meg Ryan starring as Delia's fictional counterpart, Eve. Lisa Kudrow of *Friends* fame played an amalgam of the two younger Ephron sisters (Hallie and Amy) in her portrayal of Maddy.

The script—and the sisterly love for collaboration—was soon unrecognizable. Those old wounds about their father Henry Ephron's death (and Nora's ensuing absence) that had been held together loosely by a Band-Aid for several years? They ripped wide open.

"This was my novel about my relationship with my father," Delia later explained. "I didn't want her changing my material . . . she was trying to make it hers."

The story of Nora and Henry as told by Nora, and the story of Delia and Henry as told by Delia turned out to be wildly different—so much so that the sisters stopped speaking altogether after disagreements over the first draft of the script.

ACT V

IN THE END
(2000–2012)

19 | *HANGING UP*

IN AN EFFORT TO PUT the pieces of their broken relationship back together, Nora and Delia allowed director Diane Keaton to make *Hanging Up* her own. She could relate as the eldest of three sisters herself. "Somehow when we're with our families we end up being ten years old again," she said.

As for *Friends* actress Lisa Kudrow, she realized how much Keaton had influenced her as a comedian, and said she continued to do so as they worked together on the movie.

Once Meg Ryan signed on as Eve in 1998, development moved forward quickly with financing from Sony. Working from a $40 million budget, Keaton was midway through filming the 2001 flop *Town & Country* when production started on *Hanging Up*. (The former lost its $90 million investment despite an all-star cast including Keaton, Warren Beatty, and Goldie Hawn.)

In *Hanging Up*, Walter Matthau plays a funny but mean not-too-fictionalized version of Henry in his last film role before his death, while Tracee Ellis Ross makes a cameo as Eve's assistant, Kim.

In truth, Henry was what Delia's therapist called "an uproar man," and she wrote it into the novel and the movie. He could be hysterical. He could be mean. And by the time they were adults, he had the "dwindles," as Delia called them, which meant that he was so disoriented that sometimes he didn't know what day or time it was—or who or where some of the most important people in his life were: his daughters.

"My girls left me and went to New York," Matthau says to Eve one day in the hospital.

In this version of the Ephron family story, the mother of the fictional Ephron girls isn't gone, but she's not there either. It's a poignant reminder of how excruciating it can be to have a parent who is alive but not quite him- or herself—whether from illness or alcoholism, or in Phoebe's and Henry's cases, both. When Eve goes to see her mother, Pat (Cloris Leachman) to try to convince her to come home, Pat explains that she never quite took to mothering the way others do. It's painful to watch.

Still, there are moments of joy in the movie—it's Christmastime, Nora's favorite time of the year—and there's real warmth emanating in the unabashedly sentimental moment of Ryan and Matthau searching for the perfect Christmas tree together.

In a deleted flashback sequence, many of Nora's peccadillos are on full display through Keaton's portrayal of Georgia as the sisters try to meet up for dinner in Manhattan. She, for example, requests a round table that's just right (a Nora requirement for optimal dinner conversation), and Eve and Maddy mention a few times that "Georgia will know what to do." Indeed, Eve points out why she puts up with Georgia's high-maintenance shenanigans when she says, "Suppose I got mad at her? She's the only mother I've got."

When *Hanging Up* premiered on February 16, 2000 (after being pushed back from a Christmas 1999 release), the critics weren't impressed, touched, or even amused. Nor were the studio heads when they saw the opening weekend numbers.

Hanging Up opened at No. 2 when it bowed over the Presidents' Day weekend in February 2000. Kudrow's fellow *Friends* star Matthew Perry's *The Whole Nine Yards* fared slightly better to take the lead spot. In total, the film earned just under $52 million worldwide.

Both audiences and critics seemed to either not like the movie or simply didn't understand it. One particularly negative review mentions a marketing attempt to compare itself to the 1996 film *The First Wives Club*, a comparison, in fact, that was ironic because Nora had turned down the opportunity to direct that film—as had nearly every female director in the Directors Guild of America (DGA), deeming the material "antifeminist." (However, *The First Wives Club*, which also starred Keaton, became a sleeper hit that brought in more than $181 million worldwide. It was her greatest hit of the decade.)

As for her experience working on *Hanging Up*, Keaton felt the movie's disappointing reception essentially ended her directorial career. "I didn't really pull it off," she later recalled. "When you have a failure like *Hanging Up*, people aren't going, 'Gee, can you direct my movie?' So I haven't had many other opportunities to direct again."

Roger Ebert's review focused on how the reality of growing up in the Ephron family was perhaps to blame for the story's failure to resonate on screen. "The movie doesn't really want to be all that heartbreakingly true," he wrote. "It's a facile comedy of manners, a story in which the three daughters have somehow been taught by their upbringing to put a consistent face on everything." The critical consensus on Rotten Tomatoes made an even finer point on it: "Though the screenplay and the novel it's based on were both written by the same person, critics say *Hanging Up* is an unsuccessful adaptation. The acting is praised as solid, but is ultimately unable to save the film."

While the elder Ephron sisters had managed to make up in some form or another, chaos and conflict abounded around them. The controversial 2000 presidential election would be a doozy, and the attacks on Nora's beloved New York City on September 11, 2001, weren't long off in the future.

But with Nora back in the director's chair on *Lucky Numbers*, a fun time was had by all—even if the movie wasn't fruitful by the measures of the studio, critics, or audiences at the time. The set was alive with creativity as trusted collaborators and pals including producer Sean Daniel and composer George Fenton, along with Dreyer, Lindley, and Lee. John Travolta (who starred as Russ Richards, a local weatherman) and Kudrow (as the TV station lottery girl, Crystal) riffed on funny lines and participated in the requisite Nora Ephron food contests. The gang was back together again.

In a departure from Nora's oeuvre, though, comedy writer Adam Resnick scripted the film while Nora directed. It was the only time she directed material that she didn't write or at least rewrite. Russ Richards (Travolta) is the big fish in the little pond of Harrisburg, Pennsylvania. Resnick's original script was based on the real-life story of those in Pittsburgh who had rigged the lottery.

Nora adored the script. She simply found it hilarious—and particularly appreciated how "wicked" the female lead (Crystal) was. About twenty-seven pages in, she knew Kudrow could pull that off. She brought Resnick in to participate in casting sessions and preproduction. She'd been welcomed on film sets as a writer—and she knew how helpful it could be.

To round out the cast, she added Ed O'Neill (post–*Married . . . with Children* and pre–*Modern Family*), whom she had long wanted to work with after he starred in one of her favorite films (1990's *Sibling Rivalry*, directed by pal Rob Reiner). She called him "a Shakespearean actor who happened to work in television." Tim Roth, who had worked with Travolta on Tarantino's *Pulp Fiction*, costarred alongside Michael Rapaport, while documentarian Michael Moore made a cameo. (Nora's favorite scene is when the three actors create their lottery scam in the bar. And the line: "Fuck me, no fried clams?")

She also cast a young Maria Bamford as the waitress at Denny's. She allowed for, and encouraged, improv by Bamford and all the actors. Second unit director Alfonso Gomez-Rejon came up with the footage Travolta watches on his small TV at home. He and J. J. Sacha both have cameos in the film as well. (For Gomez-Rejon, he remembers that Nora treated him "like an equal, which was impossible to even comprehend, because she's a God. But she gave me a seat at the table," he recalled.)

Originally titled *Numbers*, the Resnick-scripted screenplay was dark—and much raunchier than anything in Nora's film wheelhouse. And to this day, it appears he's still feeling bitter about how the whole thing came together.

As Resnick remembered it, Paramount hired Nora to help create a lighter version of the movie. "Nora was good at her thing, romantic comedies, but this just wasn't something for her," he recalled. "I guess she wanted to try something different. The funny thing is, the studio thought Nora would lighten it up and make it audience friendly, but she was determined to make a dark comedy—something different than what she'd done before."

Maybe the funnier thing is that neither Resnick nor those in charge of the development process seemed to have been aware of Nora's roots in the heyday of New Journalism. And for all his complaints about where the movie ended up, he did appreciate Nora's graciousness in including him throughout the process.

"I had many lunches and dinners with her so I got to witness the whole 'Nora Ephron' thing—her love of food and gossip and hanging out with other famous people," he added. "Unlike me, she seemed to be someone who really enjoyed life."

He'd provided her with location photographs during his preproduction visit to Pennsylvania and hoped the movie would maintain a "shabby realism," and after seeing the first cut of the movie, decided to send her pages of notes. But he felt hopeless. He recalled that he had hoped his frequent collaborator, Chris Elliott (*Schitt's Creek*), would be hired for the role of Detective Pat Lakewood (which ultimately went to Bill Pullman) and how he pictured George Clooney for Travolta's role.

"They eventually got another writer," he said. "My agent told me, 'Look, it might not turn out to be the movie you wanted, but Nora makes hits, so you'll be able to write your own ticket after it comes out.'"

As for Nora and a number of her favorite collaborators, when they began filming on location in Pennsylvania, they were welcomed by locals with open arms as they lined up to try to catch a glimpse of the action—or perhaps an autograph or photo with the film's star, John Travolta.

"Everyone was feeding off each other which was exciting," Nora said, "because everyone brought something to the table."

Still, even Nora's talents at both the real-life and proverbial film table couldn't save *Lucky Numbers* at the box office: it earned only $10.9 million domestically on a $63 million budget.

As had seemingly happened with *Mixed Nuts*, the mix of well-meaning studio and editorial notes along with commercial pressures to lighten the mood seemed to take what could have been a successful Coen brothers–style dark comedy and turned it into a strange, unrecognizable stepchild of the Ephron universe.

When *Lucky Numbers* premiered in late October 2000, the nation was in a state of flux. The USS *Cole* bombing, just two weeks earlier, startled the nation just as it was on the verge of electing George W. Bush as president of the United States after President Bill Clinton's two terms were coming to an end.

The opening weekend box office opened at No. 7 and brought in only a lousy $4.5 million, while Jay Roach's hit romantic comedy *Meet the Parents* hung on to its spot at No. 1 for the fourth week in a row. The following week, the megahit *Charlie's Angels*, the female-driven action comedy based on the cult favorite 1976 TV series, took over with more than $40 million in domestic receipts in its opening weekend alone.

It could be chalked up to bad timing, but sensibilities were changing—and just as the reasons why Americans went to the movies had transformed during the political upheaval and youth uprising of the 1960s so, too, had the reasons changed for the audiences of the 2000s.

Roach, coming off the success of the *Austin Powers* film franchise, was able to show "he can dial down from farce into a comedy of (bad) manners," critic Roger Ebert pointed out when *Meet the Parents* was released. "His movie is funnier because it never tries too hard; De Niro, in particular, gets laughs by leaning back and waiting for them to come to him. And Stiller is like the target in a dunk-the-clown game, smiling while the world falls out from under him."

The movie was De Niro's highest grossing, and a new generation of filmgoers were discovering him decades after Martin Scorsese's *Mean Streets* in 1973. Still, the film world is a smaller world than one might think, and Nora was in fact continuing to work on her beloved but yet-to-be-made screenplay for *Higgins & Beech* with *Mean Streets* producer Jonathan Taplin.

The former band manager for Bob Dylan, Janis Joplin, and other icons of the folk-rock movement in the late 1960s, Taplin was "naive enough to think that if I could have produced 150 concerts, I could produce a movie," he later recalled. When Scorsese, a young filmmaker, approached him about working together on his screenplay (then titled *Season of the Witch*), he raised $500,000 on his own to help bring the project to life.

Nora hoped Taplin could bring the same movie magic to *Higgins*.

But Michelle Pfeiffer soon announced she was pregnant, and the project came to a halt once again. Fox put it in turnaround. By 1997, there were talks to pick it back up again with Fox 2000, but the deal was never done, and the project was never to be picked back up in Nora's lifetime.

———

It was a sunny Tuesday morning when hijackers intentionally flew two planes into the Twin Towers of the World Trade Center in downtown Manhattan, and a third into the Pentagon in Washington, DC, on September 11, 2001. More than three thousand people died that day.

Nora was in bed when the news broke. A friend called and said, "Nora, turn on the TV." She initially thought it was a small plane that was lost before realizing the horror of what was happening. Still, she thought to herself, *This is why I live in this city.*

"The pride in how brave people were and how strong people were," she recalled in a panel discussion of September 11 on *Charlie Rose* five years later.

It was a dark time in America, and it took time to put itself back together. Nora, noticing the changing sensibilities of American movie audiences, thought about writing a play. There was always writing to do, and this time, she returned to the stage with her play *Imaginary Friends*. It was a return in the sense that her material had technically first been seen on-stage nearly six decades earlier when her parents debuted *Three's A Family*, which opened just a few weeks shy of Nora's second birthday. At twenty-three months old, she was already inspiring her parents with her wit. At sixty-one years old, she was intrigued by a theme that still resonates today: truth versus fiction—and how little we actually know about real events in other people's lives.

When the famous playwright Lillian Hellman published her memoir *Pentimento* in 1973, Nora went to Martha's Vineyard to interview the then sixty-eight-year-old writer (and Dorothy Parker pal) at her summer home for the *New York Times*—and, as Nora put it, "did not ask a tough question." After all, Hellman was the woman who'd told the House Un-American Activities Committee, "I cannot cut my conscience to fit this year's patterns." She was the kind of heroine Nora was drawn to; like Nora, she'd alternated between projects that were huge successes (her 1969 memoir, *An Unfinished Woman*, was a bestseller and National Book Award winner) and those that weren't—but somehow always found a way to pick herself back up.

By the time they met, Hellman was well into her third act. A chapter in *Pentimento* became the Academy Award–winning film *Julia* in 1977, when a young Meryl Streep made her film debut. Over the years, Nora and Hellman became friends—or at least pen pals. She'd send Nora funny letters, usually typed and always signed "Miss Hellman." She'd share recipes, too, and the pair visited one another's apartments in New York. She'd have dinners, not unlike the dinners Nora had, with vibrant conversation, stories, games, and laughter.

But Hellman, who'd dedicated *Pentimento* to Mike Nichols (also a dear friend of hers) didn't see eye to eye with Nora when she split from Carl. It essentially ended the friendship.

"She was mystified that I wouldn't forgive my husband [Bernstein] for what she saw as this thing guys do," Nora said of his infidelity. "She thought, 'what's the big deal?' She wouldn't let it go."

After seeing Michael Frayn's Tony Award–winning play *Copenhagen*, about the fraught relationship between physicists Werner Heisenberg and Niels Bohr, Nora became interested in writing about Hellman's famous feud with fellow writer and critic Mary McCarthy. The two women's mutual antagonism (read: loathing) toward one another apparently started in the 1940s, when they were both becoming famous in New York literary circles. McCarthy thought Hellman was a ridiculous liar; Hellman thought McCarthy should learn to appreciate the brilliance of drama and perhaps not take life so seriously. But when McCarthy appeared on *The Dick Cavett Show* in 1979 and said of Hellman, "Every word she says is a lie, including 'and' and 'the,'" Hellman sued her immediately for libel. The $2.25 million case wasn't dropped until after Hellman's death in 1984.

Nora workshopped the play at the Actors Studio as she made revisions and added ideas about music after seeing the Mae West biographical play *Dirty Blonde*. To explore the events in a smart and funny way, Nora imagined that the two women were stuck in the lady's room in hell together sharing stories. But jokes aside, she also thought it was important to point out how feuds like that of McCarthy and Hellman had actually impacted how many women were at the table. "What's really great about them is that they're both right and they're both wrong, so that's delicious," Nora explained later to Charlie Rose. Nora also reflected on how even in her own career, a fierce competitiveness with her female contemporaries could be both exhilarating and toxic at the same time.

One of the elements that Nora loved, but critics at the time didn't seem to appreciate, was how often she had the characters break the "fourth wall"—when they talk directly to the audience. Her 2013 play, *Lucky Guy*, followed the same convention, and numerous popular shows and directors have done the same before and since, such as *House of Cards*, Woody Allen, and the rise of the mockumentary genre in hit network comedies like *The Office* and *Modern Family*. In literature, it can be traced back as far as *The Canterbury Tales*, and to writers like Virginia Woolf.

Imaginary Friends premiered in September 2002 at the Old Globe in San Diego. Legendary composer Marvin Hamlisch provided the melodies to the show's songs while Craig Carnelia added the lyrics.

The preview in San Diego was well received. The *Los Angeles Times* gave a favorable review, writing that "her dramatization of the parallel and conflicting lives of Lillian Hellman and Mary McCarthy, is a feast of wit and language drawn from the words of her famous protagonists but smartly shaped into a serious comedy with music (a handful of songs by Marvin Hamlisch and Craig Carnelia) that grows into a hair-pulling duel even Don King could appreciate."

Directed by Jack O'Brien and starring Cherry Jones and Swoosie Kurtz in the starring roles, it ran for just over a month in San Diego before transferring to Broadway's Ethel Barrymore Theatre on December 21, 2002. Nora was devastated when it closed only two months later after seventy-six performances and twenty previews.

"My biggest flop was a play I wrote," she recalled later. "It got what are known as mixed reviews—which is to say, it got some good reviews, but not in the *New York Times*. It puttered along for a couple of months, and then it died. It lost its entire investment."

"It was the best thing I ever wrote, so it was a particularly heartbreaking experience," she added. "If I think about it for more than a minute, I start to cry."

Then, Nora shared a fantasy she still privately kept close to her heart—that one day, as she lay dying, she'd ask a favor: "Could you please do a revival of my play?"

20 | *BEWITCHED*

AS THE NATION STRUGGLED to recover from the devastation of the terrorist attacks on September 11 and an impending war in Iraq, Nora's return to the stage gave her a much-needed, but ultimately brief, reprieve from the harsh critics of Hollywood. Just a year later, she got a call from Amy Pascal (who by now was the head of Columbia) one afternoon in early 2003 that lured her back in.

"Nora, please help!" Amy said. "Nicole Kidman is coming to meet about doing *Bewitched* tomorrow morning and we don't have a plot."

From 1964 to 1972, the popular ABC fantasy sitcom *Bewitched* had featured Elizabeth Montgomery in the lead role of Samantha Stephens, a modern suburban woman who happens to be a witch. She marries a mere mortal in Darrin Stephens (played originally by Dick York and in later seasons by Dick Sargent), but often gets into trouble when she continues to perform magic by twitching her nose. Nora's challenge was to figure out how to adapt that 1960s sitcom premise to a new feature film.

By February, Nora had not only solved the plot issue (which she did that very next morning) but she'd signed on to direct and said she would write the script with Delia. The premise for the script was that it would be a movie about the making of a TV show: a remake of the original *Bewitched* in which the actress playing the fictional witch Samantha would be a witch in real life.

Amy, Nora, and Delia had found their "Samantha" in Nicole Kidman, the beautiful, tall Australian American actress who was coming off a number of critically acclaimed dramatic roles, including *The Hours*, for which she won an

Academy Award for Best Actress (the first Australian to do so), and the late Anthony Minghella's Civil War epic *Cold Mountain*. She could even wiggle her nose like Elizabeth Montgomery. But they still needed their "Darrin."

The hysterical *Saturday Night Live* fan favorite Will Ferrell was hired in October as Jack Wyatt (the actor playing Darrin Stephens in the movie's sitcom remake), and his longtime collaborator Adam McKay (with whom he later founded the *Funny or Die* video comedy skit website) signed on to work with Nora and Delia as the ninth and final screenwriter to join the project after more than a decade in development.

"It's a big, fat, fun mainstream summer movie," McKay told the *New York Times*, "that at the same time, requires some real acting skills."

As for those who could provide "real" acting skills, legendary actors Shirley MacLaine and Michael Caine signed on to star alongside Ferrell and Kidman, while Kristin Chenoweth, Jason Schwartzman, David Alan Grier, and Heather Burns played supporting roles.

Cinematographer and friend John Lindley remembered how much Nora loved the cast, especially Ferrell, despite their different approaches to humor. "Nora's humor was just so based on her intellect, sometimes simply a turn of a phrase, " Lindley told me. "Nora was really funny and smart, obviously so is Will, so they hit it off right away, being funny and smart together."

On the first day of shooting in New York, Will's character has a dream that he's on Conan O'Brien's show—sans pants. When he showed up in his teeny bikini underwear, it cracked her up. "That's not cerebral," Lindley said, "but she found it incredibly funny."

But as journalist Ed Leibowitz observed, "Even in Hollywood, where it isn't unusual for relatively simple projects to drag on for years and exhaust the efforts of many capable people, the *Bewitched* project has sometimes appeared to be, well, hexed."

Other beloved sitcoms had been adapted for film with varying levels of success, such as *The Beverly Hillbillies*, which was turned into a 1993 film of the same name that floundered at the box office, and *Dennis the Menace*, which was adapted a number of times, while *The Brady Bunch* and *The Addams Family* both spawned successful 1990s film franchises that became bona fide box office hits.

The *Bewitched* project started in 1992. While Nora was hard at work prepping for *Sleepless in Seattle*, Penny Marshall was likewise busy with postproduction on *A League of Their Own*. Her best friend and business partner, Ted Bessell (of *That Girl* fame), wanted to pursue the movie rights for the sitcom, because he considered it "a romance for the ages." "*Bewitched* was Ted's vision," Penny remembered. "He just loved the idea of giving up immortality for love."

According to Leibowitz, a former *Laverne & Shirley* writer was first brought in to help with a script, but after turning in three drafts, Bessell still didn't have quite what he had imagined. That's when British writer Richard Curtis (*Four Weddings and a Funeral*) was hired, followed by Douglas Carter Beane, who'd just found success with *To Wong Foo, Thanks for Everything! Julie Newmar* (alongside a frequent Nora collaborator, producer G. Mac Brown) in 1995.

While Ted worried about how to make sure the way of life for a witch was captured accurately, Penny was instead concerned with the emotions: "Gotta make me cry," she told Beane.

By the time spring of 1996 rolled around, Beane had submitted his script and held a reading at a Greenwich Village theater. A pre-*Sex and the City* Cynthia Nixon played Samantha. As for the big screen, casting considerations for Samantha included everyone from Gwyneth Paltrow to Jennifer Aniston, Alicia Silverstone, and Cameron Diaz. Budgets were being drawn up, and sets were being discussed. It seemed like the film might be close to becoming a reality.

"My interest in *Bewitched* was how it is actually knowing that we're mortal that forces us to create and care about people, and that the immortals are jealous of that," Beane said.

Indeed, in retrospect, the sentiment of the story's meaning could be applied to Nora's life too. She of course knew she was mortal like the rest of us, but learning that mortality was upon her just two short years later seemed to serve as even more fuel to create and care for the people she loved with even greater intensity. Despite the film's "seemingly fluff and inconsequential theme," film scholar Liz Dance writes, Nora's *Bewitched* is a "tangle of realities" that proves that life is a "combination of things." Nora's "realness of the imagined," as Dance calls it, allowed her to access meaningful relationships with those she'd lost (such as her own mother), or perhaps those she had never met (such as the chef Julia Child), in life and through her movies.

"*Bewitched* has a depth and complexity only accessible when Nora's world view is understood," Dance writes, adding that it is a "contemplation of the multiple narratives which inform daily life." Nora believed there was no such thing as fiction or nonfiction, only narrative.

In October, tragedy struck the project's most passionate advocate: Ted Bessell suffered from an aortic aneurysm and died suddenly at the age of sixty-one. Producer Douglas Wick (*Gladiator*) was brought in along with his wife and producing partner, Lucy Fisher, of Red Wagon Entertainment, and in August 2004, production finally began.

Still, it wasn't smooth sailing. The film's editor, first and second assistant directors, and some crew members left during production because of what Nora referred to as problems with communication. For Nora's part, she felt great pressure to deliver after being handed a hefty $85 million budget—the highest of her career.

"You know movies," she explained just before the film's release in June 2005. "You only have 12 weeks when you're shooting, and what you're hoping is that the people that you're working with will have easy communication."

But even though Nora was known by now for firing people on her film sets, script supervisor Dianne Dreyer explained that it was often for good reason given the high stakes involved in making a successful studio movie.

"These aren't the right muffins," Nora had said at one point, to which a prop man replied, "Yeah I couldn't find those, so I just got another brand of muffins."

Nora was flabbergasted.

"She learned to be specific about everything," Dreyer told me. "Some people would say that's harsh. But Nora would say, 'You know, somebody just gave me $25 million to make a movie. Why would I work one more day with a guy who's not taking that seriously?'"

She was organized and as precise as a surgeon when it came to the way she approached the story, her collaborators said, and on the business side, she had developed a reputation for turning in movies on time and on budget. "Nora always had a firm grasp of the story. So, every once in a while when it started to get away from the actors, she would step in and get it sorted out," Lindley told me. "She was just in the driver's seat on her movies. Sometimes with directors you feel like every day they're fighting with the process or with the material, and I never felt that with Nora."

Rehearsal time was incredibly important to Nora, and she fought hard for it. "Even though she'd come and assist on storyboarding and everything, it was a reference," Dreyer said. "It wasn't a bible. It didn't preclude the opportunity for somebody else to have a better idea." Many of the best ideas came out of those rehearsal sessions, and Nora had learned to appreciate the collaborative spirit that moviemaking permitted. "It's also a real testament to her confidence, because only people who are confident in what they're doing can make space for change like that," Dreyer added.

Willow Lindley, now in high school, was thrilled to have her father John and her dear friend and mentor, Nora, in Los Angeles for an extended shoot. She remembered spending a good deal of time hanging out on the *Bewitched* set—and, of course, participating in all things food related.

"She was in a cupcake frenzy," Willow remembered. "And she was particularly obsessed with finding the best coconut cupcake that existed. There were many taste tests and discoveries." (The winner? Joan's on Third in Los Angeles.)

The discovery of the "perfect" or "best" version of something was inherently exciting to Nora, and she loved to hunt and report back to share what

Michael Caine, Nicole Kidman, director Nora, and sister Delia on the set of *Bewitched*, 2005. © *Columbia Pictures / The Everett Collection*

she'd learned. Even better, she liked to share and watch other people discover the greatness for themselves, Dreyer remembered.

Nora had declared that Langer's, a deli in Los Angeles, made the best pastrami sandwich in the world, so one afternoon, she called ahead to place an order and arranged for a bus to take people who wanted to join her to go and try it out. Nearly the entire crew took her up on her offer.

What made the OG downtown Jewish deli's version of the pastrami sandwich so special? They put about seven ounces of pastrami on it, which as Nora put it is "the proper proportion of meat to bread." Add in the tangy Gulden's mustard and "it's an exquisite combination of textures and tastes," she wrote of it in her 2002 piece for the *New Yorker*. "It's a symphony orchestra, different instruments brought together to play one perfect chord. It costs eight-fifty and is, in short, a work of art."

Dreyer agreed. "It definitely *was* the best pastrami sandwich I've ever eaten," she said. "For all the people who had lived and breathed and grown up in Los Angeles who'd never had a Langer's pastrami sandwich, I think their life improved a tiny little bit."

Nora was likewise always on the hunt for great up-and-coming comedians. Just as she'd done in years past, she and the casting agents brought in actors like Stephen Colbert and Steve Carell to be day players on the movie.

"I always hear about Johnny Carson giving comedians a break even when they were very different from his kind of humor," the elder Lindley explained. "Not that Nora was giving Will a break, because she wasn't, but I think she had an interest in supporting other people's humor. And she could find her own way to it. That's a gift, to allow that to happen on a set, especially if you're the writer."

For others, being on set with Nora was all just part of the Nora Ephron fifteen-pound-weight-gain plan. "One of the big jokes about *Bewitched* was that everyone gained so much weight because there was cake every day, or some like insanely delicious baked good situation to the point where I think someone said, 'We have to stop,'" Willow added.

But while the complaints on set were shared in good fun, the reactions to the movie's previews weren't particularly positive. When she presented her director's cut of *Bewitched* at a "Friends & Family" screening, a friend had a strong reaction to it.

Nora was hurt.

"In a series of 'hats on hats,' the realities at work in *Bewitched* become a confusion of and a complex mingling of understandings about the narratives which underpin contemporary Western culture," Dance writes. Ironically, she says, "stories are told to create order out of confusion, the otherwise arbitrary nature of life," but in this case, Nora's movie-about-a-show seemed to be more confusing for audiences and critics than anything else.

"She read the reviews and she cared about them," J.J. told me. "And she certainly cared about what people thought. . . . Some might believe she was impenetrable, but that wasn't the case. What is true is that she was able to put it all behind her very quickly and move forward."

But there was more loss to come. In 2003, Nora had gotten a call from her dear friend Judy Corman.

"Hi, doll," Judy said.

"Hi, darling," Nora replied.

"A weird thing happened . . ."

"It did?"

"Yes. . . . There's a lump on my tongue."

Though Nora and Judy both knew they were getting older, they were both healthy and well. Less than a year later, Nora's dear Judy was gone.

21 | "I HAVE THIS BLOOD THING"

> This is for those of you who understand, in short, that
> your purse is in some absolutely horrible way, you.
>
> —*Love, Loss & What I Wore*

AS 2005 TURNED TO 2006, Nora called her sister Delia.

She wasn't home, but Delia knew something was wrong. She got the call when she and her husband, Jerry, returned from Paris, having spent New Year's Eve in a lovely apartment in the city that year, entertaining close friends. It had been the best New Year's Eve of her life.

But the mood quickly changed when she got the message.

"Are you back yet?" Nora said.

Not only was Nora ill but the doctors told her she had only six months to live. Six months.

"All I remember from that night was fear," Delia wrote in 2013. "It was in the room the way air was. We were all terrified."

For sisters as close as Nora and Delia, the news wasn't just devastating, it was earth-shattering, or as Delia put it, "as if the Earth had shifted on its axis, something unfathomable had occurred in the galaxy in which I lived."

Walking down a Greenwich Village street, she reflected on their complicated but ultimately loving relationship full of the deep devotion only sisters share. They were "Nor and Del" (pronounced like "deal"). They borrowed and shared witty one-liners like other sisters shared dresses. Most of all, they shared so much love and laughter.

I need something from her, Delia thought. *Something . . .*

Just a few days later, while they were at work on what would become the hit play *Love, Loss, and What I Wore*, there it was: Nora's pansy ring.

"You should have it," Nora said. "You love pansies."

Of course, it wasn't the first or last time the big sister would teach the younger one a lesson about gift giving. She was always teaching lessons one way or another in her trademark bossy but loving fashion. "It's not your couch that needs to be replaced, it's your lamps . . . and your chairs would be better off in the bedroom," she'd once told Delia. "The dressing room smells moldy—you should fix that," she had told a theater's management, who quickly repaired it.

She could be ruthless if not outright cruel in her writing and in her criticism. But she was also a generous, loyal, and kind friend and mentor. In moments like these, it was the sweetness that remained. (As Nora lay in the hospital years later, a bouquet of two-dozen perfectly plump peach roses would arrive at Delia's door with a note: "xx, Nora.")

As terrified as Nora was, perhaps for the first time in her life, she knew that even a careful disclosure of her diagnosis and prognosis to her loved ones and to her colleagues would have real consequences. Initially, only Nick, Delia and her husband, and friend Richard Cohen and his girlfriend Mona Ackerman knew. She told her sister Amy, too, but waited until she'd started a medication regimen that was working before telling the kids or her loyal assistant, J.J.

"I have this blood thing," she told Jacob. "I don't want to tell you the name of it because I know you'll Google it and be scared. And we don't have to be scared. I'll be OK."

She also realized that time was limited—and there were certain things she simply would have to give up (willingly) on knowing anything about. She was OK with this. The list she made at the time included: "The former Soviet Republics, the Kardashians, Twitter, all Housewives, Survivors, American Idols, and Bachelors. Karzai's brother, soccer, monkfish, Jay-Z, every drink invented since the Cosmopolitan, especially the drink made with crushed mint leaves. You know the one."

As she explained more precisely to Charlie Rose in an interview, "I'm sure Jay-zees is great, but I don't have room for him. . . . You know, he doesn't have room for me, so don't feel bad about it."

Nora was determined to find a way to go on. She and Nick pursued answers from specialists in New York and Seattle. She'd felt "punky," she told Jacob, and had started to have fevers that couldn't be explained.

The diagnosis was myelodysplastic syndrome (MDS), a rare condition that occurs when the blood-forming cells in the bone marrow become abnormal, which can lead to low numbers of one or more types of blood cells. (Writer Susan Sontag had died from complications of the same condition just two years earlier at the age of seventy-one.)

"I think she didn't want to come to me while she was feeling vulnerable or hysterical about it," Jacob explained later. "I know that she and my stepfather [Nick] got back from Seattle, where she had seen this doctor, and she really broke down, from what Nick said. But I never saw her break down over her illness, just as I never really saw her break down over anything."

———————

It was a long road to get *Love, Loss, and What I Wore* to the stage. It was a lesson in perseverance and faith that it would somehow, someday come to fruition.

"The idea of the book is if you ask women about their clothes, they tell you about their lives," Delia explained of Ilene Beckerman's bestselling memoir of the same name.

When Nora first picked it up, she felt a strong connection right away. "This is not about fashion; it is about what clothes really are to us," she said during a Q&A session in 2009 moderated by *Elle* magazine. "Those moments when we are constantly trying to find our identity through them, and either failing or succeeding,"

Never one to take on a serious issue without humor, she immediately thought the book could work as a play, adding her own comedic sensibility and her sister Delia's to Beckerman's material. "We both share half a brain," Nora added. "We both have the same historical references; we both think that the *Archie* comic books are a template for everything. We laugh at the same things."

The sisters commissioned stories from one hundred of their friends via e-mail, and some of those highlighted in the play are from the likes of Rosie O'Donnell, Annie Navasky, Nancy De Los Santos, and the late Nancy Dolman Short, among others.

"We thought of it as *The Vagina Monologues* without the vaginas," Delia explained later. "What we did was we asked all our friends to tell us the stories of their clothes, and then we did a lot of interviewing separately. And then we brought all the material together and began to craft this play."

After several unsuccessful workshops in New York and L.A. with actors together onstage, the sisters continued to work on the material. But as Delia remembers it, "Everyone hated it."

They tried it again and it didn't work. They put it away again and forgot about it.

"We left and we never spoke about it again," Delia said. "We didn't say anything to each other about it. Nothing. It was over. There was nothing to say."

But four years later, the sisters received a call from theater director Karen Carpenter, who had seen the play collecting dust on a shelf at the Old Globe in San Diego.

"Could we please try a workshop?" she asked.

"If you have Linda Lavin in it, you can," Nora replied.

"And for some reason, Linda Lavin agreed, and it worked," Delia remembered. "Fourteen years later, the play worked. We got a producer immediately and the next thing we knew it was on Broadway. And everyone thought it had happened overnight. That was 14 years. And now it's played all over the world."

The play features five women sharing monologues and ensemble pieces about memories through the lens of their clothes, often with a rotating cast of film and television actresses, and it won the 2010 Drama Desk Award for Unique Theatrical Experience.

The original off-Broadway cast included Tyne Daly in the lead role of Gingy, and Rosie O'Donnell, Samantha Bee, Katie Finneran, and Natasha Lyonne in supporting roles.

Ten years after its premiere, director Jenny Sullivan led a cast in a special one-night-only benefit performance in Santa Barbara, California. The cast included California state senator Hannah-Beth Jackson (who was actively working on legislation to protect women against abuse in the workplace), six-time Emmy nominee Meredith Baxter, Hattie Winston, Kathryne Dora Brown, and Lily Gibson.

Sullivan was handpicked by Nora and Delia to lead the show's epic run at the Geffen Playhouse in 2010—a seven-month, rotating-cast extravaganza that broke box office records for the Southern California venue. At the Geffen, the cast was led by Carol Kane, Rita Wilson, Natasha Lyonne, Tracee Ellis Ross, and Caroline Aaron, who received rave reviews.

"It's not a 'chick' play," Sullivan told me. "It's a document of a time for women, and of the collaboration of Delia and Nora."

Sullivan was a fellow child of "the business" back in Beverly Hills whose parents were Broadway actors Barry Sullivan and Marie Brown. They were close with Henry and Phoebe—both families were New York transplants—and understood the challenges of adapting to Southern California life. The Camp Tocaloma stage was a familiar stomping ground for the Ephron girls and for Sullivan every summer, too.

When *Love, Loss* first premiered off-Broadway at the Westside Theatre in New York City on October 1, 2009 (after a preview in the summer of 2008 in East Hampton, New York), it was praised for being both touching and unsentimental—that special quality the Ephron sisters had managed to pull off in the tricky romantic comedy film genre by writing and directing *Sleepless in Seattle* and *You've Got Mail*, among other classics they made both together and apart over the years.

Writer Elizabeth Segal was there for both of those collaborations, and she contributed her piece about her relationship with her boots—and with a guy—from that beautiful summer in Seattle.

"[Nora] saw the beginning of the relationship, and then she saw the end of the relationship," Segal told me. "But right at the very beginning, she was saying, 'Well, you don't actually know if this relationship is going to work out or not.' It's just so funny that she could always see the big picture in somebody else's life, that you couldn't even see yourself."

She can still hear Nora's sweet but stern nasally voice in her ear.

"Well, we *know* how this is gonna end," Nora would say.

"She was a know-it-all, but she was usually right," Segal added. "It was complicated. She knew I could be a writer. And now I make a living as a writer. And so it's like, far be it for me to push back on her then and say, well, 'I don't know if I can do this, I can do the journalism, but not the creative stuff.' And now finally, I'm doing the creative stuff."

When Nora said the play is about identity, it's easy to see how audiences recognize themselves in many of the vignettes about fashion tragedies, and in her famous "I Hate My Purse" essay from the 2006 bestselling collection *I Feel Bad About My Neck: And Other Thoughts on Being a Woman*, which makes an appearance toward the end of the play: "I tried spending quite a lot of money on a purse, the theory being that having an expensive purse would inspire me to become a different person."

One of Delia's contributions about high heels ("Heels or Think?") is likewise all too relatable, providing thoughtful fodder for the ongoing problematic relationship women have with the things they must wear, want to wear, hate to wear, and need to wear as they perform their femininity at work and at home.

The women's diverse set of twenty-eight stories are about breast cancer, the death of a parent, bad boyfriends, and prom dresses, but buried beneath the layers are many more quiet struggles that speak to a broader sense of the often difficult decisions women face alone and in silence. Most vividly, the moments of the play that touch on rape and abuse directly seem even more prescient now, in the shadow of #metoo, than perhaps they did then.

But the play is also about magical thinking. In a particularly poignant monologue, a woman remembers the electric blue robe her mother once wore.

Sisterly love: Delia and Nora pose at the after-party for the *Love, Loss, and What I Wore* 500th Performance Celebration, B. Smith's Restaurant, New York, N.Y. January 13, 2011. *Gregorio T. Binuya / The Everett Collection*

She remembers coming home and finding the side of her mother's closet empty after her death. That electric blue robe and all its details ends up being the only piece of clothing that to her evokes any meaning.

In a 2015 interview with the late author and journalist Richard Reeves, he softly revealed the quiet, aching void Nora's husband Nick still felt when he was at home in New York in the nearly three years after her death. The texture, the smell, the uniqueness of her—it's undoubtedly what he misses most.

"He refused to get rid of her clothes," Reeves told me. "They smell like her."

At its best, *Love, Loss* is about the shared humanity in the common experience of what seems trivial, pointing to the times it wasn't: who you were when you bought the thing, wore the thing, and most importantly, who or what you loved, and perhaps lost in it. The women help you remember who you were when you had to let it go . . . or perhaps who you could be if you did.

It's about relationships—not with the clothes themselves, but with the people they represent—mothers, sisters, daughters, husbands, lovers. But when that person is the one looking back at her reflection in the mirror? That's when the stories get really good—and also, at times, really difficult. (For her oldest son Jacob, a beautiful, soft cable-knit sweater from Maxfield was Nora's final gift to him six months before she died. "It took me about three years to be able to put it on," he said.)

Clothes matter to women, and what matters to women matters.

Today, the play is about the loss of Nora, too. When she died in 2012, fans the world over mourned. But her sister Delia was unable to shake her grief, trying to manage the gravity of how personal it was with the need to deal with it publicly. She wrote about their special relationship in her bestselling memoir, *Sister Mother Husband Dog* in 2013.

Then, something magical happened.

"I couldn't think or write or sleep," she wrote in an op-ed for the *New York Times* in 2017. "I realized, I'm falling in love. I am 72 years old, how is this possible?"

Nora had set Delia up with a man some fifty-four years earlier. Now the pair had a second date, and a second chance at love.

"The day of our date, I had an excellent blow-dry," Delia wrote. "I spent way too much time considering what to wear. I was tongue-tied at dinner. I believe I asked him his favorite color. My brain was jumbled by his presence, by the ghost of my husband who would only want me to be happy, but still."

In love, and loss, it all came back to her relationship with her dear sister.

"I look at Peter and wonder how this miracle happened to us. My sister, of course."

22 | A SOFTER NORA

> Whenever you cook, in some strange way, it's a form
> of time travel.
>
> —Nora Ephron

FOUR YEARS BEFORE THE PREMIERE OF *LOVE, LOSS*, just after Nora's
version of *Bewitched* hit movie theaters in the summer of 2005, Nora ran into
Meryl at a Shakespeare in the Park performance. The Central Park tradition
was one of Nora's favorites that she never missed, while Meryl had sometimes
attended as an audience member, and other times as part of the cast, having
played the role of Kate in William Shakespeare's *The Taming of the Shrew* in
1978, and as Arkadina in a Mike Nichols–directed *Seagull* in 2001 (she'd also
appear in the titular role in George C. Wolfe's production of *Mother Courage
and Her Children* in 2006).

But on this particular sweltering day, Meryl was curious what her dear
friend was up to.

"What are you working on these days, Nora?" Meryl asked.

"Actually, I'm working on a script based on Julia Child's life in France,"
Nora replied.

With that, Meryl instantly began demonstrating her Julia Child impression
complete with her high-pitched, singsongy cadence.

"*Bon appétit!*" she exclaimed.

Days later after reading the script, she called Nora right away. Nearly
twenty-five years after their first collaboration on *Silkwood*—and numerous
credits and awards later for both director and leading lady—they still found

themselves giddy at the idea of working together on something that felt particularly special.

"I thought it was absolutely beautiful," Meryl recalled. "It made me cry, the idea that what you put in front of your family, that love, those connections between people, are the real important things."

She also had a casting suggestion for Nora: Stanley Tucci should play her husband, Paul Child. The esteemed actors had just worked together in the hit comedy drama *The Devil Wears Prada* (released in 2006), and *Julie & Julia* required a certain kind of intimacy that the real-life dueling charades players and close friends felt they could pull off on-screen in an authentic way.

Tucci keyed in very quickly on how Julia's romantic bond with Paul became such a vital part of her development as a chef and author. "I think that Julia Child didn't know, necessarily, that she was a creative person, that she was in essence, an artist and a teacher because of the way she grew up," he said. "And once she was given the liberty to even think that maybe that's who she was, she was then able to execute it and choose whatever she wanted."

Born in Pasadena, California, on August 15, 1912, Julia was educated at Smith College. Not unlike Nora, she'd once moved to Manhattan after college to pursue a writing career, and she had planned to become a "famous woman novelist" before heading back home to take care of her ailing mother before her mother's death in 1937. By 1942, World War II had broken out, and she found a research job with the Office of Strategic Services (OSS), a wartime intelligence agency that preceded the CIA.

It was in Ceylon (now Sri Lanka) that she met the "bread to her butter" in Paul Child in 1944 and married him in 1946. He was a true Renaissance man—a painter, a photographer, a curator, and a cultural liaison. He opened up the world to her, quite literally, with their move to France in 1948 for his job with the American embassy in Paris—but at thirty-six, Julia wasn't quite yet Julia. And that's where Nora picked up her story as she wrote the screenplay for *Julie & Julia*. It would be a coming-of-age story that for once wasn't about a teenager, and perhaps more importantly, was about a woman in love with her husband, with food, and with life. The parallels to Nick and Nora's love story later in life couldn't be missed, Meryl later explained.

My Life in France, the late chef's 2006 memoir with her grandnephew, Alex Prud'homme, provided the backstory for half of the *Julie & Julia* story.

"When we first meet her, she and her husband Paul are living in Paris where they've been posted after the Second World War, trying to promote all good things American since he worked for the diplomatic corps," Meryl said. "She was very bright, but the expectations for women at that point were not necessarily to have a career and find their life's work."

But it was Julia's "relentless appetite and curiosity for all sorts of things," as Meryl put it, that helped revolutionize the way Americans would cook for decades to come.

Simply put, Julia "made cooking fun," and she inspired millions of Americans to overcome their fear of the kitchen and to appreciate the joy of making and eating fine cuisine. After falling in love with French food and discovering that there weren't really any cookbooks about French food written in English, she joined her colleagues Simone Beck, and Louisette Bertholle, who'd been working on creating one and needed an American collaborator.

At their cooking school, L'École des trois gourmandes, the Cordon Bleu-trained trio would test and prototype their recipes while teaching their students—each of whom paid five dollars per lesson—and they worked hard to ensure the ingredients and instructions would be available and accessible for the "servant-less" chef in the United States. (*Gourmet* magazine's French recipes offered throughout the 1950s were often meant for those who indeed had servants to prepare them.)

For Nora, it was Julia's gift for teaching that she appreciated most—even as a fearless chef herself. "I'm a good cook, and I look at something like *Iron Chef* and think, 'It's a good thing I already know how to cook'—because I would never think I could do it, if I watched these shows," she told NPR's Linda Wertheimer when the film was released. "She made you know you could do it."

Back in 1962, when Nora first moved to New York following graduation from Wellesley College, she'd bought a copy of Child's *Mastering the Art of French Cooking* (as she tells it, "everybody" was doing it). Though her friends from college were there in real life, she found a friend in Julia—an imaginary friend—who provided comfort through food.

"It was a way of saying you were intelligent and therefore you were going to cook in a way that a smart person was going to cook," she later explained. "So Julia Child became an imaginary friend for me and for the millions of women who bought this cookbook, and, years later, I think the same thing was true for Julie Powell."

With Streep and Tucci on board, Nora turned to casting the movie version of Powell, whose bestselling 2005 memoir *Julie & Julia: 365 Days, 524 Recipes, 1 Tiny Apartment Kitchen* would inform the other half of the film. Nora looked to Amy Adams because "among the many things I liked about her was that I believed that she was smart enough to be a writer," Nora explained. "And she's funny."

For both Nora and Meryl, cooking with Julia Child through the eyes of a young Julie Powell was also a way to reconnect with and even honor their late mothers.

"[My mother] was somebody who turned the lights on when she came into a room," Meryl said. "I have a much more reserved side. But I've always wanted to be more like her, so playing Julia gave me the chance."

"My out is that I'm not really 'doing' Julia Child, I'm Julie Powell's idea of who she was," Meryl said in another interview. "So while I felt a responsibility to her memory and legacy of the great work she did, and to the essence of her character, I didn't feel I was replicating her."

Nora tapped actor Chris Messina, who'd played a small but important role as an ill-informed Fox Books employee in *You've Got Mail*, to play the film version of Powell's husband, Eric.

The movie might have been a small indie film had it not been for Nora, according to Julie. "Initially, the rights (to my book) were bought by Eric Steel," she said. "Then Nora popped up and said, 'Oh I'll do it.' So it suddenly became this big movie."

In truth, one of the first advocates for the project was Amy Robinson, who'd seen a biography on A&E about Julia and Paul Child and was inspired along with Steel to bring the idea to Amy Pascal.

"I'm buying this," she said almost immediately.

"Don't you want to hear our ideas?" Robinson asked.

"No, I'm buying this," Pascal replied, "and Nora should direct it."

There was a time when Steel asked if Montreal would do as a stand-in for Paris, which Nora simply pretended not to hear. Filming would *have* to take place in Paris, she thought. It played a key role in the film just as much as the actors and the food.

With a reported $40 million production budget—a healthy amount, but about half of what she'd had on *Bewitched* four years earlier—principal photography began in March 2008. At the time, Nora's blood condition, MDS, made her feel tired, but being on set still seemed to make her as happy as it always had.

Meryl's instincts about Nora—and vice versa—had never failed her, except perhaps now. When it came to recognizing her longtime friend and collaborator's illness, this time Nora was the one pulling off the most believable acting performance of all.

"She never sat down," Meryl Streep later recalled.

Others noticed something was a bit off about their usually bright and fearless leader, but no one wanted to question her. At the beginning of filming, Don Lee noticed she wasn't her usual energetic self. He was worried but wanted to respect Nora's privacy.

"I'm not going to ask, because if she wanted me to know what was going on, she would tell me," he told Delia.

But after the first two weeks she was back to her usual self, and everyone was relieved, not yet realizing the gravity of her illness.

Amy and Meryl had just finished filming *Doubt* two weeks earlier, so although there was little time for much prep in between, the consummate professionals—one still on the cusp of greatness after starring in the indie *Junebug* and winning a Special Jury Award at Sundance in 2005, and the other having already garnered fifteen Oscar nominations and two wins for her work in *Kramer vs. Kramer* (1980) and *Sophie's Choice* (1983)—arrived on set ready to bring both gravitas and authenticity to their respective real-life heroines.

But as much as Julia Child was larger than life, Meryl said it was more intimidating playing another venerable real person with her watching—on the set of *Heartburn* in 1983, when she played a fictionalized version of Nora.

Nora, on the other hand, highly recommends having Meryl play you—not just in the movies but in life too:

> I highly recommend having Meryl Streep play you. If your husband is cheating on you with a carhop, get Meryl to play you. You will feel much better. If you get rear-ended in a parking lot, have Meryl Streep play you. If the dingo eats your baby, call Meryl. She plays all of us better than we play ourselves, although it's a little depressing

knowing that if you went to audition to play yourself you would lose out to her. Some days when I'm having a hard day, I call up Meryl and she'll come and she'll step in for me. She's so good people don't really notice. I call her at the end of the day to find out how I did and inevitably it's one of the best days I've ever had.

One day on set, Messina began to complain about the amount of food he was expected to consume. It was Lobster Thermidor day, and multiple takes meant that he was already approaching delirium and was unsure he could continue. But never one for weakness, the fearless foodie director got him refocused with one simple sentence yelled in from the other room:

"Robert De Niro would do it!" Nora said.

With that, he was ready for yet *another* seven lobsters. (It was, as they say, a rough day at the office.)

"I know that sounds so crazy to say, but Mr. Messina is a brilliant eater," Amy said. "I don't know how he does it. He eats like a man, yet he doesn't make it look grotesque. It's a talent."

Award-winning costume designer Ann Roth—who'd begun her partnership with Meryl and Nora decades earlier on *Silkwood*—was tasked with bringing America's favorite French chef to life through the details of her clothing, including girdles, gloves, and, of course, a crisp toque blanche (chef's hat).

"It was all about height," Roth explained later in an interview with *Variety*. "I had the shoemaker make me three pairs of spectator shoes that made Meryl, who is 5 feet 6 inches, look taller." She added that the counters and stoves were built at a lower height to accentuate the illusion of a towering Child, who in real life was six foot two.

As for Amy's wardrobe, Roth remembered that New Yorkers, still in a post-9/11 haze, weren't very concerned with fashion, or at least weren't as fussy as they once were before the attacks. She expressed this in a bleak way in the film, showing Julie and other actors in the background in drab clothing to capture the mood of the time.

Even with the incomparable Meryl Streep on set as Julia, there was one powerful role that needed to be cast arguably just as carefully: the food. From the early scene of sole sizzling in butter that greets Julia Child in mid-twentieth-century Paris to the final presentation of Julie's pièce de résistance meal for her friends on the rooftop of her Queens apartment, it had to be perfect.

"The food had its own presence," Mark Ricker, the production designer on the film, told *Variety*. "I had to provide a foundation for it. I designed the kitchens to be as usable as possible in order to support the food itself."

Based on detailed photographs of Child in her kitchen in Paris practicing recipes and by a visit to real-life Julie Powell's small apartment in Queens, Ricker was able to recreate sets that were both authentic and functional. Prop master Diana Burton "was the glue that held it all together," Ricker said, handling everything from Le Creuset pots to silverware to ensure the perfect presentation of the food. He even found an old suitcase that once belonged to Paul Child and used it in the opening scene as the couple arrives in Paris.

At the time of Julia's real-life transformation into a world-renowned chef, she and Paul had settled into the top two floors of 81, rue de l'Université, or as they liked to call it, "Rue de Loo." Most of the interiors of the replicated apartment were shot at Silvercup Studios in Queens, and an entire tent was set up there for cooking—food stylist and cookbook author Susan Spungen and chef Colin Flynn had a real working kitchen complete with running water and a working stove (actually, they had several). Spungen, a former food editor at *Martha Stewart Living*, helped ensure the actors worked with the food and tools in a believable way. "If it didn't look right when they sharpened a knife, I would say, 'hold it like this,'" she said.

"My job is not making food look good but making it look delicious," she added. "[Julie] is a home cook, still learning. We didn't want things to look too good, and we did a lot of messing up in the kitchen to make it look real."

As for the real food left behind between takes? That was happily taken care of by the cast and crew—although complaints did abound on certain days, like when Messina had so much bruschetta he thought he'd never eat again, or when Nora's assistant and associate producer J. J. Sacha said he gained fifteen pounds from "taste testing."

"Nora made me the official taste tester of every dish you see in the movie," he told me. "Susan Spungen had a kitchen on whatever set we were on. And I always got to taste things. Everything. And it wasn't just a taste, I should add. Susan had to make multiple versions of everything, as you might imagine. I took home a lot of great food from that set. Lobster thermidor was a dish I remember loving. I had never had that before and haven't since. You just don't see it anywhere. It is outstanding."

Nora's trusted collaborators joined her on the set of what would be her last film, *Julie & Julia*, in 2009: associate producer J. J. Sacha, script supervisor and coproducer Dianne Dreyer, Meryl Streep, and director Nora. *Jonathan Wenk / © Columbia Pictures / The Everett Collection*

That's how executive producer Don Lee remembered it too. For him, doing a foodie project with Nora was a dream come true. "It was so fun to make *Julie & Julia* because not only did we have a food consultant but we had a full-time chef because we were making food constantly for camera," he told me. "And also we would bring in outside food trucks and things."

One day, there was a scene where Julie makes a chocolate cream pie. The recipe was Nora's. As Julie makes it in the film, she recalls one of Nora's earlier observations from *Heartburn*: "After a long day, when nothing makes sense, you mix cream and butter and it takes."

Lee said they'd also, for good measure, brought in a pie truck on that particular day. "So that was the joke: that it was the only film that had a pie appetizer before a pie entree," he said. "And that would be typical."

But even with all the goodies to sustain the cast and crew, would Nora be able to sustain herself during the shoot? Would willpower—and plenty of butter—be enough to overcome the reality of her worsening MDS?

23 | BUTTER

You can never have too much butter, that is my belief.
If I have a religion, that's it.

—Nora Ephron

NORA'S MDS DIAGNOSIS (or perhaps the treatments that helped control it) seemed to, ironically, have invigorated her even more. She was eager to work, and eager to mentor. Coming off the disappointment of *Bewitched* just a couple of years earlier she knew her next film project needed to be a hit—not just for the powers that be but for her own sanity and sense of accomplishment.

What had never failed her throughout the ups and downs of Hollywood or life itself? Her writing. She could always return to her writing. And she could seemingly always find a way to laugh at herself—even as she navigated what she considered to be some of the most dreadful parts of aging. Her witty collection of essays, *I Feel Bad About My Neck: And Other Thoughts on Being a Woman*, was released to critical acclaim in July 2006, and by September was listed at No. 1 on the *New York Times* nonfiction bestseller list.

"When she says that she can trace the history of the last 40 years through changing trends in lettuce, she isn't kidding," Janet Maslin wrote in a review for the *Times*. "Some things don't change. It's good to know that Ms. Ephron's wry, knowing X-ray vision is one of them."

It was that X-ray vision that had been piqued just a few years earlier when Nora read about Powell, then just a blogger in Queens, in another *Times* article by food writer Amanda Hesser. On the verge of turning thirty, Julie was cooking her way through Julia Child's famed 1961 *Mastering the Art of French Cooking* cookbook, one recipe and one day at a time.

Nick and Nora had a ritual in the mornings. They'd wake up, make coffee, and read the newspapers. Before long, Nora was at her desk writing—and Nick was typing away at his.

"Nick said he would be downstairs at [home in] East Hampton and he would hear the footsteps," Martin Short told me. "Now that she's up, she's had her coffee, and right to the desk and typing."

But on this particular day, Wednesday, August 13, 2003, the Hesser piece had caught her eye. A RACE TO MASTER THE ART OF FRENCH COOKING, the headline read.

The bravery of Powell's act astonished Nora. After all, she knew how incredibly time consuming and complex some of the recipes were—and she also knew more than a little something about using cooking to get through life events over which we don't have any control.

Powell found a friend in Julia just like Nora did. Not just any friend—someone to help her believe in herself. "I was drowning in the ocean and she rescued me," the fictional Powell tells her husband in the movie.

Like a thick stew, the ingredients of what would become *Julie & Julia* were slowly coming together.

"It's always hard to combine two stories," Nora told *Variety*. "But I was inspired by *The Godfather: Part II*. I consider this film a ninth cousin to that movie."

In truth, she was also inspired by *The Hours*. She initially thought it was a movie about a book, and then told food writers it was about food, "and I told the people at the Smithsonian that it was a movie about America," she explained to Charlie Rose.

That spring, Nora had run into actress Jane Lynch at the premiere of the Christopher Guest mockumentary *A Mighty Wind*. "Maybe we'll work together someday," Nora said.

Then, just a few years later, Lynch got a call. It was Nora.

"You're the tallest person I know," Nora told her. "How would you like to go to Paris and shoot a movie?"

"Oh, I would love to!" Jane replied.

Playing Julia Child's sister, Dorothy, Jane had a few seemingly tiny, but ultimately very important scenes to film alongside Meryl.

For producer Laurence Mark, who'd worked with Nora on *Cookie* back in 1989, it was about the sisters: Julia and Dorothy, and Nora and Delia. "The only scene we ever reshot in the entire movie was this tiny, tiny scene in front of the mirror where the two of them are getting ready for the party," he remembered. "She wanted to get it perfect."

"Pretty good," Julia says at the sight of herself and her sister dressed up in the mirror, "but not great."

For J.J., it's one of the scenes that personifies Nora most: it's about sisters and the way a few words can mean so much.

But as with any project Nora took on, the subject matter, and her signature warm delivery of it, was completely personal.

"I love food," Nora said. "I'm obsessed with food. I think about it constantly." She had a lifelong love affair with food, yes, but being in the kitchen was also a way of connecting to her past—and a way to perhaps make time stand still when there wasn't quite enough of it left.

In the script for *Julie & Julia*, Julie explains to her husband how when her mother made boeuf bourguignon when Julie was growing up it seemed that "everything was going to be all right." Could it have been the same feeling Nora had as a little girl herself—when Phoebe would dress up the table with her finest silver, and sing, and laugh?

Nora may have bristled at the notion that she was a typical child of alcoholics, but the gift of time travel of a taste or a familiar smell, to bring her mother back to her, is shared so beautifully and captured in this film in a

Nora at home in Manhattan as she prepares an apple tart with writer John Horn from Julia Child's recipe, July 2009. © *Jennifer S. Altman. All Rights Reserved*

way that's both personal and sweet without being excessively sentimental. She continued to make three recipes from Child's cookbook throughout her life: lamb stew, boeuf bourguignon, and chicken breasts with a cream-and-port-based mushroom sauce.

"I actually think whenever you cook in some strange way it's a form of time travel," Nora told NPR shortly after the film's debut in August 2009. "When I used to cook from Julia's cookbook, I had long imaginary conversations with her. And I used to think maybe she would come to dinner, even though I had never met her, and never did."

In truth, Nora actually *was* once invited to have lunch with the real Julia Child back in her early magazine journalism days. She never did make it to Boston for a visit, though, something she came to regret later.

Regrets aside, from the early scene of sole sizzling in golden butter, Nora was perhaps most proud of the fact that the movie celebrated what to her was a sacred part of life, love, and lunch: butter. "You can never have too much butter, that is my belief," Nora said. "If I have a religion, that's it."

And when Paul Child says, "You are the butter to my bread," that's about Nick, Amy Pascal said. When asked to provide life advice in six words or less, Nora simply replied: "Secret of life: marry an Italian."

"It's a kind of marriage that actually exists," she explained of both Julia Child and perhaps herself on *Charlie Rose*. "Thank *god* it does or people would accuse me of making this up. But there *are* guys who really do take enormous pleasure in their wives' growth."

With Nick, she was truly happy. "And happiness, even more than journalism, screenwriting, directing, cooking, blogging, was Nora's gift to her fans and to her friends," wrote family friend and writer Alessandra Stanley in the *New York Times*. "In 1986, when a Newsweek cover put a metaphorical bullet through the single career women over 40, she refuted all by herself the fear that powerful women repel men, that funny girls go home to their cats, that having it all means enjoying it alone."

———

As Nora would also say, there are no long days in Paris. Somehow, no matter what challenges might come up, you always end up at dinner. So finding the

Nick and Nora glowing at
the Westwood, Los Angeles,
premiere of *Julie & Julia*,
July 2009. *Photo by Michael
Germana / The Everett Collection*

proper restaurant, bistro, brasserie, or café *pour dîner* while shooting *Julie &
Julia* was crucial.

At night, it was Lee's job to coordinate and book large dinners for the
group to attend together after wrapping for the day. While the seven-day
shoot had gone extraordinarily well, arranging the dinners was in some ways
an even higher-pressure situation. After reviewing Nora's approved list (Nora
recommended the famed bar and brasserie at the Hôtel Lutetia on the Left
Bank, for example), he worked with his French counterparts to secure the
perfect setting.

"We would bring forty to fifty people to dinner once a week," he told me.
"That's the beauty of Nora, she was so inclusive. She'd invited everybody. We
had forty Americans we brought over, we brought the core crew over and then
you bring the French crew on too—she would invite everybody to dinner. How
many people do that?"

These were the rules at a typical Nora dinner: at certain points, she'd tap
her glass and the guests would have to shift down a seat in a sort of highly
sophisticated version of musical chairs.

"Everybody would talk to everybody," Lee explained. "Everybody was there. We always worked hard to try to have a happy set."

As for the actors, Stanley and Meryl got along so well—and were such quintessential masters of their respective crafts by that time—that they were able to ad lib together in various scenes.

"What is it that you *really* like to do?" Stanley Tucci's Paul Child asks his wife.

"Eat," she replies.

"And you're so *good* at it!" Paul exclaims. Nora was experienced enough to know to keep the sweet moment in the final cut.

And eat they did—both on set and behind the scenes.

Chris Messina loved that the actors had a chance to "play," and thought Nora's ingenious "and let's do one just for fun" technique brought out a great sense of creativity among the cast.

In rehearsal, especially, Meryl and Stanley had a great time "throwing out a lot of little nonsense" since Nora let them know the door was open to new ideas.

"Julia is given the [book] *Larousse Gastronomique* for her birthday, for her fiftieth birthday, in fact, it's what started her cooking," Nora explained. "And she and Stanley are in bed, about to go to bed about to make love. And she's reading aloud from the cookbook . . . Meryl found a chicken recipe in it, and it was all arranged in the script that Julia Child couldn't really speak French and that Paul Child was much better at it. And, I'm going to ruin this line, but she says, 'I don't know what this means?' 'Wash the thighs' Stanley said. And then Stanley said, 'And then stuff the hen until she just can't take it anymore.'"

Nora laughed—and jotted it down to be added to the final draft.

"That's the beauty," Tucci added. "You know, when you walk away from a movie and you say, Oh my God, that was so much fun. You know that things like that were allowed to happen. And that there is ultimately a trust that everyone has with each other."

And while the film is a love story about food and reinvention, it's also a tribute to the perseverance and unbelievable tenacity required to publish a book.

Back in Paris, in one of Nora's favorite scenes in the film, Julia has just learned that Houghton Mifflin doesn't want to publish her cookbook. She shares the letter with Paul. He suggests teaching, or perhaps teaching on television, which Nora calls "an astonishing" idea for the time.

Her admiration and adoration for these two actors is evident. She says she could just watch the scene over and over again, not for the writing, but for the acting.

"Somebody is going to read your book and realize what you've done," Paul tells Julia. "Because your book is amazing . . . (a beat) . . . fuck them!"

Cut to: the offices of Alfred A. Knopf. Judith Jones, a young editor, as she receives Child's book. The first recipe she tries? Julia's boeuf bourguignon. "Yum," she says.

Child's sturdiness can be felt in the book itself. Sacha said that Nora kept it on her desk as she wrote the script, frequently flipping through its pages for inspiration, and Jones, who became Child's venerable editor, even provided notes on early drafts of the script.

When it came time to create the director's cut of the movie, the late editor Richard Marks and first assistant editor Shelly Westerman were invited to join Nora in the Hamptons from May until September. They'd spent the previous months traveling from their Manhattan cutting room to where they were shooting in Brooklyn to watch dailies with Nora.

"I thought, I don't eat seafood, but if I'm ever going to do it, it's the time to do it," Shelly told me. "So [Nora] encouraged me."

After indulging in her very first soft-shell crab at Nick & Toni's in East Hampton, Nora said, "Tell me all about it," adding, "I remember the first time I had soft-shell crab. I was working in the Kennedy White House . . ."

It wasn't just the gift of food that Nora was sharing—it was how to eat, or more precisely, how to live.

"It's not just like you learned about food," Shelly said. "It's like you learned the value of if you're going to eat something, make it really good. Of making really nice choices and not being afraid to treat yourself once in a while to something good."

The following year, Shelly and Richard ("Richie") did another film together for director James L. Brooks, *How Do You Know* starring Reese Witherspoon.

They found themselves stuck in Philadelphia shooting for five months when Shelly e-mailed Nora for her emergency foodie expertise.

"Richie and I are miserable," she wrote. "All there is is shitty cheesesteaks. What should we do? Please help!"

"I will hear none of this. Stand by," Nora replied. Almost instantly, she enlisted all her friends who were local to the area and promptly sent a list of food recommendations. (She'd naturally done the same for Alfonso Gomez-Rejon when he went to Rome for the first time, and for Willow Lindley when she traveled to Paris.)

———————

At a private White House screening in 2009, Nora, Stanley, and Meryl met the Obamas—President Barack Obama and First Lady Michelle Obama. As the director, actors, and first family settled into the upholstered forty-seat, narrow storied family theater room in the East Wing, Nora was, in a way, back home again. It was a fitting full-circle moment for the esteemed filmmaker since she had begun her career in the White House as an intern some four decades earlier.

She likewise was having a blast promoting the movie and basking in her identity as an OG foodie in more ways than one. Just before *Julie & Julia* premiered that summer, Hesser cofounded the food blog *Food52*. Nora later became a secret blogger for the site—a hobby she found delightful—by signing her posts as "mrsp," a.k.a. Mrs. Pileggi. The voice is instantly recognizable.

Julie & Julia opened at No. 2 behind *G. I. Joe: Rise of Cobra* in August 2009, ultimately bringing in more than $94 million domestically and nearly $130 million worldwide. It remains her fourth-highest grossing film as a director behind *Sleepless in Seattle* ($270.5), *You've Got Mail* ($210.7), and *Michael* ($184.3) when adjusted for inflation.

It was generally well received by most critics too. David Denby of the *New Yorker* proclaimed that "*Julie & Julia* is one of the gentlest, most charming American movies of the past decade," while *Los Angeles Times* critic Kenneth Turan said, "[*Julie & Julia*] does it right. A consummate entertainment that echoes the rhythms and attitudes of classic Hollywood, it's a satisfying throwback to those old-fashioned movie fantasies where impossible dreams do come true. And, in this case, it really happened. Twice."

The warmth emanated through the screen. At a press screening in Los Angeles, a longtime film critic who'd always been wary of mixing business with friendship recalled how the doors swung open as the credits rolled, and there was Nora—arms wide open, ready for a hug—and he felt compelled to go for it.

And it was the second time Nora and Meryl's work together resulted in Meryl's recognition for an Academy Award for Best Performance by an Actress in a Leading Role (the first was for *Silkwood* in 1983). The Oscar went to Sandra Bullock for *The Blind Side*.

At the Los Angeles premiere, Nora wore her signature head-to-toe black and a crisp white jacket, while Meryl chose a belted lipstick-red dress, and Amy looked ethereal and youthful in white. In New York, the film premiered at the now-shuttered Ziegfeld Theatre on West Fifty-Fourth Street in Manhattan. Internationally renowned chefs mingled with actors and Hollywood executives at the after-party at the Metropolitan Club.

Just as she'd been doing for decades at home, Nora had seemingly effortlessly pulled together such culinary aficionados as Martha Stewart, the late Anthony Bourdain, and Nobu restaurateur Drew Nieporent for an official celebratory evening alongside Sony's top brass, such as Amy Pascal, Michael Lynton, Howard Stringer, and Jeff Blake, and actors such as Patricia Clarkson and Sam Rockwell.

In the fall of that year (2009), Nick and Nora, Mike Nichols and his wife Diane Sawyer, and other famous friends such as musician Carly Simon and playwright Neil Simon were the unfortunate victims of a Ponzi scheme perpetrated by Kenneth Starr, their business manager. In total, he reportedly swindled an estimated $59 million through fraud and money laundering. But Nora was nonetheless ready with a witty one-liner about the incident when it was time to write her tribute to Mike as he received the American Film Institute Life Achievement Award.

"I had to call Mike a couple of weeks ago on the occasion of the accountant he had referred me to being arrested," she quipped. "And he couldn't talk because he was at the White House getting an award for being a Jew. Who knew that there was an award for this? But that's what he said. At least none of us had to speak at it—only the president."

Mike laughed along with the rest of the star-studded crowd as he took out his handkerchief and wiped away his happy tears.

"Anyway, all of us could be a Buñuel movie," she continued, "a pack of people who owe Mike everything and are therefore doomed to spend eternity giving him awards. Love you!"

Mike got Nora, and Nora got Mike. Their shared love of food, of words, of theater, and of comedy was enough to keep their friendship fresh for decades.

A year later, Nora was already at work on another project: a biopic of Peggy Lee with Reese Witherspoon. Reese and Nora had gotten to know one another when Nora took it upon herself to help Reese following her split from actor Ryan Phillippe.

Although the screenplay was completed, Nora didn't get the chance to finish the project, and it was put on hold indefinitely after her death in 2012. Then, in 2014, a new draft was picked up by Pulitzer Prize–winning playwright Doug Wright, but it stalled again for several more years.

The project was revived again in early 2021 when it was announced that Michelle Williams would star while Todd Haynes would direct and Witherspoon would stay on as a producer.

There was another script too. The Columbia Pictures project *Lost in Austen* was being developed as Nora's comedic update on the 2008 British ITV series in which a modern woman in Brooklyn, Amanda, finds herself suddenly transported into the world of Jane Austen's *Pride and Prejudice*. Nora had signed on to write and direct, and Don Lee remembers that she had a draft of the screenplay done. They were already scouting locations in London, thinking about budget, and discussing casting when he got an unusual late-night e-mail from Nora.

"Don, I have to drop out of this thing," she wrote.

"That's when I knew something was up," he told me. "We were talking about London, of course, and talking about taking the train to Paris on the weekends."

Still, he said, it was bittersweet to have ended their work together on *Julie & Julia*. "We ended our collaboration in Paris, which was one of her favorite places, and got to shoot and eat our way through France. So how bad could it be?"

24 | MORE WRITING THAN EVER

> It's very important to have your last meal before it is
> your last meal. Otherwise, you could squander it on
> something like a tuna melt.
>
> —Nora Ephron

SOME SAY THAT IT OFTEN TAKES a terminal diagnosis to get someone's attention to start living. But for someone like Nora, she seemed to always lead her life with a sense of clarity that left many in awe.

In her now seemingly prophetic 1986 *New York Times* essay "Revision and Life: Take It from the Top Again," Nora wrote of how her transition from reporting to essay writing to fiction in her thirties changed her view of revision—both in writing and in life. "It was becoming clear that I had many more choices than had occurred to me when I was marching through my 20's," she wrote. "I no longer lost sleep over what I should have said. Not that I didn't care—it was just that I had moved to a new plane of late-night anxiety: I now wondered what I should have done. Whole areas of possible revision opened before me. What should I have done instead? What could I have done? What if I hadn't done it the way I did? What if I had a chance to do it over? What if I had a chance to do it over as a different person?"

"By the time you reach middle age, you want more than anything for things not to come to an end; and as long as you're still revising, they don't," she continued. "I'm sorry to end so morbidly—dancing as I am around the subject of death—but there are advantages to it. For one thing, I have managed to move fairly effortlessly and logically from the beginning of this piece

207

through the middle and to the end. And for another, I am able to close with an exhortation, something I rarely manage, which is this: Revise now, before it's too late."

By 2010, Nora knew her time to revise might be limited. But to continue to make revisions—to continue to write—was her best hope for survival.

Still, there was the business of living and loving, and she did her best to make time for family, friends, and even strangers who needed a helping hand. Especially if food was involved.

When her friend Nancy Dolman Short died in August 2010, Nick and Nora arrived with food for Martin "Marty" Short and his kids. And then they came back with more the next day. And the one after that.

On the third day, Nora arrived with a large platter of chicken.

"Nora, we have *so* much food," Marty said.

"And now you have *more* food," she replied.

The kids, who were all close with Nora, were comforted by her presence and her all-knowing sense of what to do when nothing made sense at all.

She'd lost other dear friends too: John Gregory Dunne, who died suddenly from a heart attack in 2003 (memorialized so beautifully by his wife, the late Joan Didion, in *The Year of Magical Thinking*), and her beloved Judy Corman to cancer a year later in 2004.

As she went out to promote what would be her final essay collection, *I Remember Nothing*, Nora didn't really let on that anything was wrong with her own health. At least not to the naked eye. But there were hints along the way. Every so often, she'd confide to Richard Cohen, "[I] don't have much time left."

Nora and Martin "Marty" Short smile together in a casual snapshot. *Courtesy of Martin Short*

The book, which was dedicated to Richard and Mona (who was herself battling cancer), ended with two telling essays: "What I Won't Miss," and "What I Will Miss."

First, in "What I Won't Miss," Nora lists "dry skin, email, bras, funerals, illness everywhere . . . email, panels on Women in Film, and taking off makeup every night" as things she wouldn't mind doing without.

In "What I Will Miss," which closes out the collection: "my kids, Nick, Spring, Fall, waffles, the concept of waffles, bacon, a walk in the park, the idea of a walk in the park, the park, Shakespeare in the park, the bed . . . twinkle lights, butter, dinner at home just the two of us . . . Thanksgiving dinner, one for the table, the dogwood, taking a bath, coming over the bridge to Manhattan, pie."

Eleven years earlier, Nora became intrigued by a story about a local tabloid newspaper columnist who'd won a Pulitzer Prize as he was dying from cancer. His name was Mike McAlary.

In 1999 Nora first started working on the script for *Stories About McAlary*, which was originally conceptualized as a feature film, then as a television film for HBO. At the time, Tom Hanks was coming off the success of *Saving Private Ryan*, Steven Spielberg's acclaimed World War II epic that earned eleven Academy Award nominations and took home five of them at the Oscars ceremony in March. It's widely considered one of the greatest films of all time—and some of its most technically challenging sequences are taught in film schools around the world. (Hanks, who was nominated for Best Actor, lost to Roberto Benigni for *Life Is Beautiful*.)

But even when Nora and Hanks weren't directly collaborating on a project, Nora's influence, particularly as a journalist, loomed large.

"Nora covered the Beatles every time they flew into JFK (Idlewild!) as both a news story and as *the Idea* [*sic*]," Hanks told me. "The facts are what make fiction so worthwhile. She recommended [the Library of America collection] *Reporting World War II* ('The greatest journalism writing ever!') and it altered *Saving Private Ryan* for me and led to everything since."

He said Nora told him, and taught him by example, that his fascination with history "was a storyteller's fascination with human behavior, and that behavior has never, ever, changed."

Of another book she'd gifted him, *The Aspirin Age: 1919–1941*, he said, "There are ten movies in that book and they are all movies she could have made. I wish she had. I'd have been in five of them."

As for Nora, she was focused on getting *Stories* made. By 2009, it was being reconceptualized as a play rather than a movie. Hanks, the bona fide movie star, wasn't yet sure if he was ready to return to Broadway. Jon Hamm was reportedly interested in the role, and at a reading in 2010, Hugh Jackman read for the part of Mike McAlary as Mike Nichols directed.

Nora didn't know that she would one day share more than just an interest in New York's gritty journalism scene with McAlary. But that came later.

Finally, with George C. Wolfe as director, and Hanks starring, the pair kept asking her, "Nora, what's this play about?"

"This play is about somebody who has more luck than talent," she told Wolfe. "And I know something about that."

They were aghast. Nora—a beneficiary of luck? That hardly explained it.

More precisely, Wolfe explained, "to me at the end of the day I think what *Lucky Guy* is about is about a human being who replaces ambition for grace."

Lucky Guy opened on Broadway on April 1, 2013. To be able to perform in Nora's final act while coping with his grief, Hanks said, was a gift.

"The half a year of the play was spending every day and evening with Nora herself," he told me. "George Wolfe and I heard Nora in every line and every moment of every rehearsal and performance, like we were having a three-way conversation with her."

Hanks and Wolfe ran to each other as soon as the curtain came down on opening night, "and there in the greenroom we wept like two of the luckiest and saddest men in the world. We wept the same way the night we closed. We missed her so and yet had her to ourselves from February through June of 2013."

The show was a financial success, garnering mostly warm critical reviews and receiving six Tony Award nominations, including a posthumous nomination for Nora for Best Play. The production ended up winning two awards,

Best Performance by a Featured Actor in a Play for Courtney B. Vance (*American Crime Story: The People v. O. J. Simpson*) and Best Lighting Design.

Short pointed out how Nora's last two collections, *I Feel Bad About My Neck* and *I Remember Nothing*, were like taking a cross-country flight with her right next to you. "She totally wrote in her own voice," he told me. "And that was a gift of a great writer."

It was another gift she gave Hanks too. As he considered trying his hand at writing, he consulted Nora. "Is this a thing?" he'd asked her of his prose. "Indeed, it is," she said.

And there were the dinner parties. The always spectacular, wonderful, lively dinner parties at Nick and Nora's.

One evening at Nick and Nora's home in Beverly Hills, California, Short asked the group of ten esteemed guests seated at the round table—just as Nora liked it—"Who's the biggest prick that anyone has ever worked with?"

"Oh, I love this game!" Nora said.

It started with Short, who named someone, then his wife, Nancy, then David Geffen, and on to Tom Brokaw and his wife, Meredith. The Brokaws, and Nicole Kidman, seated next to them, struggled with the prompt. "I can't really think of anyone," she said.

Nora grew irritated.

"Didn't you sue your manager?" Nora asked.

"Well, yes, but he was a nice bloke, not a prick," Kidman replied.

Finally, they got around to Nick.

"I can't think of anyone," he said.

"Nick! You work with murderers!" Nora said.

"Yeah, but they're not pricks!"

"I cannot believe you all," she said impatiently. "I've had a list of nine, I've been trying to whittle it down."

It's an example of one of many of the purest "Nick and Nora" moments—two people who really loved and understood one another, but who genuinely remained exactly who they were in the process.

"That's such a Nick answer," Don Lee explained to me. "Nick and I liked to talk about from whence we came. I grew up in Pittsburgh, I'm the grandson of Irish immigrants and Scottish blah-blah, and he's the son of Italian immigrants from Calabria, and we're just grateful for the opportunities and where we are, and we're just enjoying it."

Then, he said, Nora would just look at them with her classic pursed lips and maybe a trademark eye roll.

"*Borrring!*" she'd say.

"Then we'd laugh and quit talking about it," Lee said. "Nora wasn't having any of it so that would really make us laugh."

She simply only had time for what was good. And she wanted everyone else to have it too. The night after she died, Lee, Brokaw, and Nichols found themselves sharing an elevator up to her apartment, where she'd planned a small memorial to take place.

"What will we do now?" Mike asked, wiping away his tears, "without her?"

———————

It's gut-wrenching to hear Nora's response to a question from the host of a local PBS program in Seattle in 2010, knowing what we know now—and what she likely knew then.

"What will you do next? Will you make more movies?" the host innocently asked.

There was a beat before she replied, "Maybe . . . but mostly I'm going to cook."

Nora met up with her longtime editor and friend Bob Gottlieb at Knopf, to talk about putting together her next collection of works, *The Most of Nora Ephron*. Ever since 1975, after the publication of *Wallflower at the Orgy*, he'd worked with her on all her books. The idea was to "celebrate the richness of her work, the amazing arc of her career, and the place she had come to hold in the hearts of so many readers," he wrote in the book's introduction.

After a while, they'd set it aside. She was busy at work on *Lucky Guy*, but there were other, more painful, reasons too. Had she begun to see the book as a memorial? An uncomfortable, tangible reminder that her time was indeed being cut short, and that she might not be around to finish it?

It's possible, Gottlieb wrote. In publishing the collection posthumously on behalf of her estate, he also shared that "I think I know what she would have wanted this book to be, and her family allowed me to shape it. My immediate reward was having a professional excuse to reread everything she ever wrote. No other editorial job I've ever performed has been so much fun."

Meanwhile, Nora's friends noticed how she'd become more forgiving, tender, and more tolerant with the bad news of her worsening illness. Most of them may not have known why, exactly, but they could see and feel a difference. She was "easier and easier about her own flaws, she laughed easier about things," Meg Ryan said. "She just got so porous."

When they met up at Balthazar for lunch, Nora didn't look well, Meg remembered, but she didn't ask. "I don't know if she would have told me," she said. "I regret not asking, 'Are you OK?' Maybe she would have confided in me."

In November 2011, Nick and Nora joined dear friend Calvin "Bud" Trillin, Serious Eats founder Ed Levine, and his wife Vicky for dinner. In her thank-you note e-mailed to Levine the next day, Nora wrote: "That was so much fun and so delicious. Thanks to you and Vicky. . . . I am still thinking about that lemon cake. And the beans. Omigod the beans. Congratulations again on the book. It's just terrific. xxx n&n"

Nora and J.J. even joined Levine at the Serious Eats offices on West Twenty-Seventh Street to test biscuits. Illness notwithstanding, she reviewed and evaluated them with the same gusto she'd always had, but she'd grown even more thin.

About six months before she died, she sent a late-night e-mail to Rosie O'Donnell, who'd also become a dear friend ever since their work together on *Sleepless.*

"Just sitting here in LA today thinking I miss you and I love you," Nora wrote.

There were many, many lunches and dinners—and conversations with "odd silences" as Nichols put it. "I was too stupid to notice that it was a goodbye lunch," he said later.

As for Lee, he'd joined her for dinner one night at Locanda Verde. She ordered wine and, for the most part, managed to keep her secret. She may have become softer about her friends, but she was still Nora—she didn't think the garlic chicken was "up to par that night," as he remembered it.

At the Whitney Museum, Nora met up with Marcia Burick for lunch. Nora spoke about her latest project—the biopic of Peggy Lee—and, in a rare hint that something was off, she asked Marcia about her father's illness. He had died in 1986.

"Tell me again what your father died of?" Nora asked.

"Acute myeloid leukemia," Marcia said.

Nora and J. J. Sacha engage in a very academic biscuit dialogue with Ed Levine and model biscuits at the Serious Eats offices in New York in 2009. *Photo by Robyn Lee for Serious Eats / courtesy of the photographer*

"Are you afraid you're going to get it?"

"Of course not . . . it's not genetic." Marcia paused. "What's going on?" she asked.

"Nothing," Nora said.

As their fiftieth reunion approached at Wellesley in May, Marcia called Nora to see if she'd be coming with her as usual.

"You really should come," she said.

"I don't think I can," Nora said from her hospital bed, "but call me and tell me everything when you get back."

Just two days earlier, she and Marie Brenner met up for a four-hour lunch. "Let's get cheesecake," she said. It was as if she didn't want the lunch to end.

"I'm having a little health crisis," Nora told Jacob. It was just before Memorial Day when he got the call. The crisis was more serious than she let on: her MDS had turned into leukemia, and a painful course of chemotherapy would be necessary right away. And even with that, she had less than a 50 percent chance of survival.

"What should I tell people?" Richard Cohen remembers her asking him. "Tell them you have leukemia and you're going to beat it," he said.

The next thing he knew, the line was "We aren't telling anyone anything."

Jacob immediately grabbed a cab to join her at New York-Presbyterian Hospital. Max and his then girlfriend (now wife), Rachel, hopped on a plane from Los Angeles. When Jacob arrived that night, what he found was a rare sight: his mother was crying.

"There she was, in her Chanel flats and her cream-colored pants and her black-and-white-striped blouse, looking so pretty and so fragile as she dabbed her eyes with a Kleenex," he remembered. "I finally understood what she meant when she said she was a bird—that she wasn't just talking about her looks but something inside as well."

"I want to live to be 100," she told him. "I want to see how things turn out for you and Max."

At night, they watched episodes of *Curb Your Enthusiasm*, and in the daytime, Nora and Delia would write. Binky Urban and Richard and Mona would visit and bring treats, like ice cream or milkshakes. Nick made peanut butter and jelly sandwiches to sustain the morning-to-night visitors.

But as Jacob remembered, the long days turned into long weeks, and it soon became clear that the chemotherapy wasn't working.

"In out, in out," she said to Cohen. "So it's happening."

Ever the reporter and observer, Nora was noting the process, even as she went in and out of consciousness. Sitting with her husband and sisters and sons at her hospital bedside, family and friends drifted in and out of the room, each taking turns holding her hand.

"Mom, I'm going to miss you so much," Max said.

"Miss me?" she replied, "I'm not dead yet."

But just a few days later, on June 26, 2012, she slipped away. Nora's obituary made the front page of the *New York Times* on June 27, 2012, just below the latest foreign affairs headlines—and above the fold.

But even some of her closest friends and collaborators were the last to find out she was ill. Amy Pascal, Rob Reiner, Barbara Walters, actor Bob Balaban, Rosie O'Donnell: all felt blindsided by the news. "It was an ambush," Meryl Streep said.

Every last detail for her memorial had been planned—and Delia, J.J., Richard, Nick, and the children helped carry out her wishes impeccably. She asked that each speaker in her chosen lineup, starting with Richard, kindly keep their remarks to under five minutes if possible, and to essentially "get it over with."

It was called "A Gathering for Nora" when luminaries from film and journalism, friends, family, and colleagues gathered on a hot summer afternoon in July. Guests received a program that included recipes and quotes from friends and family, including her kids, Max and Jacob, Nichols, and others. The whole affair cost an estimated $100,000 and included Arpeggio catering for $20,000 and her favorite pink champagne. (A lucky few close friends and colleagues had also received "Nora's Cookbook," a self-published white spiral-bound 174-page collection that "blends Ephron's wry observations about throwing a great dinner party and using clarified butter with relatively simple recipes for dishes like chicken salad, monkey bread and pot roast.")

Patricia Bosworth wrote of attending the service in *Vanity Fair*: "[It] ended with Rosie O'Donnell reading Nora's essay "I Hate My Purse," which is from the play *Love, Loss, and What I Wore*, written by Nora and her sister Delia. It is extremely funny, but it made me cry."

For the first time, Nora was wrong about one thing: the venue was too small. The service was moved to Alice Tully Hall at Lincoln Center, just a block from where her first apartment stood. An estimated eight hundred esteemed guests showed up to pay their respects, and somehow, almost all of them truly had a genuine connection to her.

It was a New York death—but not the lonely, unnoticed one she'd imagined as a young woman on the cusp of starting her life after Wellesley. It was the death of a woman who was beloved around the world and left us wanting more.

But as Tom Hanks so eloquently put it: "Like the great influences in a life, and a great love once shared, Nora is never far away."

EPILOGUE

America Post-Nora (2012–Present)

RICHARD COHEN, despite all his years spent reporting on politics and hard news in New York and Washington, was softened by the tiny, but mighty, tour de force that was Nora. They were best friends for nearly forty years—seeing one another through marriages, divorces, job changes, career changes, aging, and illness.

"There was then and always an air about Nora of great wisdom—not merely, if I may correct myself, of great wisdom, but of *greater* wisdom," Cohen writes of her in *She Made Me Laugh: My Friend Nora Ephron*. "She was smart, very smart, and knowledgeable, very knowledgeable, but beyond that she had an inerrant touch for the best of almost anything."

It made the loss of Nora to acute myeloid leukemia (brought on by complications of her MDS) all that much more painful. Nora directed films, but she also directed the lives of the people she loved most. Her specific instructions—even for the kind of sandwiches to be served at the reception the day after her death (cucumber tea sandwiches from William Poll, the tiny Upper East Side store)—were outlined neatly in a file on her computer called EXIT.

She was an advocate and mentor for aspiring writers and filmmakers; a fiercely loyal woman who loved throwing dinner parties and cooking at home and on the set; and a devoted mother to sons Jacob and Max. And she was in one of the greatest real-life love affairs of all time with Nick for nearly thirty years.

"I told her how much she was loved, about all the love in the room," Cohen writes of those final days in room 242. "She raised herself and looked

219

out the window, south to the skyline. She extended her left arm and scooped Manhattan into her. "'And out there,'" she said.

And out here, we were mourning too. When Nora transitioned from essayist to screenwriter and film director, she became more than just a source of wisdom for a generation of rom-com fans—she became a popular-culture force to be reckoned with. Nora wrote a total of thirteen screenplays that were developed (three of which were nominated for Academy Awards) and made nearly twenty films. She wrote countless essays and articles, and several bestselling books during a career that spanned more than five decades.

But Nora's legacy will live on for the next generation in the many writers, filmmakers, and artists she influenced and mentored along the way—as long as we show them our support.

We lost Nichols just two years later in November 2014. Nichols and Nora were hopelessly devoted to the art and craft of writing and making good movies that told the "stories of our lives," as Nichols put it, in interesting, often funny, compelling, and heartwarming ways. Creative collaboration—and mutual respect—between writers, actors, and directors was essential to their success, and led to some of the most significant contributions to cinematic art in the past half century either directly or indirectly.

Having come from theater, Nichols was accustomed to having the playwright on hand while staging and rehearsing a play. He had worked with Neil Simon and Elaine May, among other legendary writers, to help bring their words to life on stage and screen, earning him the elusive "EGOT"—Emmy, Grammy, Oscar, and Tony awards—for his work over six decades.

In the early 1980s, Nora had brought Nichols the screenplay for *Silkwood*, based on the real-life story of whistleblower Karen Silkwood, who died under suspicious circumstances. After signing on to direct, he invited her (and coscreenwriter Alice Arlen) to come along to watch him make the movie on location in Oklahoma.

It was clear to Nichols that Nora was meant to be a director. "I knew big time that this charming, brilliant writer who wants to be a movie director, will be, because she was out and out studying it," he said of working with her on *Silkwood*.

There's this beautiful space-time continuum in cinema, where the lines between art and life, past and present, can become blurred and remixed into something wonderful.

Greg, the protagonist in *Me and Earl and the Dying Girl*—winner of the 2015 Sundance Grand Jury Prize and Audience Award—recalls Benjamin Braddock's anything-but-suave attempts to start an affair with Mrs. Robinson in *The Graduate*—which is no accident. Director Alfonso Gomez-Rejon was inspired by Nichols's iconic coming-of-age film from Hollywood's New Wave in the 1960s, and many others from his world-class mentors as he conceptualized how to shoot the film.

Gomez-Rejon (*The Current War*) began his career as an assistant to legends such as Martin Scorsese, Robert De Niro, and Alejandro González Iñárritu, and most notably, for Nora—who in turn invited him into her world and introduced him to everyone in it (including Nichols). He went on to direct the second unit for Nora's *Lucky Numbers*, *Bewitched*, and *Julie & Julia*, González Iñárritu's *Babel*, and Ben Affleck's Oscar Best Picture winner *Argo*.

But he soon found himself searching for an outlet to cope with the emotional pain of the loss of both Nora and his father, and that was when he came across the *Me and Earl* screenplay in 2013. "The script was funny in an unusual and unpredictable way," he said. "I felt that if I could make this film, I'd be able to express my own personal losses and transform them through humor."

Based on the bestselling novel of the same name by Jesse Andrews, its brilliance is in the way the directing, the writing, the acting, and the music each come together to make you truly ache for its quirky characters, who are just trying to deal with real-life problems in real time—not in a clean, Hollywood-packaged, box office thriller kind of way, but in an inconvenient story line and cinematic style that takes us back in time—to an era when being still, and sometimes silent, mattered.

There's a sweet tenderness to the way Greg fumbles around and constantly says the wrong thing. "I'm actually here because my mom's making me," he tells Rachel upon finding out she has cancer. How is he (or anyone?) to know what to say to a dying girl? (He's just a guy, after all.)

Me and Earl is a return to days gone by—to the romanticism of real friendship, the kind you yearn and fight for (not *swipe* or "like" for), and it is a testament to how art can be both transcendent and transformative, maybe even more than we'd like to admit. The film invites us into Greg's world to take an offbeat look at our own relationship with life and death, and the important, tiny details that make up all the spaces in between.

Nora, of course, was known for "caring about detail in a big, big way," as Dianne Dreyer had once put it. There's a scene in her Academy Award–nominated script for *Sleepless in Seattle*, for example, where Meg Ryan is peeling the apple at the table exactly the same way Tom Hanks's fictional late wife did.

To get that texture sans unnecessary sentiment (Greg actually reminds us several times that this is, in fact, not a "touching romantic story," whereby his eyes would meet with Rachel's—the smart, charming "dying" girl of the title, played by Olivia Cooke—and "suddenly we'd be furiously making out with the fire of a thousand suns"), Gomez-Rejon worked directly with Andrews (as did producer Dan Fogelman of *This Is Us* fame) to adapt the novel into one of the most flawless screenplays in recent memory.

The sharp, witty, authentic dialogue, hilarious situations—and the raw emotional moments that all these things evoke—have Nichols and Nora written all over them. One such moment that stuck with Gomez-Rejon when he first read the script, and that ultimately led him to fight for the chance to direct the movie, is the one where Greg and his teacher-mentor Mr. McCarthy have a one-on-one chat about this very notion of "tiny details" that can unfold and reveal themselves to you even after you lose someone you love—"as long as you pay attention." It's evidence that Nichols and Nora's ethos has seeped into our contemporary cinema and into the veins of the next generation of talented filmmakers in more ways than one.

The gravity of the loss of Nora in 2012—but also the gift of her friendship and mentorship—have had a profound influence on Gomez-Rejon. "Nora's a big part of the reason I can call myself a director, because she got me into the [Directors Guild of America] DGA by insisting that the studio hire me as her second unit director, even though I had no second unit experience; she simply believed in me," he said. "She's set the bar so high as a human being and as a filmmaker. "

Like his film's protagonist, and like Benjamin Braddock, Gomez-Rejon said a lost boy often needs both art and love, admiration, or friendship (hopefully all three) to push him forward. For him, that woman—that constant—had been Nora. He was first introduced to her by Nick when Gomez-Rejon was working for Scorsese on *Casino* in 1995.

She promptly hired him as her assistant on *You've Got Mail* in 1998. His first opportunity to show Nora what he could do came when he created a shot list for the AOL dial-up sequence. "She asked me to direct a two-day second unit still shoot, photographed by the legendary Ken Regan," Gomez-Rejon said, noting that the scene eventually ended up on the cutting room floor.

Patience has been one of his most valued allies during the rough times in Hollywood in the 2000s. Through the ups and too many downs, Nora would make time for him even when his old friends from back home wouldn't. A self-described "late bloomer"—a trait he shares with many iconic women, including Julia Child and his mentor Thelma Schoonmaker, the legendary film editor—Gomez-Rejon has never been too concerned about time.

But he still hears Nora's voice as he lives and works. "I always wonder, 'What would Nora think of this? Would she think this is OK?' Because she's seen it all." (Hanks echoed the sentiment: "Rita [Wilson] and I think 'What would Nora make of this?' And we can hear her answer, her cadence beginning with 'Well, I mean . . .'")

"She was so special to me," Gomez-Rejon added. "It's an amazing thing to have someone like Nora treating you like a colleague, like an equal, introducing you to some of the greatest people on the planet. She gave me advice on everything from love life to what scripts and books to read. Her influence on me as a human being can't be overstated. I continue to learn from her, even now."

The way Gomez-Rejon lives and works is a testament to those who came before him and taught him not only how to make movies but how to do it right. As Nichols said, "Making movies is like making love; you wonder, is this how everyone else is doing it?"

Gomez-Rejon and his work seem to come from another era. He wants to make movies that matter and that move people, even if on a small budget or short time frame. He has somehow been able to fuse his scrappiness with his talent to become a true artist in the purest (and least pretentious) sense of the word. (The Tribeca Film Festival Nora Ephron Prize winners have done much the same these past several years.)

Still, as executive producer Don Lee told me, "There's not going to be another Nora because the stars aligned. The world that she came from no longer exists, and it won't exist. That's why you're not going to have another Nora."

But Nichols has said that movies are metaphors—and the best ones are driven by what's actually happening in our own lives. To direct well, he has said, is to just allow that which is naturally occurring to happen, then to say "Action." For those she loved, mentored, and collaborated with, the naturally occurring events in life had seemingly always been directed by Nora.

"When I fly into NYC for any length of time—for work or leisure—I always assume I'll be having dinner that night with Nora, and looking forward to it," Hanks told me, adding that "Mike [Nichols] would be there too. . . . Then, I come up short."

Back in 2012, there was a story that had been hidden too well in all the metaphors and glossy covers. Nichols was forced to fumble around with the stunning bad news that his beloved Nora lay dying in a New York hospital without so much as a hint that she had been ill throughout their weekly conversations, dinners, and lunches over the previous six years.

Along with the sandwiches she had outlined in her Exit file was her list of speakers for her memorial service. Cohen was there. Nichols was there. Hanks was there. And though she'd "hoot at the idea of her spiritual presence," as Hanks put it, Nora was, in a way, still there—"on the set . . . in the kitchen, and at the movies"—as Nichols poignantly and prophetically put it during his AFI Life Achievement Award acceptance speech in 2010.

Indeed, John Lindley, the cinematographer on four of Nora's films—*Michael, You've Got Mail, Lucky Numbers*, and *Bewitched*—said Nora seemed to exist in a different time, so that she somehow always knew what to do. And yet, she also knew how to keep things fresh. Even today, many of her scripts and essays read as if they were written in the present moment. Somehow, she was able to acutely observe changes happening in real time, while drawing on times gone by and writing and living as a visionary for the future—all at once.

All the greats were like that, though. *The Graduate* is revered not just for Nichols's landmark visual style but for his use of popular music to evoke nostalgia—something no one else had done before in film. More than fifty years later, it now stands out as a reminder of the sounds of silence a generation of young people wouldn't forget in the backdrop of the Vietnam War and the civil rights movement.

We have to know where we've been to know where we're going.

Nora was obsessed with old films, and like Ryan's character in *Sleepless*, she knew all the words to many of them, according to *New York* magazine colleague Richard Reeves. She loved old books and was a devoted Jane Austen fan. She reread *Pride and Prejudice* every year and encouraged her friends to do the same.

"Nora lives on in her movies," Cohen told me. "Movies have a kind of permanency because they're about love. Love doesn't go away."

As they prepped for the film *Michael*, John Lindley recalled what Nora said to him: "To me, what this movie is about is that Heaven is on Earth." Nora wasn't ill at the time, but now that she's gone, her words are painfully bittersweet.

ACKNOWLEDGMENTS

I must start by expressing with my immense gratitude to those who shared their time and precious memories (and some never-before-seen photos and mementos) of Nora with me so generously via phone, e-mail, and Zoom and in person—some of them speaking about Nora publicly for the first time in these pages—including Caroline Aaron, Carole Bayer Sager, Martha Bewick, Marcia Burick, Richard Cohen, Dianne Dreyer, George Fenton, Alfonso Gomez-Rejon, Dan Greenburg, Tom Hanks, Mark Harris, Nancy Krim, Donald J. Lee Jr., Ed Levine, John Lindley, Willow Lindley, Audrey Lord-Hausman, Patricia K. Meyer, Victoria Riskin, J. J. Sacha, Elizabeth Segal, Martin Short, Nicholas Stoller, Jenny Sullivan, Jonathan Taplin, Shelly Westerman, and the Wellesley class of 1962. And thank you to those who shared their comments and memories anonymously or on background.

I'm grateful to Dan Greenburg for sharing such personal one-of-a-kind photos and letters with me, as did several others. Much gratitude to Marjorie Bribitzer for kindly arranging an unofficial Zoom call with some of the Wellesley class of 1962, and for the generosity of spirit, connections, and candid reflections many of the women shared during and after the call. Thank you, Martha Bewick, for your diligence in helping to make it possible for some of those special connections and photos to be included in the book. And thank you, dear Marcia Burick, for your incredible generosity and trust in sharing some of your favorite memories (and archives!) from your lifelong friendship with Nora.

The inspiration for this book began with my 2015 master's thesis at USC Annenberg, but the encouragement for my writing began long ago. My teachers and professors, especially Miss Sullivan, Ms. Schwarz, Mary Murphy, Joe Saltzman, Dr. Laura Castañeda, Sandy Tolan, Barbara Nance, Karen Lowe, Kenneth Turan, Sasha Anawalt, Richard Reeves, Dr. Todd Boyd, Dr. Henry

Jenkins, Michael Parks, Geoff Cowan, and Willow Bay, all provided support and new ways of thinking about the intersections of Nora's work—and many of them became and remain treasured mentors.

Professor Mary Murphy, who served as my thesis chair, instantly connected me with the wonderful late Professor Richard Reeves, and both of them spent hours talking with me about their memories of Nora in the magazine journalism heyday of the 1970s. I will always be so thankful for those conversations, and for the opportunity to sit with our beloved Professor Reeves as he shared his incredible stories, laughter, and elegant, warm, buttery voice with me as a student and long afterward. I'm also grateful to USC Cinematic Arts screenwriting professor Barbara Nance for her course on Nora Ephron's works, which allowed me to not only study and learn more about Nora as a screenwriter but also to meet and talk to some of her esteemed colleagues, such as Lynda Obst, John Lindley, Meg Wolitzer, and others. Thank you to Dr. Alison Trope for sharing insights about Nora's legacy in popular culture.

Though I started my project in 2014, to me this book humbly stands on the shoulders of several subsequent works, including Liz Dance's wonderful scholarly book *Everything Is Copy: Nora Ephron* and Nora's son Jacob Bernstein's extraordinary, moving documentary *Everything Is Copy*, as well as *I'll Have What She's Having* by Erin Carlson and *She Made Me Laugh* by Richard Cohen. Erin and Richard, thank you both for your support in helping to make this book a reality. I am also indebted to authors Marsha McCreadie and Rachel Abramowitz for their research, reporting, and writing on women in Hollywood in their respective books *The Women Who Write the Movies* and *Is That a Gun In Your Pocket?*

This book also would not have been possible without the talent, support, and years-long dedication of my research assistants, Tamara Rosenblum, Abigail Barr, Haley Ray, and Holly Thomas, who helped me not only comb through hundreds of hours of transcripts, photos, and archival material but also reassemble a timeline for Nora's life in the context of six decades of change in America. As well, I am indebted to Laura Clos at Harvard, and to the librarians and archivists at USC's Cinematic Arts Library, especially Ned Comstock; the Wellesley College Archives; the Writers Guild Foundation; and the Academy of Motion Pictures Arts and Sciences' Margaret Herrick Library.

And my sincerest thanks to Holly Van Leuven, whom I found on this crazy yellow-brick-road journey (along with other amazing women at Quilt in Los Angeles) to be a modern-day Avis DeVoto of sorts to my more-than-inferior Julia, and a constant source of sanity, strength, and light; and to the wonderful folks at the *Los Angeles Review of Books*, especially Tom Lutz, Laurie Winer, Boris Dralyuk, Medaya Ocher, and Evan Kindley. To Kara Rota, my incredible editor, whose enthusiasm and belief in this project have sustained me through some challenging moments; Devon Freeny, who meticulously shepherded the manuscript through production; my publisher, Cynthia Sherry; and the team at Chicago Review Press. To my agent, Betsy Amster, for patiently keeping me going. And to my students and colleagues at Loyola Marymount University, especially Dean Scheibel, Craig Rich, Barbara Rico, Michele Hammers, and Evelyn McDonnell, for their kind support.

Lastly, I am so thankful for the support of my family and friends, especially my parents, Robin and John, and my grandmother Thelma Marguerite Graves, from whom I received not only a beautiful middle name but also a lifelong love of words, literature, and learning. To my siblings, Jennifer, Sarah, and Matthew, whose attendance at my "bookstore" parties growing up came with only a few complaints, and whose Nora-like devotion to wonderful art, food, and laughter continues to lift me up. And hugs and kisses to my beloved doggies, Brie Bentley and Scout "Cubby," who provided immeasurable company and endless waggy tails, the secret ingredients to surviving book writing.

And thank you, most of all, to Nora, for living an extraordinary life more than worthy of celebration.

BOOK CLUB
QUESTIONS

1. Nora had a game she'd play while waiting for tables in restaurants, where you have to write the five words that describe you on a piece of paper. What are the five words you'd use to describe yourself today? What are the five words you'd like to use in five years?

2. Nora said, "I try to write parts for women that are as complicated and interesting as women actually are." How would Nora write about you? How would you like to be written?

3. Nora liked to bring people together at the table with good food and good conversation. Who would you invite to make your perfect table?

4. Nora's mother taught her that "everything is copy"—that anything that happens is writing material. As painful as something might be, you can eventually write it funny. What have you experienced that could, one day, become funny material?

5. Nora drew inspiration from authors like Jane Austen and witty writers like Dorothy Parker. Who inspires you and your work or art?

6. Nora said: "I look out the window and I see the lights and the skyline and the people on the street rushing around looking for action, love, and the world's greatest chocolate chip cookie, and my heart does a little dance." What makes your heart do a little dance?

7. Nora said her idea of a perfect day "is a frozen custard at Shake Shack and a walk in the park. (Followed by a Lactaid.) My idea of a perfect night is a good play and dinner at Orso. (But no garlic, or I won't be able to sleep.)" What's your perfect day or night? How can you make time for more such days or nights?

8. Nora, though incredibly independent in her thinking, believed strongly in the power of collaboration. Who do you depend on when seeking advice on your most important work or art?

9. Nora said, "Reading is escape, and the opposite of escape; it's a way to make contact with reality after a day of making things up, and it's a way of making contact with someone else's imagination after a day that's all too real." What was the last book you read for fun? What are the books on your current to-read list?

10. Nora wrote in her bestselling novel *Heartburn*: "What I love about cooking is that after a hard day, there is something comforting about the fact that if you melt butter and add flour and then hot stock, it will get thick! It's a sure thing! It's a sure thing in a world where nothing is sure." What are your go-to recipes or foods to eat when nothing feels sure?

NOTES

Author's Note: Why Nora Ephron (Still) Matters

"Don't be frightened": Ephron, "Nora Ephron '62 Addressed the Graduates," https://www
.wellesley.edu/events/commencement/archives/1996commencement.

calls an "aca-fan": Henry Jenkins, "Acafandom and Beyond: Week Two, Part One (Henry
Jenkins, Erica Rand, and Karen Hellekson)," *Confessions of an Aca-fan* (blog),
June 20, 2011, http://henryjenkins.org/blog/2011/06/acafandom_and_beyond
_week_two.html.

"because in the great rushing": Meg Wolitzer, "Feminist, Foodie, Filmmaker—
Ephron Did It All, and Wrote About It, Too," *All Things Considered*, NPR,
November 1, 2013, https://www.npr.org/2013/11/06/242086848/feminist-foodie
-filmmaker-ephron-did-it-all-and-wrote-about-it-too.

"after dinner at L'Ami Louis": Nora Ephron, Proust questionnaire, *Vanity Fair*, December
1996, via Wellesley College Archives.

"One of the things you discover": "All About Nora," TCM Festival, April 13, 2019.

Prologue: Not An Heiress

It all started with a telephone call: Nora Ephron, "My Life as an Heiress," *New Yorker*,
October 4, 2010, https://www.newyorker.com/magazine/2010/10/11/my-life
-as-an-heiress.

"The hardest thing about writing": Nora Ephron, quoted in the "In Memoriam" video
tribute at the 85th Academy Awards ceremony, February 24, 2013.

"In fifteen minutes": Ephron, "My Life as an Heiress."

"EXTERIOR. NEW YORK STREET CORNER": Nora Ephron, *When Harry Met
Sally . . .* (screenplay) (New York: Knopf, 1990), 15.

"We bought a dogwood": Ephron, "My Life as an Heiress."

Act I: Growing Up Ephron (The Early Years: 1941–1958)

Growing Up Ephron: Hallie Ephron used this phrase as the headline of the print version of her 2013 article for *O, the Oprah Magazine*. "Saving Memories with Old New Borrowed Redo," *Jungle Red Writers*, February 20, 2013, https://www.jungleredwriters.com/2013/02/saving-memories-with-old-new-borrowed.html.

1. The Goddess

"learned to write in the womb": Cohen, *She Made Me Laugh*, 22.

Phoebe Ephron was a mysterious: Ephron refers to her mother as a "goddess" in "The Legend" in *I Remember Nothing*, 38.

"I remember her teaching": Nora Ephron quoted in the epilogue of *We Thought We Could Do Anything*, by Henry Ephron, 209.

"By the end": Delia Ephron recounts the story of her parents' first date in *Everything Is Copy*, dir. by Bernstein.

"Nora was lovable and quick": Henry Ephron, *We Thought We Could Do Anything*, 6.

"It was a great way to learn": "Nora Ephron Cooks with Food Critic Jeffrey Steingarten," *Vogue*, accessed September 29, 2021, https://www.vogue.com/video/watch/test-kitchen-nora-ephron-cooks-with-food-critic-jeffrey-steingarten.

if "butter" is your religion: Nora Ephron, interview by Linda Wertheimer, *Morning Edition*, NPR, August 7, 2009, https://www.npr.org/transcripts/111543710.

"What I love about cooking": Nora Ephron, *Heartburn* (New York: Vintage, 1996; orig. publ. 1983), 133.

It's fitting: Doidge, "It's Not Just About Harry," 16.

"It is about the passion": Cohen, *She Made Me Laugh*, 272.

"She is her mother's daughter": Dance, *Everything Is Copy*, 43.

"Above all, be the heroine": Ephron, "Nora Ephron '62 Addressed the Graduates," https://www.wellesley.edu/events/commencement/archives/1996commencement.

"What was the truth?": Nora Ephron, "The Legend," in *I Remember Nothing*, 38.

"I was invested in": Ephron, 38.

2. The Camp Years

It was May 26, 1950: Bernstein, dir., *Everything Is Copy*.

"Nora has always been": Bernstein, dir., *Everything Is Copy*.

"out of a Tracy-Hepburn movie": Abramowitz, *Is That a Gun in Your Pocket?*, 223.

"everything had gone downhill": Abramowitz, 224.

"The thing that really breaks my heart": Delia Ephron, interview by Terry Gross, *Fresh Air*, NPR, December 9, 2013, https://www.npr.org/programs/fresh-air/2013/12/09/249747271/.

"It was all very civilized": Abramowitz, *Is That a Gun in Your Pocket?*, 224.

"The competition for airtime": Hallie Ephron, "Coming of Age with the Ephron Sisters—and Their Mother," *O, the Oprah Magazine*, March 2013, http://www.oprah.com/spirit/nora-ephrons-mother-hallie-ephron-essay/all.

"every single summer": Nora Ephron to the *New York Observer*, quoted in "Famous Survivors of Summer Camp," *News & Record* (Greensboro, NC), July 16, 1993, https://greensboro.com/famous-survivors-of-summer-camp/article_ace2988c-0468-55e0-b666-09db6a8187c7.html.

"The ethos of this camp": Riskin, interview by the author.

"What kind of letters?": Henry Ephron, *We Thought We Could Do Anything*, 210.

"[My mother] wrote the most fantastic": Ephron, 210.

"I would just like to say": Nora Ephron, "Me and My Gun," *Huffington Post*, February 14, 2006, https://www.huffpost.com/entry/me-and-my-gun_b_15673.

she was given a teakettle: "Famous Survivors of Summer Camp," *News & Record*, 1993, https://greensboro.com/famous-survivors-of-summer-camp/article_ace2988c-0468-55e0-b666-09db6a8187c7.html.

3. Beverly Hills High

"Mr. Lubitsch wants to see you": Henry Ephron, *We Thought We Could Do Anything*, 18.

they could help translate a book: Ephron, 37.

"Read the book": Ephron, 19.

One night in 1933: Ephron, 19.

they began writing and working together: Ephron, 33.

It was a difficult labor: Ephron, 6.

"It was truly an upside down": Ephron, 6.

ran for 495 performances: Abramowitz, *Is That a Gun in Your Pocket?*, 224.

"a lifelong love of the Democratic party": Nora Ephron, The Drexel InterView, 2010, via YouTube, https://www.youtube.com/watch?v=D5qUhbosSv4.

House Un-American Activities Committee: Shelley Stamp, "HUAC Timeline," University of California, Santa Cruz, 2018, https://people.ucsc.edu/~stamp/134A/FILM_134A/Hand-Outs_files/HUAC%20Timeline.pdf.

supported Norman Thomas: Hallie Ephron, "Coming of Age," http://www.oprah.com/spirit/nora-ephrons-mother-hallie-ephron-essay/all.

"Phoebe, vy you a Communist?": Ephron, "My Life as an Heiress."

their screenwriting credits weren't restored: Stamp, "HUAC Timeline," https://people.ucsc.edu/~stamp/134A/FILM_134A/Hand-Outs_files/HUAC%20Timeline.pdf.

"She had contempt for women": Abramowitz, *Is That a Gun in Your Pocket?*, 224.

the one responsible for Phoebe's: Henry Ephron, *We Thought We Could Do Anything*, 104.

"Mother, why won't you": Ephron, 104.

the first woman since Mary Pickford: Elizabeth Winder, "The Secret Career Genius of Marilyn Monroe," *Marie Claire*, July 26, 2017, https://www.marieclaire.com/celebrity
/a28305/marilyn-monroe-career-woman/.

"At a time when the studios wielded": Winder, https://www.marieclaire.com/celebrity
/a28305/marilyn-monroe-career-woman/.

the glamorous Robinson's department store: Chris Nichols, "A Look Back at Robinson's
as the Glamorous Beverly Hills Store Is Demolished," *Los Angeles*, July 23, 2014,
https://www.lamag.com/theclutch/a-look-back-at-robinsons-as-the-glamorous
-beverly-hills-store-is-demolished/.

"Slip on a banana peel": Nora Ephron, quoted in various sources.

"There wasn't a whole lot": Bernstein, dir., *Everything Is Copy*.

"I don't think Mom ever said": Bernstein, dir., *Everything Is Copy*.

"There she was, reading The Wizard of Oz": Nora Ephron, eulogy for Phoebe Ephron,
1971, in *We Thought We Could Do Anything*, by Henry Ephron, 209.

Act II: The Wellesley Years (1958–1962) & New Journalism (1962–Mid-1970s)

4. *Take Her, She's Mine* (Nora at Wellesley)

"Are you any relation to Phoebe?": Anecdote provided anonymously.

"Wellesley was one of the best places": Nora Ephron, acceptance speech for her Alumni
Achievement Award, 2006, via Wellesley College Archives.

Phoebe and Henry were eager: Henry Ephron, *We Thought We Could Do Anything*, 144.

"The kids are growing up": Ephron, 144.

"coldest, most delicious milk": Nora Ephron, "The Story of My Life in 3500 Words or
Less," in *I Feel Bad About My Neck*, 99.

WELLESLEY ELECTS DICK NIXON: *Wellesley News* cover, via Wellesley College Archives.

Nora covered it: Nora Ephron's *Wellesley News* pieces, via Wellesley College Archives.

"I was more different than the same": Nancy Collins, "Nora Ephron: The 'Us' Interview,"
US Weekly, February 1999, via Wellesley College Archives.

"You've worked so hard": Ephron, "Nora Ephron '62 Addressed the Graduates," https://
www.wellesley.edu/events/commencement/archives/1996commencement.

"looked like distilled Velveeta": Nora Ephron, "Me and JFK: Now It Can Be Told," in *I
Feel Bad About My Neck*, 89. First appeared in the *New York Times*.

Friday afternoon in the Rose Garden: Ephron, *I Feel Bad About My Neck*, 88.

"No wife of mine will ever": Ephron, "My Life in 3500 Words or Less," 100.

"One day she wasn't an alcoholic": Ephron, "The Legend," 37.

her *"remarkable mother"*: Ephron, 37.

Nora lay awake worried: Ephron, 38.

"Alcoholic parents are so confusing": Ephron, 38.

"She is not just the mother": Nora Ephron, eulogy for Phoebe Ephron, 211.

"the Phoebe Ephron family plan": Ephron, 211.

writer Santha Rama Rau: "Alumnae Achievement Awards 1971: Santha Rama Rau '45," Wellesley College official website, accessed September 29, 2021, https://www .wellesley.edu/alumnae/awards/achievementawards/allrecipients/santha-rama-rau-45.

5. Mail Girl

If I can just get back to New York: Ephron, *I Remember Nothing*, 97.

"horrible brand-new white-brick building": Ephron, 18.

she *"might never find a way"*: Ephron, 18.

"Why do you want to work here?": Ephron, 17.

"epiphany after epiphany": Nora Ephron, "You've Got Rapture," *O, the Oprah Magazine*, June 2002, https://www.oprah.com/omagazine/nora-ephrons-books -that-made-a-difference/all.

"At the center of the strike": "The Great Newspaper Strike of 1962–1963," *On the Media*, August 8, 2013, https://www.wnycstudios.org/podcasts/otm/segments /311624-great-newspaper-strike-1962-1963.

her *"proper place in the city"*: Cohen, *She Made Me Laugh*, 52.

"If I was home alone at night": Nora Ephron, "Serial Monogamy," *New Yorker*, February 5, 2006, https://www.newyorker.com/magazine/2006/02/13/serial-monogamy

"What do you know about Leonard Lyons?": Ephron, "Journalism: A Love Story," in *I Remember Nothing*, 25.

"Don't be ridiculous": Ephron, 25.

"By the way, there are 1,511 raisins": Ephron, quoted in "Ephron's First Scoops Were for the Post," *New York Post*, by Andy Soltis, June 28, 2012, https://nypost .com/2012/06/28/ephrons-1st-scoops-were-for-the-post/.

"I loved the city room": Ephron, *I Remember Nothing*, 31.

"You see that girl": Greenburg, interview by the author.

6. Wallflower

the Cuban Missile Crisis: "Cuban Missile Crisis," John F. Kennedy Presidential Library and Museum, accessed September 29, 2021, https://www.jfklibrary.org/learn /about-jfk/jfk-in-history/cuban-missile-crisis.

"Hi, my name is Nora": Greenburg, interview by the author.

"*There would be conversation*": Bernstein, dir., *Everything Is Copy.*
"*I always thought that Nora*": Bernstein, dir., *Everything Is Copy.*
"*Write as if you're sending*": Nora Ephron, eulogy for Phoebe Ephron, 210.
"*Bladder. Whimsy. Dailies*": Nora Ephron, "Yossarian Is Alive and Well in the Mexican Desert," *New York Times*, March 16, 1969, https://archive.nytimes.com/www.nytimes.com/books/98/02/15/home/heller-yossarian.html.
"*Whether 'Catch-22' will be a masterpiece*": Ephron, https://archive.nytimes.com/www.nytimes.com/books/98/02/15/home/heller-yossarian.html.
"*a picture about dying*": Ephron, https://archive.nytimes.com/www.nytimes.com/books/98/02/15/home/heller-yossarian.html.
demonstrations against the draft: "Timeline of Conscription (Mandatory Military Enlistment) in the U.S.," NewsHour Extra, PBS official website, 2001, https://www.pbs.org/newshour/extra/app/uploads/2014/03/Timeline-of-of-conscription.pdf.
"*My mother loved Thanksgiving*": Nora Ephron, "The Mink Coat," *Esquire*, December 1975.
"*I found it unbearable*": Ephron, "The Mink Coat."
"*Nora,*" she said. "*You're a reporter*": Ephron, "The Mink Coat."
"*I hope you never tell anyone*": Delia Ephron, interview by Amy Dickinson, Chicago Humanities Festival, 2013, via YouTube, https://www.youtube.com/watch?v=trVwlCvpRWQ.
"*We're all born into a family*": Delia Ephron, interview by Dickinson, https://www.youtube.com/watch?v=trVwlCvpRWQ.
"*I'm going to give the nurse*": Ephron, "My Life in 3500 Words or Less," 103.
"*My mother died of cirrhosis*": Ephron, 103.
"*She was tough*": Nora Ephron, eulogy for Phoebe Ephron, 209.
"*My first husband is a perfectly nice person*": Ephron, "My Life in 3500 Words or Less," 104.
"*Don't be crazy*": Ephron, 104.
"*you know, people in my*": Greenburg, interview by the author.

7. After *Wallflower* (Women's Issues)

"*She thought she was the most interesting*": Doidge, "It's Not Just About Harry," 6.
Esquire's editor, Harold Hayes: *Smiling Through the Apocalypse*, directed by Tom Hayes (First Run Features, 2013).
"*Well, what is it you want*": *Smiling Through the Apocalypse*, dir. by Hayes.
Nora fulfilled it with vigor: Doidge, "It's Not Just About Harry," 6.
"*Postwar affluence and a rapidly developing*": Brian Clarey, "A Beast of an Editor," *Triad City Beat*, June 25, 2014, https://triad-city-beat.com/a-beast-of-a-editor-the-harold-hayes-papers/.

"Ephron, as a columnist": Yardley, "Nora Ephron's 'Crazy Salad,'" https://www.washing tonpost.com/wp-dyn/articles/A17418-2004Nov1.html?nav=rss_artsandliving /books/columns/jonathanyardley/secondreading.

"[Hayes] had the exact thing": Frank DiGiacomo, "The Esquire Decade," *Vanity Fair*, December 20, 2006, https://www.vanityfair.com/culture/2007/01/esquire 200701.

Nick fell into journalism: Michele Willens, "Pileggi, the Fella Behind 'Goodfellas,'" *Los Angeles Times*, March 22, 1991, https://www.latimes.com/archives/la-xpm -1991-03-22-ca-593-story.html.

"I'd literally check in": Willens, "Pileggi."

"as close to it as": Nora Ephron, "A Star Is Born," *New York*, 1973, via Wellesley College Archives.

"If you take the job": Ephron, "A Star Is Born."

"I thought what she was saying": Ephron, "A Star Is Born."

"I had no jealousy": Ephron, "A Star Is Born."

"I figured there are worse things": Ephron, "A Star Is Born."

"she was a bit of an acquired taste": Doidge, "It's Not Just About Harry," 6.

"She was the first person to write": Doidge, 6–7.

"so fresh you could smudge": Freeman, "Nora Ephron Taught Me All About Feminism," https://www.theguardian.com/commentisfree/2013/aug/05/a-book-that -changed-me-nora-ephron.

"It's certain that fine women eat": W. B. Yeats, "A Prayer for my Daughter," 1921, via poets.org, https://poets.org/poem/prayer-my-daughter.

as the women's movement was taking shape: Doidge, "It's Not Just About Harry," 10.

"sympathetic but mischievous and occasionally": Yardley, "Nora Ephron's 'Crazy Salad,'" https://www.washingtonpost.com/wp-dyn/articles/A17418-2004Nov1 .html?nav=rss_artsandliving/books/columns/jonathanyardley/secondreading.

"Fight for the cream soda": Doidge, "It's Not Just About Harry," 11.

"I can't come up to see you": Marie Brenner, interviewed in *Everything Is Copy*, dir. Bernstein.

"I was dazzled": Carl Bernstein, interviewed in *Everything Is Copy*, dir. Bernstein.

"maybe the single greatest reporting": Gene Roberts, quoted in *Pulitzer's Gold*, by Roy J. Harris Jr. (Columbia: University of Missouri Press, 2007), 233.

"She turned on me": Richard Cohen, in his speech at Nora's memorial in July 2012, quoted in "Richard Cohen to Pen a Nora Ephron Biography," by Lindsey Weber, *Vulture*, December 9, 2013, https://www.vulture.com/2013/12/richard-cohen-to -pen-a-nora-ephron-biography.html.

"Richard, this will be": Cohen, *She Made Me Laugh*, 28.

"She extended her hand": Richard Cohen, speech at Nora's memorial, https://www
.vulture.com/2013/12/richard-cohen-to-pen-a-nora-ephron-biography.html.

Act III: Bernstein and Bernie (1976–1987)

8. Ms. Ephron Goes to Washington

the blockbuster era: Tom Shone, *Blockbuster* (London: Simon & Schuster, 2004), 27–40.

"The men who cover wars": Nora Ephron, interview by Robert Cromie, *Book Beat*, WTTW,
1975, via WTTW official website, https://interactive.wttw.com/playlist/2017
/03/13/archives-nora-ephron.

"Nora, you can't go there": Ephron, interview by Cromie.

her heroine, Dorothy Parker: Nora Ephron, radio interview by Studs Terkel, July 28,
1975, via Studs Terkel Radio Archive, https://studsterkel.wfmt.com/programs
/nora-ephron-discusses-feminism-and-her-book-crazy-salad.

"I want to tell you that it's magic": Mildred Newman and Bernard Berkowitz, *How to
Be Your Own Best Friend* (New York: Random House, 1973).

chic but sweet black-and-white photo: *People*, May 3, 1976.

"This wedding had to be wedged": Notes on People, *New York Times*, April 16, 1976,
https://www.nytimes.com/1976/04/16/archives/notes-on-people-bernstein
-coauthor-of-nixon-books-weds.html.

"I just married Carl Bernstein": Burick, interview by the author.

where "everybody is nobody": David Remnick, "The Shuttle," *Washington Post*, October
6, 1985.

the five most important things: Ephron, "Nora Ephron '62 Addressed the Graduates,"
https://www.wellesley.edu/events/commencement/archives/1996commencement.

"Our class was actually at the edge": Martha Reardon Bewick, e-mail correspondence
with the author.

"I can pretend that I have come back": Nora Ephron, reunion piece in *Esquire*, 1972, via
Wellesley College Archives.

"potential resource for Wellesley": Betty Diener to Mrs. Gordon, October 1972, via Wellesley College Archives.

told the new graduates to "make trouble": Nora Ephron, 1979 commencement speech,
quoted in the *Boston Globe*, via Wellesley College Archives.

"I am bulging, laden, sloggy": Nora Ephron, "Having a Baby After 35," *New York
Times*, November 26, 1978, https://www.nytimes.com/1978/11/26/archives/having
-a-baby-after-35-having-a-baby.html.

"How do you feel about": Ephron, "Having a Baby."

"Why are you having a baby now?": Ephron, "Having a Baby."

"I had not wanted a child": Ephron, "Having a Baby."

"I have thought of [my mother]": Ephron, "Having a Baby."

9. When Nora Met Jacob . . .

"Jacob is like a dish of ice cream": Bernstein, dir., *Everything Is Copy*.

"The women's movement didn't prepare us": Dana Micucci, "Ephron Likes Director's Chair Because It's the Driver's Seat," *Chicago Tribune*, May 17, 1992, via Wellesley College Archives.

how happy he and Nora seemed: Ken Auletta, quoted in *Everything Is Copy*, dir. by Bernstein.

"Writing this scoop makes me": Dolly Langdon and Martha Smilgis, "Can Carl Handle Deep Troth? Nora Ephron Leaves Him over an Ex-P.M.'s Daughter," *People*, January 14, 1980, https://people.com/archive/can-carl-bernstein-handle -deep-troth-nora-ephron-leaves-him-over-an-ex-p-m-s-daughter-vol-13-no-2/.

thought of naming him "Early": Langdon and Smilgis, "Can Carl Handle Deep Troth?"

"Nora could forgive him": Langdon and Smilgis, "Can Carl Handle Deep Troth?"

his "skirt-chasing" ways: Langdon and Smilgis, "Can Carl Handle Deep Troth?"

"She isn't trying to play it off": Michelle Markowitz, "I Think About This Photo of Nora a Lot," *New York*, February 12, 2018, https://www.thecut.com/2018/02/i -think-about-this-photo-of-nora-ephron-carl-bernstein.html.

"no one is betting against": Langdon and Smilgis, "Can Carl Handle Deep Troth?"

"Like a cat": Mike Nichols, quoted in *Everything Is Copy*, dir. Bernstein.

"The real reason was that": Matthew Gilbert, "When Nora Went to Hollywood," *Boston Globe*, August 12, 1990.

"What Nora and I did right": Paul Chi, "How Would Nora Ephron Describe Her Son's Documentary About Her? 'It's Almost Good,'" *Vanity Fair*, March 16, 2016, https://www.vanityfair.com/hollywood/2016/03/nora-ephron-everything-is-copy -documentary.

"M.F.?": Gillian Brockell, "Deep Throat's Identity Was a Mystery for Decades Because No One Believed This Woman," *Washington Post*, September 27, 2019, https:// www.washingtonpost.com/history/2019/09/27/deep-throats-identity-was -mystery-decades-because-no-one-believed-this-woman/.

"For many years, I have lived": Nora Ephron, "Deep Throat and Me," *Huffington Post*, May 31, 2005, https://www.huffpost.com/entry/deep-throat-and-me-now -it_b_1917.

"It was a great way to learn": *Irish Times*, 2007, via Wellesley College Archives.

"a horrible television movie": *Irish Times*, 2007.

"I honestly believed that": Nora Ephron, "Moving On, a Love Story," *New Yorker*, May 29, 2006, https://www.newyorker.com/magazine/2006/06/05/moving-on-nora -ephron.

"One afternoon": Ephron, "Moving On, a Love Story."

10. Rescued by a Building

"Would you like to meet": Abramowitz, *Is That a Gun in Your Pocket?*, 230.

"The original impulse was": Abramowitz, 230.

Alice Reeve Albright: Robert D. McFadden, "Alice Arlen, Screenwriter and Collaborator with Nora Ephron, Dies at 75," *New York Times*, February 29, 2016, https://www.nytimes.com/2016/03/01/arts/alice-arlen-screenwriter-with-premier -journalistic-pedigree-dies-at-75.html.

"a rebel and a writer": McFadden, "Alice Arlen, Screenwriter."

"What was great is that": William Murphy, "Alice Arlen Dead; Author, Niece of *Newsday* Founder Was 75," *Newsday*, March 2, 2016, https://www.newsday.com /long-island/obituaries/alice-arlen-dead-author-niece-of-newsday-founder-was -75-1.11531733.

"You're always looking for a moment": Abramowitz, *Is That a Gun in Your Pocket?*, 231.

"I love that movies have a way": Mary Swerscek, "Screenwriter Nora Ephron Keeps Audience Sleepless in Salomon," *Brown Daily Herald*, 1997, via Wellesley College Archives.

eager to "get into the movies": *Los Angeles Times*, April 10, 1977, referenced in "*Silkwood* (1983)," AFI Catalog of Feature Films, accessed September 30, 2021, https://catalog .afi.com/Catalog/moviedetails/58079.

a massive library of information: *Silkwood* production notes, via Cinema Library Archives, University of Southern California.

Silkwood estate had filed: *Silkwood* production notes.

all got involved in the case: *Silkwood* production notes.

three-month Silkwood v. Kerr-McGee Corp. trial: *Silkwood* production notes.

"he began to play hardball": *Fame* magazine profile of Bernstein, quoted in "Ephron by the Numbers: Lunch and More with All the Noras," by Jeff Simon, *Buffalo (NY) News*, July 30, 1989, https://buffalonews.com/news/ephron-by-the-numbers-lunch -and-more-with-all-the-noras/article_1a88cc84-8334-56ae-9776-1e928475 cd94.html.

"I'd just come out of this experience": *Fame* magazine profile of Bernstein.

either "negligently or purposefully": Richard L. Rashke, *The Killing of Karen Silkwood: The Story Behind the Kerr-McGee Plutonium Case*, 2d ed. (Ithaca, NY: Cornell University Press, 2000), 56–62.

By 1986, the original judgment: Rashke, 56–62.

"tie the entire thing up": "Silkwood—Was the Reality Uglier?," *LA Weekly*, January 6–12, 1984, via Cinema/AFI/Mayer Library Clipping File, University of Southern California.

"a highly fictionalized Hollywood dramatization": "Silkwood," *LA Weekly*.

the producers struck a deal: *Silkwood* production notes.

"she was out and out studying": Bernstein, dir., *Everything Is Copy*.

"One of the things Mike teaches": Nora Ephron, interview by American Academy of Achievement, 2007, via YouTube, https://www.youtube.com/watch?v=3HhXgLux6iw.

"You don't see [Meryl]": Jazz Tangcay, "Meryl Streep Collaborator Ann Roth on How Costumes Helped Inform 'Silkwood,' 'Julie & Julia,' 'Doubt' and 'The Post' Roles," *Variety*, June 18, 2020, https://variety.com/2020/artisans/production/meryl-streep-costumes-1234640730/.

"I looked at photographs of Karen": Tangcay, "Meryl Streep Collaborator Ann Roth."

"They both had that ability": Kristin Marguerite Doidge, "Poetic and Real: A Conversation with Mark Harris," *Los Angeles Review of Books*, March 20, 2021, https://lareviewofbooks.org/article/poetic-and-real-a-conversation-with-mark-harris/. First published in *LA Review of Books*.

"Even when he leaves movies": Doidge, "Poetic and Real."

"For me, that's one of the things": Doidge, "Poetic and Real."

11. When Nick Met Nora . . .

when Nick officially met Nora: Cohen, *She Made Me Laugh*, 182–183.

"Richard," she said. "You must come": Cohen, 182–183.

"It was one of those things": *Boston Herald* article, 1993, via Wellesley College Archives.

"A by-the-book feminist interpretation": Nell Beram, "The Troubled Marriage That Inspired Nora Ephron," *Salon*, August 18, 2013, https://www.salon.com/2013/08/18/the_troubled_marriage_that_inspired_nora_ephron/.

"effective self-publicizer": Books of the Times, *New York Times*, April 8, 1983, https://www.nytimes.com/1983/04/08/books/books-of-the-times-085275.html.

"Giving Nichols Heartburn": Mark Harris, *Mike Nichols: A Life* (New York: Penguin, 2021), 396.

"He was moved by the way": Harris, 397.

"I can't believe you're": Harris, 397.

"Much better than the book!": Dan Bronson, memo to Jeffrey Katzenberg, Paramount Pictures, via Special Collections, Margaret Herrick Library, Academy of Motion Picture Arts and Sciences.

a "woman's Annie Hall": Bronson, memo to Katzenberg.

the right to review and approve: *Screen International*, July 6, 1985, referenced in "*Heartburn* (1986)," AFI Catalog of Feature Films, accessed September 30, 2021, https://catalog.afi.com/Film/57348-HEARTBURN.

"*This is not happening*": Harris, *Mike Nichols*, 401.

"*steam came out of her ears*": Bernstein, dir., *Everything Is Copy*.

"*Nora was always there*": Harris, *Mike Nichols*, 401.

"*She would get inside of the head*": Roger Friedman, "Carly Simon on Nora Ephron," *Showbiz411*, June 27, 2012, https://www.showbiz411.com/2012/06/27/exclusive-carly-simon-on-nora-ephron-she-would-get-inside-the-head-of-the-character. Courtesy of / printed with permission from Roger Friedman.

"*And then the dreams break*": Ephron, *Heartburn*, 174.

"*I guess it was the restrictions*": Abramowitz, *Is That a Gun in Your Pocket?*, 310.

Act IV: Nora the Filmmaker (1989–2000s)

12. What Nora's Having

"*No,*" *Nora said*: Ephron and Reiner, "It All Started Like This" featurette.

"*it started before it*": Ephron and Reiner, "It All Started Like This" featurette.

"*This is a talk piece*": Nora Ephron, introduction to *When Harry Met Sally...* (screenplay), xi.

"*funny but extremely depressed*": "Making of" featurette, *When Harry Met Sally...*, directed by Rob Reiner (MGM Home Entertainment, 2001), DVD.

"*I'll have the avocado*": Nora Ephron, introduction to *When Harry Met Sally...* (screenplay), x.

Once when Nora was on an airplane: "Making of" featurette, *When Harry Met Sally...*

"*Rob fell in love*": Abramowitz, *Is That a Gun in Your Pocket?*, 312.

long line of popular young actors: Abramowitz, 312.

"*I don't think Tom*": Abramowitz, 312.

"*God, it's too bad*": Abramowitz, 312.

"*nurse each other through*": Abramowitz, 311.

"*We've told you all this*": Ephron, interview by Academy of Achievement, https://www.youtube.com/watch?v=3HhXgLux6iw.

"*we honor the script*": Ephron and Reiner, "It All Started Like This" featurette.

"*The director is constantly trying*": Abramowitz, *Is That a Gun in Your Pocket?*, 311.

"*We had a huge battle*": Abramowitz, 312.

"*And I know just who*": Ephron and Reiner, "It All Started Like This" featurette.

"It ended up being the funniest": Bruce Weber, "Estelle Reiner, 94, Comedy Matri-
arch, Is Dead," *New York Times*, October 29, 2008, https://www.nytimes.com
/2008/10/30/movies/30reiner.html.

"It's hard to imagine that": Ephron and Reiner, "It All Started Like This" featurette.

This movie is going to be so fabulous: Ephron and Reiner, "It All Started Like This"
featurette.

"I'm a fixer": Nora Ephron, interview by Terry Lawson, *Dayton (OH) Daily News*, August
27, 1989, via University of Southern California Archives.

"What could I do?": Stanley, "Hollywood Ending," https://www.nytimes.com
/2012/06/28/fashion/nora-ephrons-hollywood-ending.html.

13. *My Blue Heaven*

"I'd like the chef salad": Ephron, *When Harry Met Sally . . .* (screenplay), 10.

"At times we would look": David Marchese, "Meg Ryan on Romantic Comedies, Celebrity and Leaving It All Behind," *New York Times Magazine*, February 15, 2019,
https://www.nytimes.com/interactive/2019/02/15/magazine/meg-ryan-romantic
-comedy.html.

"When you write a script, it's like": Ephron, *The Most of Nora Ephron*, 381–382.

"If you want to know how we got": Mark Harris, "When 'Harry' Met 'Annie,'" *Grantland*, July 21, 2014, http://grantland.com/features/when-harry-met-sally-woody
-allen-roomcom-week-25-years/.

"modern Muslim spin": Brent Lang and Matt Donnelly, "Mindy Kaling, Amazon Studios Adapting Novel 'Hana Khan Carries On' as Film," *Variety*, August 11,
2021, https://variety.com/2021/film/news/mindy-kaling-hana-khan-carries-on
-movie-1235039244/.

"When Harry Met Sally is kind of a dark": "Nora Ephron Movies: Quotes from Her
Films, from 'When Harry Met Sally' to 'Sleepless in Seattle,'" *Huffington Post*,
June 26, 2012, https://www.huffpost.com/entry/nora-ephron-movies-quotes-when
-harry-met-sally_n_1628026.

"When each character hits rock bottom": Harris, "When 'Harry' Met 'Annie,'" http://
grantland.com/features/when-harry-met-sally-woody-allen-roomcom-week
-25-years/.

On this particular day: Michael Mewshaw, *The Lost Prince: A Search for Pat Conroy*,
(Berkeley: Counterpoint Press, 2019), 151–153.

"Nora, how could I ever thank you": Mewshaw, "The Time I Crashed at Nora Ephron's."

she wouldn't have voted for herself: Andrea King, "Ephron Wild About 'Harry' Nom,"
Hollywood Reporter, March 26, 1990, via Cinema Library Archives, University of
Southern California.

"Herb Ross could turn": Matthew Gilbert, "This Is Her Life," *Boston Globe*, March 1, 1992, via Wellesley College Archives.

Korean War love story Higgins & Beech: Newhouse News Service, 1990, via Wellesley College Archives.

"very good taste": Nora Ephron, *Sleepless in Seattle* press conference, via Library Archives, Academy of Motion Picture Arts & Sciences.

"It was a picture of him walking": Matthew Gilbert, *Boston Globe*, August 12, 1990, via Wellesley College Archives.

"slender and spirited" Nora: "Ephron Got Lucky as a Screenwriter," Newhouse News Service, September 9, 1990, via Wellesley College Archives.

commanded more than $1 million: "Ephron Got Lucky as a Screenwriter," Newhouse News Service.

"most interesting and revealing films": Dance, *Everything Is Copy*, 112–113.

reportedly even lent Hill money: Stanley, "Hollywood Ending," https://www.nytimes.com/2012/06/28/fashion/nora-ephrons-hollywood-ending.html.

"When I was working for New York magazine": Adams, "Nicholas Pileggi," *Guardian*, https://www.theguardian.com/tv-and-radio/2013/feb/03/nicholas-pileggi-vegas-nora-ephron.

"tossed away on this sketchy outline": Caryn James, "When Heaven Turns Out Not to Be," *New York Times*, August 18, 1990, https://www.nytimes.com/1990/08/18/movies/review-film-when-heaven-turns-out-not-to-be.html.

"nutball idiosyncrasies almost manage": Duane Byrge, review of *My Blue Heaven*, directed by Herbert Ross, *Hollywood Reporter*, August 20, 1990.

14. *This Is My Life*

"where everything is copy": Claudia Eller, "Ephron, Obst Are Linked for 'Life,'" *Hollywood Reporter*, August 25, 1989, via Cinematic Arts Library, University of Southern California.

"You've got such great taste": Meyer, interview by the author.

"tonally, there was no other": Meyer, interview by the author.

"Nora, Dawn, and I are girls": Meyer, interview by the author.

"Everybody comes at everything": Abramowitz, *Is That a Gun in your Pocket?*, 363.

"The Red Sea was made": Nora Ephron, eulogy for Phoebe Ephron, 210.

It can't get any worse: Abramowitz, *Is That a Gun in Your Pocket?*, 363.

"You should try the chicken": Abramowitz, 364.

"I think the movie would have done better": Ephron, interview by Academy of Achievement, https://www.youtube.com/watch?v=3HhXgLux6iw.

"It was a very funny script": Ephron, interview by Academy of Achievement.

"I said, 'Julie'": Hilary de Vries, "'Darling! Listen to me!'" *New York Times*, January 26, 1992, https://www.nytimes.com/1992/01/26/magazine/darling-listen-to -me.html.

"a person who is very selfish": De Vries, "'Darling!'"

"What if you give someone a note": Abramowitz, *Is That a Gun in Your Pocket?*, 364.

15. Sleepless

a reported $10 million: Peter Travers, review of *This Is My Life*, directed by Nora Ephron, *Rolling Stone*, February 21, 1992, https://www.rollingstone.com/movies /movie-reviews/this-is-my-life-105716/.

bringing in only $2.9 million: "This Is My Life," Box Office Mojo, accessed September 30, 2021, https://www.boxofficemojo.com/movies/?id=thisismylife.htm.

"A ROOMFUL OF MEN": Alice Arlen and Nora Ephron, *Higgins and Beech* (screenplay draft, 1989), Brian E. Lebowitz Collection of 20th Century Jewish-American Literature, University of Colorado Boulder.

"I was dying to work with": Lawrence Frascella, "On the Front Lines of the Sexual Battlefield," *Rolling Stone*, July 8, 1993.

"It had all these weird, wonderful ideas": Frascella, "On the Front Lines."

"There I was, a hopeless teenage girl": Frascella, "On the Front Lines."

informed much of Nora's work for decades: Dance, *Everything Is Copy*, 23.

"make a movie about how movies": Richard Maltby, *Hollywood Cinema* (Oxford: Wiley, 2003), 53.

"a bumpy two-year stretch": *Austin American Statesman*, June 28, 1993, quoted in "Sleepless in Seattle (1993)," AFI Catalog of Feature Films, accessed September 30, 2021, https://catalog.afi.com/Film/59663-SLEEPLESS-INSEATTLE.

"I was looking for a happy ending": Carlson, *I'll Have What She's Having*, 112.

that Arch deemed "terrible": Carlson, 114.

"I didn't have my choice": Carlson, 118.

"This Is My Life also marks": Travers, review of *This Is My Life*, https://www .rollingstone.com/movies/movie-reviews/this-is-my-life-105716/.

"It was a geographically accurate": Cohen, *She Made Me Laugh*, 192.

described himself as "persnickety": Cohen, 192.

credited Tom with his "wonderful work": David Hunter, "When Nora Met Romance," *LA Village View*, June 25–July 1, 1992.

quite literally—out of the picture: Hunter, "When Nora Met Romance."

"Hello, Nora?": Carlson, *I'll Have What She's Having*, 124.

"This is the woman who understands": Carlson, 124.

"Go out and hire": Ephron, *Sleepless in Seattle* press conference.

"Nora was the greatest food orderer": *Sleepless in Seattle* screening talk, TCM Festival, April 2019.

"When Nora showed up in Seattle": Cohen, *She Made Me Laugh*, 198.

"She was protecting the movie": Cohen, 199.

the young boy's mother, Linda Watt: Carlson, *I'll Have What She's Having*, 155.

"I remember it being outside": Carlson, 155.

"Nora, you are sixteen years old": Nora Ephron, eulogy for Phoebe Ephron, 209.

"Tom [Hanks] made it": Doidge, "It's Not Just About Harry,"13.

"It was like the scene": Doidge, 13.

"We live in a place called the United States": Hunter, "When Nora Met Romance."

16. After *Sleepless*

sneak upstairs to pinch her: Henry Ephron, *We Thought We Could Do Anything*, 40.

"My first memory of Nora": Bernstein, dir., *Everything Is Copy*.

"My father had died": Bernstein, dir., *Everything Is Copy*.

"I'm sure she thinks": Bernstein, dir., *Everything Is Copy*.

"You always think that a bolt": Ephron, *I Remember Nothing*.

met with film scholar Marsha McCreadie: Marsha McCreadie, acknowledgments, *The Women Who Write the Movies* (Secaucus, NJ: Carol Publishing Group, 1994), ix.

"She spontaneously broke in": McCreadie, ix.

between $20 and $29 million: "*Mixed Nuts* (1994)," AFI Catalog of Feature Films, accessed September 30, 2021, https://catalog.afi.com/Film/60398-MIXED-NUTS.

"The last thing I wanted": Bob Strauss, "Hot Line to Success?" *L.A. Daily News*, December 20, 1994, via Cinema Library Archives, University of Southern California.

"[He] kept us in stitches": Rita Wilson, Facebook status update, December 20, 2019, https://www.facebook.com/RitaWilson/posts/2647476195337248?comment _id=2647489332002601.

"I love having a group of people": Hilary de Vries, "Raw, Salted and Roasted: What's on the Table when Nora Ephron and Steve Martin Get Together?," *Los Angeles Times*, December 18, 1994.

A replica (empty) elevator shaft: *Los Angeles Times*, May 29, 1994, via "*Mixed Nuts* (1994)," AFI Catalog of Feature Films, https://catalog.afi.com/Film/60398-MIXED -NUTS.

the artwork of Laura Levine: *Vanity Fair*, December 1994, via "*Mixed Nuts* (1994)," AFI.

printing a fake press pass: "Post-punk's Visual Chronicler," RockCritics.com, January 21, 2009, https://rockcritics.com/2009/01/21/post-punks-visual-chronicler -interview-with-laura-levine-part-1/.

"She was amazing": Fenton, interview by the author.

"outstanding women who": "WIF Awards Retrospective," Women in Film official website, accessed November 11, 2021, https://womeninfilm.org/updates/wif-awards-retrospective/.

"That part was spontaneous": Madeline Kahn and Rita Wilson, HFPA *Sleepless In Seattle* press conference, via Library Archives, Academy of Motion Picture Arts & Sciences.

"My real occupation": Strauss, "Hot Line to Success?"

"I may satirize": Strauss, "Hot Line to Success?"

What could I have done differently?: Nora Ephron, "Flops," in *I Remember Nothing*, 107.

"Two or three hundred people": Ephron, 109.

"She read the reviews": Sacha, interview by the author.

escalating quickly to $43 million: Josh Young, "New Line Cinema: It Was a Very Good Year," *New York Times*, September 18, 1994, https://www.nytimes.com/1994/09/18/archives/film-new-line-cinema-it-was-a-very-good-year.html.

17. *Michael*

"I saw this angel": *Michael* production notes, Turner Pictures, via Cinema Library Archives, University of Southern California.

"John has that amazing ability": *Michael* production notes.

"Every chance he has": *Michael* production notes.

"I always saw it as a story": Monica Roman, "'Michael' Takes Flight for Turner, New Line," *Variety*, October 21, 1996, via Cinema Library Archives, University of Southern California.

"I asked Universal": Roman, "'Michael' Takes Flight."

Travolta's reported $8 million: Roman, "'Michael' Takes Flight."

"Nora is smart": Roman, "'Michael' Takes Flight."

a "lucrative" back end: Dan Cox, "MacDowell, Hurt in 'Michael,'" *Variety*, November 2, 1995.

"When Andie came in to read": *Michael* production notes.

"This was one of the best scripts": *Michael* production notes.

"This is [1994]": Carlson, *I'll Have What She's Having*, 211.

"I have an idea who could": Carlson, 211.

"a dash of unexpected magic": *Michael* production notes.

"I very much wanted": *Michael* production notes.

"What she cared about": John Lindley, interview by the author.

"What is it you like about this place?": John Lindley, interview by the author.

seemed to speak in their "own language": Doidge, "It's Not Just About Harry," 16.

"The powerful thing": *Michael* production notes.

"Nora had an approach": Dreyer, interview by the author.

"Everyone who was there": *Michael* production notes.

"I didn't know until I got there": Ethan Alter, "John Travolta Recalls Dancing the Night Away with Princess Diana," Yahoo, December 6, 2019, https://www.yahoo .com/entertainment/john-travolta-recalls-dancing-night-away-with-princess -diana-nancy-reagan-140058674.html.

a *"highlight of his life"*: "How John Travolta Got into Character to Play Mob Boss John Gotti," ABC News, September 26, 2016, https://abcnews.go.com/Entertainment /john-travolta-character-play-mob-boss-john-gotti/story?id=42089444.

influenced *"every one of her movies"*: "Nora Ephron," *Studio 360*, PRI, November 19, 2005, https://www.pri.org/stories/2005-11-19/nora-ephron.

grossing more than $95 million: "Domestic 1996 Weekend 52," Box Office Mojo, accessed September 30, 2021, https://www.boxofficemojo.com/weekend/1996W52/.

"winsome, wafer-thin": Stephen Holden, "Being an Angel Doesn't Guarantee You're a Saint," *New York Times*, December 24, 1996, https://www.nytimes .com/1996/12/24/movies/being-an-angel-doesn-t-guarantee-you-re-a-saint.html.

"insipid and flavorless": Emanuel Levy, "Travolta Takes Wing in 'Michael,'" *Variety*, December 22, 1996, https://variety.com/1996/film/reviews/travolta-takes-wing-in -michael-1200447965/.

"beguiling, joyous holiday comedy": Kevin Thomas, "'Michael': Inspired Blend of Fantasy, Comedy," *Los Angeles Times*, December 25, 1996, https://www.latimes.com/archives /la-xpm-1996-12-25-ca-12362-story.html

18. *Mail*

"We shot that [sequence]": Lindley, interview by Nance.

"I think the alchemy of film": Fenton, interview by the author.

"We had quite a big orchestra": Fenton, interview by the author.

"jot down ideas as actors": Carlson, *I'll Have What She's Having*, 248.

"She'd work in a story of her own": Carlson, 248.

Nora gave Chappelle the freedom: "14 Secrets About *You've Got Mail*," E! Online, May 19, 2021, https://www.eonline.com/uk/photos/26369/secrets-you-might-not-know -about-you-ve-got-mail.

"He proved to be a delight": Carlson, *I'll Have What She's Having*, quoted in "14 Secrets," E! Online.

sneak into a nearby bar: Carlson, *I'll Have What She's Having*, 256.

$2 billion in combined box office: "Adam Sandler," The Numbers, accessed September 30, 2021, https://www.the-numbers.com/person/126870401-Adam-Sandler.

called "poetically unfiltered": Justin Tinsley, "Dave Chappelle's Intimate New Netflix Specials Are Brilliant," *Undefeated*, March 20, 2017, https://theundefeated.com/features/dave-chappelle-netflix-specials/.

"It was a cultivated but casual": Erin Carlson, "You've Got Nora: A Valentine's Day Tribute to Nora Ephron," *Vanity Fair*, February 13, 2015, https://www.vanityfair.com/hollywood/2015/02/youve-got-mail-oral-history.

"not a step forward": Ephron, "Nora Ephron '62 Addressed the Graduates," https://www.wellesley.edu/events/commencement/archives/1996commencement.

"When you see You've Got Mail": John Lindley, interview by the author.

"dark commentary on capitalism": Amanda Hess, "'You've Got Mail' Is Secretly a Tragedy, Too," *New York Times*, December 19, 2018, https://www.nytimes.com/2018/12/19/movies/youve-got-mail.html.

"Did You've Got Mail, in fact": Hess, "'You've Got Mail' Is Secretly a Tragedy."

"Ephron's work hearkens back": Doidge, "It's Not Just About Harry," 7.

Delia had the clever idea: Nora Ephron, director's commentary, *You've Got Mail* (Warner Home Video, 2008), DVD.

"taken bits and pieces": Dance, *Everything Is Copy*, 75.

"When these romantic movies": Bernstein, dir., *Everything Is Copy*.

"sheer force of her personality": Cohen, *She Made Me Laugh*, 195.

"ripped right out of society": Hanks, interview by the author.

"Nora was a REPORTER": Hanks, interview by the author.

"Remember this moment": Bernstein, dir., *Everything Is Copy*.

Only fifty-seven women: Annenberg Inclusion Initiative, *Inequality in 1,300 Popular Films: Examining Portrayals of Gender, Race/Ethnicity, LGBTQ & Disability from 2007 to 2019* (Annenberg Foundation, September 2020), http://assets.uscannenberg.org/docs/aii-inequality_1300_popular_films_09-08-2020.pdf.

decided to bring in a director: Carlson, *I'll Have What She's Having*, 272.

"This was my novel": Bernstein, dir., *Everything Is Copy*.

Act V: In the End (2000–2012)

19. *Hanging Up*

"Somehow when we're with": "HBO First Look: Getting Connected, the Making-Of *Hanging Up*" featurette.

"Georgia will know": Deleted scenes, *Hanging Up*, dir. by Keaton, DVD.

deeming the material "antifeminist": Abramowitz, *Is That a Gun in Your Pocket?*, 421.

"I didn't really pull it off": Matt Mueller, "Golden Icon Winner Diane Keaton Gets Real at Zurich Film Fest," *IndieWire*, October 3, 2014, https://www

.indiewire.com/2014/10/golden-icon-winner-diane-keaton-gets-real-at-zurich-film-fest-190758/.

"*The movie doesn't really want*": Roger Ebert, review of *Hanging Up*, *Chicago Sun-Times*, February 18, 2000, via RogerEbert.com, https://www.rogerebert.com/reviews/hanging-up-2000.

"*Though the screenplay and the novel*": "*Hanging Up*," Rotten Tomatoes, accessed October 1, 2021, https://www.rottentomatoes.com/m/hanging_up.

"*a Shakespearean actor*": Nora Ephron, director's commentary, *Lucky Numbers* (Paramount Pictures, 2001), DVD.

"*like an equal, which was*": Alfonso Gomez-Rejon, interview by Kristin Marguerite Doidge, April 30, 2015, *Me and Earl and the Dying Girl* teleconference and Q&A, Fox Entertainment Group.

"*Nora was good at her thing*": Mike Sullivan, "How a Good Script Becomes a Bad Movie: The Inside Story of 'Lucky Numbers,'" *Vulture*, September 1, 2015, https://www.vulture.com/2015/09/how-a-good-script-becomes-a-bad-movie-the-inside-story-of-lucky-numbers.html.

"*Everyone was feeding*": Ephron, director's commentary, *Lucky Numbers*.

"*he can dial down from farce*": Roger Ebert, review of *Meet the Parents*, *Chicago Sun-Times*, October 6, 2000, via RogerEbert.com, https://www.rogerebert.com/reviews/meet-the-parents-2000.

"*naive enough to think*": Pauline Kael, The Current Cinema, *New Yorker*, October 8, 1973.

By 1997, there were talks: Michael Fleming, "Ephron Revives 'Beech' with Fox 2000 Talks," *Variety*, January 12, 1997, https://variety.com/1997/voices/columns/ephron-revives-beech-with-fox-2000-talks-1117433733/.

"*Nora, turn on the TV*": Nora Ephron, interview by Charlie Rose, *Charlie Rose*, September 11, 2006, https://charlierose.com/videos/27384. Courtesy of Charlie Rose Inc.

"*The pride in how brave*": Ephron, interview by Rose.

"*did not ask a tough question*": Ephron, *I Remember Nothing*, 83.

"*She was mystified that I wouldn't*": Laura Sandler, "Enemies: A Love Story," *Elle*, December 2002, 148, via Wellesley College Archives.

"*Every word she says*": Dick Cavett, "Lillian, Mary, and Me," *New Yorker*, December 9, 2002, https://www.newyorker.com/magazine/2002/12/16/lillian-mary-and-me.

the $2.25 million case wasn't dropped: Frances Kiernan, *Seeing Mary Plain: A Life of Mary McCarthy*, excerpted in *New York Times*, 2000, https://archive.nytimes.com/www.nytimes.com/books/first/k/kiernan-mary.html.

"*What's really great about them*": Nora Ephron, interview by Charlie Rose, *Charlie Rose*, January 16, 2003, https://charlierose.com/videos/16544. Courtesy of Charlie Rose Inc.

"her dramatization of the parallel": Sean Mitchell, Last Chance, *Los Angeles Times*, October 31, 2002, https://www.latimes.com/archives/la-xpm-2002-oct-31-wk-last chance31-story.html.

"My biggest flop was a play": Ephron, *I Remember Nothing*, 111.

20. Bewitched

"Nora, please help!": Nora Ephron and Will Ferrell, interview by Charlie Rose, *Charlie Rose*, June 15, 2005, https://charlierose.com/videos/10101.

"It's a big, fat": Ed Leibowitz, "Hexed in Hollywood: How a Film Mirrors Its Subject," *New York Times*, May 8, 2005, https://www.nytimes.com/2005/05/08/movies/moviesspecial/hexed-in-hollywood-how-a-film-mirrors-its-subject.html.

"Even in Hollywood": Leibowitz, "Hexed in Hollywood."

"a romance for the ages": Leibowitz, "Hexed in Hollywood."

"Gotta make me cry": Leibowitz, "Hexed in Hollywood."

"seemingly fluff and inconsequential": Dance, *Everything Is Copy*, 124.

"realness of the imagined": Dance, 126.

"You know movies": Leibowitz, "Hexed in Hollywood."

"These aren't the right muffins": Dreyer, interview by the author.

"Nora always had": John Lindley, interview by the author.

"Even though she'd come": Dreyer, interview by the author.

"the proper proportion": Nora Ephron, "A Sandwich," *New Yorker*, August 19 & 26, 2002, https://www.newyorker.com/magazine/2021/09/06/magazine20020819a-sandwich.

"It definitely was the best": Dreyer, interview by the author.

"I always hear": John Lindley, interview by the author.

"One of the big jokes": Willow Lindley, interview by the author.

"In a series of 'hats on hats'": Dance, *Everything Is Copy*, 125.

"Hi, doll," Judy said: Nora Ephron, "Considering the Alternative" in *I Feel Bad About My Neck*, 133–134.

21. "I Have This Blood Thing"

Nora called her sister: Delia Ephron, *Sister Mother Husband Dog*, 30.

"All I remember from that night": Ephron, 31.

"as if the Earth had shifted": Ephron, 30.

she reflected on their complicated: Ephron, 14.

"You should have it": Ephron, 32.

"It's not your couch that needs": Ephron, 30.

"The dressing room smells moldy": Ephron, 19.

"xx, Nora": Ephron, 5.

"I have this blood thing": Bernstein, dir., *Everything Is Copy.*

"The former Soviet Republics": Ephron, "I Remember Nothing" in *I Remember Nothing*, 10.

"I'm sure Jay-zees": Nora Ephron, interview by Charlie Rose, *Charlie Rose*, December 3, 2010, https://charlierose.com/videos/20433. Courtesy of Charlie Rose Inc.

myelodysplastic syndrome (MDS): "What Are Myelodysplastic Syndromes?," American Cancer Society, January 22, 2018, https://www.cancer.org/cancer/myelodysplastic-syndrome/about/what-is-mds.html.

"I think she didn't want": Jacob Bernstein, interview by Terry Gross, *Fresh Air*, NPR, March 31, 2016, https://www.npr.org/2016/03/31/472534582/in-everything-is-copy-nora-ephrons-son-tries-her-philosophy.

"The idea of the book is": Delia Ephron, interview by Dickinson, https://www.youtube.com/watch?v=trVwlCvpRWQ.

"This is not about fashion": Douglas MacKaye Harrington, "Nora Ephron Brings Laughs to Madison Avenue," Hamptons.com, December 18, 2009, http://www.hamptons.com/Out-And-About/Top-Stories/9633/Nora-Ephron-Brings-Laughs-To-Madison-Avenue.html (page discontinued).

"We thought of it as": Delia Ephron, interview by Dickinson, https://www.youtube.com/watch?v=trVwlCvpRWQ.

"Could we please try": Ephron, interview by Dickinson.

"And for some reason, Linda": Ephron, interview by Dickinson.

Love, Loss is about the shared: Doidge, "Nora & Delia Ephron's 'Love, Loss, and What I Wore.'" First published in *LA Review of Books.*

"It took me about three years": Jacob Bernstein, "All About Nora," TCM Festival, April 13, 2019.

unable to shake her grief: Doidge, "Nora & Delia Ephron's 'Love, Loss, and What I Wore.'"

"I couldn't think or write": Delia Ephron, "After 54 Years, We Fell in Love. After Five Months, I Got Leukemia," *New York Times*, May 27, 2017, https://www.nytimes.com/2017/05/27/opinion/sunday/delia-ephron-love-leukemia.html.

"I look at Peter and wonder": Ephron, "After 54 Years."

22. A Softer Nora

Whenever you cook: Ephron, interview by Wertheimer, https://www.npr.org/transcripts/111543710.

"What are you working on": *Julie & Julia* production notes, via Cinema Library Archives, University of Southern California.

"I thought it was absolutely beautiful": *Julie & Julia* production notes.

"I think that Julia Child didn't": Nora Ephron, Meryl Streep, and Stanley Tucci, Times Talks Q&A, July 30, 2009, via YouTube, https://www.youtube.com /watch?v=Ifk4MgoZZhA.

"famous woman novelist": "Julia's Life: 1935," Julia Child Foundation, accessed October 1, 2021, https://juliachildfoundation.org/timeline/.

Meryl later explained: Meryl Streep in Bernstein, dir., *Everything Is Copy.*

"When we first meet her": *Julie & Julia* production notes.

"made cooking fun": Julia Child Foundation, accessed October 1, 2021, https://juliachild foundation.org/.

the "servant-less" chef: David Strauss, *Setting the Table for Julia Child: Gourmet Dining in America, 1934–1961* (Baltimore: Johns Hopkins University Press, 2011), 233.

Gourmet magazine's French recipes: Strauss, *Setting the Table*, 221–222.

"I'm a good cook": Ephron, interview by Wertheimer, https://www.npr.org/transcripts /111543710.

"It was a way of saying": Ephron, interview by Wertheimer.

"among the many things I liked": *Julie & Julia* production notes.

"[My mother] was somebody who turned": Marisa Fox, "Ladies Who Lunch," *Ladies' Home Journal*, August 2009.

"My out is that I'm not": *Julie & Julia* production notes.

"Initially, the rights": Addie Morfoot, "'Julie and Julia' Preem One Tasteful Affair," *Variety*, August 3, 2009, https://variety.com/2009/film/news/julie-and-julia-preem -one-tasteful-affair-1118006855/.

"I'm buying this": "Secret Ingredients: Creating *Julie & Julia*" featurette, *Julie & Julia*, dir. Nora Ephron (Columbia Pictures / Sony Pictures Entertainment, 2009), DVD.

a time when Steel asked: Ephron, Streep, and Tucci, Times Talks Q&A, https://www .youtube.com/watch?v=Ifk4MgoZZhA.

"She never sat down": Bernstein, dir., *Everything Is Copy.*

"I'm not going to ask": Lee, interview by the author.

"I highly recommend having Meryl": Nora Ephron, speech at American Film Institute Life Achievement Award presentation to Meryl Streep, 2004, via YouTube, https:// www.youtube.com/watch?v=M4Moh-Sw7xE.

"Robert De Niro would do it!": *Julie & Julia* production notes.

costume designer Ann Roth: Tangcay, "Meryl Streep Collaborator Ann Roth," https:// variety.com/2020/artisans/production/meryl-streep-costumes-1234640730/.

"It was all about height": Tangcay, "Meryl Streep Collaborator Ann Roth."

As for Amy's wardrobe: "Secret Ingredients: Creating *Julie & Julia*" featurette, *Julie & Julia*, dir. Nora Ephron, DVD.

"The food had its own presence": Peter Caranicas, "Crafty Culinary Work on 'Julia' Set," *Variety*, August 11, 2009, https://variety.com/2009/film/markets-festivals /crafty-culinary-work-on-julia-set-1118007146/.

"If it didn't look right": *Julie & Julia* production notes.

23. Butter

"You can never have too much": Ephron, interview by Wertheimer, https://www .npr.org/transcripts/111543710.

No. 1 on the New York Times: Best Sellers, *New York Times*, September 10, 2006, https://www.nytimes.com/2006/09/10/books/arts/best-sellers-september-10 -2006.html.

"When she says that she can trace": Janet Maslin, "Oh, the Indignity: Nora Ephron Confronts Aging and Other New York Battles," *New York Times*, July 27, 2006, https://www.nytimes.com/2006/07/27/books/27masl.html.

A RACE TO MASTER THE ART: Amanda Hesser, "A Race to Master the Art of French Cooking," *New York Times*, August 13, 2003, https://www.nytimes .com/2003/08/13/dining/a-race-to-master-the-art-of-french-cooking.html.

"It's always hard to combine": Morfoot, "'Julie and Julia' Preem," https://variety .com/2009/film/news/julie-and-julia-preem-one-tasteful-affair-1118006855/.

"and I told the people at the Smithsonian": Ephron and Streep, interview by Rose, https://charlierose.com/videos/15908.

"Maybe we'll work together": June Thomas, "Jane Lynch's Favorite Kind of Character," *Slate*, November 2, 2020, https://slate.com/culture/2020/11/jane-lynch-acting -glee-julie-and-julia.html.

"You're the tallest person": Thomas, "Jane Lynch's Favorite Kind."

"The only scene we ever reshot": Bernstein, dir., *Everything Is Copy*.

"I love food": Ephron and Streep, interview by Rose, https://charlierose.com /videos/15908.

"I actually think whenever you cook": Ephron, interview by Wertheimer, https://www .npr.org/transcripts/111543710.

Nora actually was once invited: Ephron and Streep, interview by Rose, https://charlierose .com/videos/15908.

"You can never have too much": Ephron, interview by Wertheimer, https://www .npr.org/transcripts/111543710.

"You are the butter": Amy Pascal, quoted in *Everything Is Copy*, dir. by Bernstein.

"Secret of life": Rachel Fershleiser and Larry Smith, eds., *Not Quite What I Was Planning: Six-Word Memoirs by Writers Famous and Obscure* (New York: Harper Perennial, 2008).

"It's a kind of marriage that actually": Ephron and Streep, interview by Rose, https://charlierose.com/videos/15908.

"And happiness, even more": Stanley, "Hollywood Ending," https://www.nytimes.com/2012/06/28/fashion/nora-ephrons-hollywood-ending.html.

"throwing out a lot": Ephron, Streep, and Tucci, Times Talks Q&A, https://www.youtube.com/watch?v=Ifk4MgoZZhA.

"Julia is given the [book]": Ephron, Streep, and Tucci, https://www.youtube.com/watch?v=Ifk4MgoZZhA.

Nora kept it on her desk: "Nora would flip through the cookbook quite a lot as she wrote the script. The book was always on her desk," J. J. Sacha told me in an interview.

even provided notes on early drafts: Ephron, Streep, and Tucci, Times Talks Q&A, https://www.youtube.com/watch?v=Ifk4MgoZZhA.

"Richie and I are miserable": Westerman, interview by the author.

"Julie & Julia is one of the gentlest": *"Julie & Julia,"* Rotten Tomatoes, accessed October 1, 2021, https://www.rottentomatoes.com/m/julie_and_julia/reviews.

At a press screening in Los Angeles: Anecdote provided anonymously.

unfortunate victims of a Ponzi scheme: Harris, *Mike Nichols*, 569–570.

"I had to call Mike": Nora Ephron, speech at American Film Institute Life Achievement Award presentation to Mike Nichols, 2010, via YouTube, https://www.youtube.com/watch?v=zkFEmVD3qw4.

a biopic of Peggy Lee: Jacob Bernstein, interview by AOL BUILD, 2016, via YouTube, https://www.youtube.com/watch?v=ybWbA_YbLys.

new draft was picked up: Tatiana Siegel, "Reese Witherspoon's Peggy Lee Film Lands Director," *Hollywood Reporter*, September 8, 2014, https://www.hollywoodreporter.com/news/general-news/reese-witherspoons-peggy-lee-film-731156/.

revived again in early 2021: Joey Nolfi, "Michelle Williams to Play Peggy Lee in Todd Haynes' New Biopic," *Entertainment Weekly*, February 5, 2021, https://ew.com/movies/peggy-lee-biopic-michelle-williams/.

24. More Writing than Ever

"It was becoming clear that": Nora Ephron, "Revision and Life: Take It from the Top—Again," *New York Times*, November 9, 1986, https://www.nytimes.com/1986/11/09/books/revision-and-life-take-it-from-the-top-again.html.

"Nora, we have so much food": Short, interview by the author.

"[I] don't have much time left": Bernstein, dir., *Everything Is Copy*.

"dry skin, email, bras": Ephron, "What I Won't Miss," in *I Remember Nothing*, 132–133.

wasn't yet sure if he was ready: James T Harding, "Tom Hanks Unsure About Bway Role in STORIES ABOUT MCALARY," Broadway World, April 11, 2012,

https://www.broadwayworld.com/article/Tom-Hanks-Unsure-about-Bway-Role
-in-STORIES-ABOUT-MCALARY-20120411.

"Nora, what's this play about?": Bernstein, dir., *Everything Is Copy*.

"and there in the greenroom we wept": Hanks, interview by the author.

"Is this a thing?": Hanks, interview by the author.

"Who's the biggest prick": Short, interview by the author.

"What will we do now?": Lee, interview by the author.

"What will you do next?": Nora Ephron, interview by Enrique Cerna, *Conversations*, KCTS 9, June 28, 2011, via YouTube, https://www.youtube.com/watch?v=SXiNEgO-wxo.

"celebrate the richness": Robert Gottlieb, introduction to *The Most of Nora Ephron*, by Nora Ephron, x–xi.

"easier and easier about her own flaws": Bernstein, dir., *Everything Is Copy*.

"I don't know if she would have": Marchese, "Meg Ryan on Romantic Comedies," https://www.nytimes.com/interactive/2019/02/15/magazine/meg-ryan-romantic -comedy.html.

"That was so much fun": Ed Levine, "My Friend Nora Ephron Is Dead," Serious Eats, August 10, 2018, https://www.seriouseats.com/my-friend-nora-ephron-is -dead-the-world-of-se.

"Just sitting here in LA": Bernstein, dir., *Everything Is Copy*.

"Tell me again": Burick, interview by the author.

"You really should come": Burick, interview by the author.

"Let's get cheesecake": Marie Brenner, quoted in *Everything Is Copy*, dir. by Bernstein.

"I'm having a little health crisis": Bernstein, "Nora Ephron's Final Act."

"What should I tell people?": Bernstein, dir., *Everything Is Copy*.

"There she was, in her": Bernstein, "Nora Ephron's Final Act."

"I want to live to be 100": Bernstein, "Nora Ephron's Final Act."

"In out, in out": Bernstein, "Nora Ephron's Final Act."

"It was an ambush": Meryl Streep, quoted in *Everything Is Copy*, dir. Bernstein.

"get it over with": Bernstein, "Nora Ephron's Final Act."

"blends Ephron's wry observations": John Horn, "Nora Ephron's 'Cookbook' Showcases Passion for Food, Prose," *Los Angeles Times*, June 28, 2012, https://www.latimes .com/entertainment/movies/la-xpm-2012-jun-28-la-et-mn-ephron-cookbook -20120628-story.html.

"[It] ended with Rosie O'Donnell": Patricia Bosworth, "Nora Ephron's New York Memo- rial: A Gathering with a Hostess's Touch," *Vanity Fair*, July 9, 2012, https://www .vanityfair.com/news/daily-news/2012/07/nora-ephron-new-york-memorial

"Like the great influences in a life": Hanks, interview by the author.

Epilogue: America Post-Nora (2012–Present)

"There was then and always": Cohen, *She Made Me Laugh*, 8.

"I told her how much": Cohen, *She Made Me Laugh*, 2.

"I knew big time": Bernstein, dir., *Everything Is Copy*.

"The script was funny": Me and Early and the Dying Girl production notes, Twentieth Century Fox, 2015.

"caring about detail": Carlson, "You've Got Nora," https://www.vanityfair.com /hollywood/2015/02/youve-got-mail-oral-history.

"tiny details" that can unfold and reveal: Gomez-Rejon, interview by Doidge.

"Nora's a big part": Gomez-Rejon, interview by the author.

"She asked me to direct": Gomez-Rejon, interview by the author.

"I always wonder": Gomez-Rejon, interview by the author.

Hanks echoed the sentiment: Hanks, interview by the author.

"Making movies is like": Nora Ephron, interview by Charlie Rose, *Charlie Rose*, December 18, 1998, https://charlierose.com/videos/2857. Courtesy of Charlie Rose Inc.

To direct well: Mike Nichols discusses the value of the unconscious in film directing in *Becoming Mike Nichols*, dir. by Douglas McGrath (HBO Documentary Films, 2016).

"When I fly into": Hanks, interview by the author.

"hoot at the idea": Hanks, interview by the author.

"on the set . . . in the kitchen": Mike Nichols, acceptance speech at American Film Institute Life Achievement Award, 2010, via YouTube, https://www.youtube.com /watch?v=09NSBMgUwkg.

"Nora lives on": Cohen, interview by the author.

"To me, what this movie": Doidge, "It's Not Just About Harry," 16.

Book Club Questions

"What I love about cooking": Nora Ephron, *Heartburn*, 133.

SELECTED
BIBLIOGRAPHY

Original Interviews

Aaron, Caroline
Bayer Sager, Carole
Bewick, Martha Reardon
Burick, Marcia
Cohen, Richard
Dreyer, Dianne
Fenton, George
Gomez-Rejon, Alfonso
Greenburg, Dan
Hanks, Tom
Harris, Mark
Krim, Nancy
Lee, Don
Levine, Ed
Lindley, John
Lindley, Willow
Lord-Hausman, Audrey
Meyer, Patricia K.
Obst, Lynda*
Reeves, Richard*
Riskin, Victoria
Sacha, J. J.
Segal, Elizabeth
Short, Martin
Stoller, Nicholas
Sullivan, Jenny
Taplin, Jonathan

Trope, Alison, PhD*
Wellesley Class of 1962
Westerman, Shelly
* Original interviews conducted for the author's master's thesis

Other Sources

Abramowitz, Rachel. *Is That a Gun in Your Pocket?: Women's Experience of Power in Hollywood*. New York: Random House, 2000.

Adams, Tim. "Nicholas Pileggi: The Mob, Nora Ephron's Death and Vegas." *Guardian*, February 3, 2013. http://www.theguardian.com/tv-and-radio/2013/feb/03/nicholas-pileggi-vegas-nora-ephron.

Bernstein, Jacob, dir. *Everything Is Copy*. HBO Documentary Films, 2015.

———. "Nora Ephron's Final Act." *New York Times*, March 06, 2013. https://www.nytimes.com/2013/03/10/magazine/nora-ephrons-final-act.html.

Bettinger, Brendan. "Reese Witherspoon to Play Peggy Lee in Biopic Scripted/Directed by Nora Ephron." *Collider*, August 10, 2010. https://collider.com/reese-witherspoon-peggy-lee-biopic-nora-ephron-marc-platt-legally-blonde/.

Carlson, Erin. *I'll Have What She's Having: How Nora Ephron's Three Iconic Films Saved the Romantic Comedy*. New York: Hachette, 2018.

Cohen, Richard. *She Made Me Laugh: My Friend Nora Ephron*. New York: Simon & Schuster, 2016.

Dance, Liz. *Nora Ephron: Everything Is Copy*. Jefferson, NC: McFarland, 2015.

Doidge, Kristin Marguerite. "It's Not Just About Harry." Master's thesis, University of Southern California, 2015.

———. "Nora & Delia Ephron's *Love, Loss, and What I Wore*, 10 Years Later." *Los Angeles Review of Books*, May 27, 2018. https://blog.lareviewofbooks.org/reviews/nora-delia-ephrons-love-loss-wore-10-years-later/.

———. "'She Made Me Laugh' Is a Nora Ephron Tribute Every Woman Should Read." *Bustle*, January 4, 2017. https://www.bustle.com/articles/201321-she-made-me-laugh-is-a-nora-ephron-tribute-every-woman-needs-to-read.

Ephron, Delia. *Sister Mother Husband Dog*. New York: Penguin, 2013.

Ephron, Henry. *We Thought We Could Do Anything: The Life of Screenwriters Phoebe and Henry Ephron*. New York: Norton, 1977.

Ephron, Nora. *Crazy Salad: Some Things About Women*. New York: Vintage Books, 1975.

———. *I Feel Bad About My Neck: And Other Thoughts on Being a Woman*. New York: Alfred A. Knopf, 2006.

———. *I Remember Nothing: And Other Reflections*. New York: Alfred A. Knopf, 2010.

———. *The Most of Nora Ephron*. New York: Alfred A. Knopf, 2013.

———. "Nora Ephron '62 Addressed the Graduates in 1996," Wellesley College official website, accessed September 29, 2021, https://www.wellesley.edu/events/commencement/archives/1996commencement.

———. *When Harry Met Sally . . .* (screenplay). New York: Knopf, 1990.

Ephron, Nora, dir. *Julie & Julia.* Columbia Pictures / Sony Pictures, 2009.

———. *Lucky Numbers.* Paramount Pictures, 2000.

———. *Michael.* Turner Pictures / New Line Cinema, 1996.

———. *Mixed Nuts.* TriStar Pictures / Sony Pictures, 1994.

———. *Sleepless in Seattle.* TriStar Pictures, 1993.

———. *This Is My Life.* Twentieth Century Fox, 1992.

———. *You've Got Mail.* Warner Bros., 1998.

Ephron, Nora, and Meryl Streep. Interview by Charlie Rose. *Charlie Rose,* August 7, 2009, https://charlierose.com/videos/15908. Courtesy of Charlie Rose Inc.

Ephron, Nora, and Rob Reiner. "It All Started Like This" featurette. *When Harry Met Sally . . . ,* collector's ed. DVD. Directed by Rob Reiner. MGM Home Entertainment, 2008.

Freeman, Hadley. "Nora Ephron Taught Me All About Feminism—and About Sharp Writing." *Guardian,* August 5, 2013. http://www.theguardian.com/commentisfree/2013/aug/05/a-book-that-changed-me-nora-ephron.

Keaton, Diane, dir. *Hanging Up.* Columbia Pictures / Sony Pictures, 2000.

Lindley, John. Interview by Barbara Nance, March 3, 2015.

Nichols, Mike, dir. *Heartburn.* Paramount Pictures, 1986.

Obst, Lynda. Interview by Barbara Nance, February 24, 2015. Quoted in "It's Not Just About Harry" by Kristin Marguerite Doidge.

Reiner, Rob, dir. *When Harry Met Sally . . .* Castle Rock / Nelson Entertainment / Columbia Pictures, 1989.

Stanley, Alessandra. "Nora Ephron's Hollywood Ending." *New York Times,* June 27, 2012. https://www.nytimes.com/2012/06/28/fashion/nora-ephrons-hollywood-ending.html.

Thomas, June. "What Makes Jane Lynch's Characters Pop Onscreen." *Slate,* November 2, 2020. https://slate.com/culture/2020/11/jane-lynch-acting-glee-julie-and-julia.html.

Wolitzer, Meg. Interview by Barbara Nance, February 10, 2015. Quoted in "It's Not Just About Harry" by Kristin Marguerite Doidge.

Yardley, Jonathan. "Nora Ephron's 'Crazy Salad': Still Crisp." *Washington Post,* November 1, 2004. http://www.washingtonpost.com/wp-dyn/articles/A17418-2004Nov1.html.

INDEX

Italicized page references indicate illustrations